"Vicki Hearne is the most important animal thinker since Konrad Lorenz."
Donald McCaig

VICKI HEARNE

Victoria Elizabeth Hearne was born in Austin, Texas, in 1946, and grew up in California.

She received a B.A. from the University of California, Riverside, in 1967, and in 1969 was a Stegner Fellow in Poetry at Stanford University.

She was a lecturer in creative writing at U.C. Riverside from 1980 to 1984, an assistant professor of English at Yale University from 1984 to 1986, and a visiting fellow at the Institution for Social and Policy Studies at Yale from 1989 to 1995.

Ms. Hearne began training dogs and horses in 1967. In recent years, her "Dog Training Arts," which she operated with her husband Robert Tragesser, was located in Westbrook, Connecticut, where she lived. A website, www.dogtrainingarts.com is devoted to her training methods and writings.

Her first published book was *Nervous Horses* (1980), a collection of poetry. Two other collections followed: *In the Absence of Horses* (1984), for which she won the Academy of American Poets Peter I. J. B. Lavan Award, and *The Parts of Light* (1994).

Her other books were: *Adam's Task: Calling Animals by Name* (1986; reissued in A COMMON READER EDITION, 2000), which was selected by *Audubon* magazine as one of the 20th century's most important books on the natural world; *The White German Shepherd* (1988), a novel; *Bandit: Dossier of a Dangerous Dog* (1991; reissued in A COMMON READER EDITION, 2002); and *Animal Happiness* (1994), a collection of essays.

Her involvement in the "Bandit case" is the subject of *A Little Vicious* (1992), an Academy Award-nominated documentary by Immy Humes.

Among Ms. Hearne's many other writings is the essay "Oyez À Beaumont" (1993), which was reprinted in 2002 in *The Pushcart Book of Essays*, an anthology of the best work to have received the Pushcart Prize over the last twenty-five years.

In 1992, Ms. Hearne received an American Academy and Institute of Arts and Letters Award for distinguished achievement, and in 1994 she received an Ingram Merrill Foundation Award, also for distinguished achievement. Her outstanding contributions to dog welfare were recognized in 1989 by the Endangered Breeds Association.

She was married twice, and had one daughter.

Vicki Hearne died in August 2001.

By the same author in
A COMMON READER EDITION:

Adam's Task: Calling Animals by Name

Bandit

DOSSIER OF A
DANGEROUS DOG

Vicki Hearne

*With a new Introduction by John Hollander
and Postscript by Donald McCaig*

A COMMON READER EDITION
THE AKADINE PRESS
2002

Bandit
Dossier of a Dangerous Dog

A COMMON READER EDITION published 2002 by The Akadine Press Inc.,
by arrangement with the author.

A COMMON READER EDITION and fountain colophon
are trademarks of The Akadine Press, Inc.

ISBN 1 58579 046 X

10 9 8 7 6 5 4 3 2 1

The world was conquered through the understanding of dogs; the world exists through the understanding of dogs.

—NIETZSCHE

My lord, my liege lord, my dear
lord, what I desire is
my own and not your kindness.

A poor man is better than a liar,
dear my lord, suppose the
desire of a man is his kindness.

—DONALD DAVIE

Contents

INTRODUCTION   *by JOHN HOLLANDER*

ACKNOWLEDGMENTS

AUTHOR'S NOTE

	Prolegomena	1
ONE	Why I Did It	5
TWO	Biting the Hand That Feeds Him	31
THREE	Bandit Himself	57
FOUR	Bandit Himself: What He Is Not	79
FIVE	"This Isn't an Animal Rights Case, Professor Wizner"	95
SIX	Some Notes on Dog Bites (Just Before the Just City)	135
SEVEN	Guarding the Just City: A Pastoral	157
EIGHT	The Pit Bull Who Founded Rome	174
NINE	Beastly Behaviors	201
TEN	Whereas	240
	Coda: A Thousand Dollars	282

EPILOGUE

POSTSCRIPT   *by DONALD McCAIG*

Introduction

WHEN *Bandit: Dossier of a Dangerous Dog* first appeared almost a decade ago, one reviewer appropriately characterized it as "not only a dog story but also a deeply eccentric lesson in justice, linguistics, racism and teleology." The "dog story" can be told briefly: in July of 1987 Mr. Lamon Redd's dog, Bandit, was provoked into biting by a neighbor who trespassed on Mr. Redd's property and attacked Mr. Redd with a broom. The State of Connecticut impounded Bandit for a time, during which he was so ineptly handled that his behavior changed radically for the worse—so much so that upon his return to his master Bandit bit him. Bandit was again put under the care of the state's canine control officer, but this time the state sought to have him killed. In opposing the state's "disposal order," Mr. Redd's lawyer called upon Vicki Hearne, a dog trainer and the author of *Adam's Task: Calling Animals by Name,* as an expert witness; Hearne so overwhelmed the court with her knowledge and eloquence that she was allowed to take Bandit herself and rehabilitate him, discovering in the process that he was in fact a well-mannered and obedient dog. He was committed to her care thereafter.

The book that tells this story is a digressive one, but never irrelevantly so, since the demonization of a provoked dog raised, for as passionate an intellectual as Hearne, many questions about nomenclature and taxonomy (e.g., what, in fact, is a "pit bull"), about the nature of "expert testimony" in a legal proceeding, and even about the nature of "civility."

And yet for all its explorations of backgrounds and substructures, legal and moral issues, and matters of public policy and personal relations (in this case, between humans and their dogs), the story of Bandit is also rather like the tip of an intellectual iceberg. What underlies this energetic and exciting book is the life's work of a uniquely fascinating mind and spirit. As Hearne might herself have delighted in pointing out, hers is a body of work in which practice, theory and allegory—the concerns of the trainer, the thinker and the poet—always worked together as a dog works with an owner. For although she was best known as a trainer of animals—horses and, more recently, dogs—Hearne was also a poet of extraordinary gifts and surprising resources, and it was through her poetry that she drew the devoted attention of Harold Bloom and the English poet and critic Donald Davie (even as her prose in *Adam's Task* engaged the notice of the major American philosopher Stanley Cavell). Her poetry precisely reflects just how her whole working and thinking life confounded clichés of expectation. Her writing in verse is always as vibrant with direct knowledge of animals, both domesticated and wild, as is her speculative and practical prose.

But Vicki Hearne was also a philosophically-oriented thinker for whom modes of thought—in such matters, say, as the so-called "private language" discussed in Wittgenstein's *Philosophical Investigations*, or Plato's fable of horse and rider, or Renaissance training manuals, or even the folklore of modern handlers—all fall like shadows over actual animals, modeling, rather than darkening, them. Her concerns were both theoretical and practical, and for a true poet this is a crucial issue, for poems are not short pieces of exposition in verse, but instances of profound figuration. Hearne's particular poetic world is one framed by a mutual inter-representation of people and domestic animals, each a potential metaphor of the other. Her mythmaking occurs in this realm; and it extends analogously to other worlds as well: she can write magnificently when confronting philosophical arguments, or the making of sculpture, or the consequences of meditating upon Roger Van der Weyden's depiction of St. Luke painting the Virgin.

Just as her views, deployed throughout *Bandit*, about civic deportment between people and dogs, and about the limits of institutional interference, give no comfort to Humane Societies, Hearne's poetry gives no comfort to the ninnies of so-called "Direct Experience," whether they oversimplify relations of language to the rest of reality, or brutally sentimentalize relations between the human Self and the animal Other. As a poet, Hearne always writes in opposition to all of the wrong sorts of literalists. Her poems are intense, passionate and drenched in thought, engaging major moral and epistemological concerns. She rejoices in what might be called the Art of Domestication—meaning not only the craft of the animal trainer, but the high aesthetic occasion which is the engagement of an unspeaking animal with the constructions of human language and thought. Aware of the traditional philosophical problems posed by the minds of others—of how and what we know of others' thoughts and feelings—she treats the otherness of animals as at once intimate and terrifying. These animals' consciousness, a beautifully hypothetical entity which keeps flickering in and out of interest the more we know and are with them, comes up in much of her work. Her poems form a kind of romance in which our worries about how we ought sensibly to talk, and what the skilled experience of training animals leads one to feel and intuitively to say, are engaged in a dialectical sparring-match.

From the outset of her writing career, Vicki Hearne was particularly concerned to avoid the way in which so much contemporary verse sets up an unacknowledged and unexplored realm of thought inhabited by crude polarities of subject and object, experience and image. "The Metaphysical Horse," from *Nervous Horses*, her first book of poems, is a fine meditation on coming to terms with one's own metaphors:

> Circling elegantly we
>
> Glimpse the ways receding
>
> True proposal in the glass
>
>
> And join the horses, who dance,
>
> Tremors of exactitude
>
> Flaming, still fresh on their limbs.

Hearne's practical experience of horses was at one not only with her interest in their mythologies, but with her work as a trainer of the elements of discourse. For a real poet, language has a kind of life of its own, and the complex "exactitude" of both precision and elicited exertion resonates in the concerns of work, art and moral imagination.

I got to know Vicki Hearne when we started corresponding about matters of poetry some thirty years ago, and met her on a visit to the University of California at Riverside a few years later. I was prepared to meet a fan (although of the kind one always prays for, whose knowledge of literature, taste and judgment make her or his approval a blessing rather than an embarrassment). When I asked her what she worked at aside from writing, she told me that she trained animals, and I suppose I responded in a somewhat leaden way; but she immediately began talking of her interest in the relation between behavioristic accounts of what an animal was doing when it was learning to respond to a command or signal, and the very different kinds of stories that those who actually train animals would tell themselves about what was happening—and of why believing those stories helped the trainers work immeasurably better. I hesitantly mentioned that more general concerns of just that nature had been of interest to twentieth-century philosophers. But before I could finish she was discussing particular passages of the *Philosophical Investigations*, then turned to her own observations on the history of theories of training horses from Xenophon through the Renaissance, the relationship between humane societies and Tory politics in England, the cultural construction of breeds (with such exemplary stories as that of the demonization, as a "Nazi dog," of the Doberman in the later 1930s), and a host of other tales, issues, problems, questions and enigmas. It was a good many months after this meeting and some subsequent correspondence that she sent me a few poems to read, being too intelligent and mannerly to have thrust them upon me at the time. I found them impressive, framing those profound connections between form and fable that all true poetry must exhibit; but they also spoke of the passionate knowledge and wonder of the—what should I call her: The Compleat Trainer?—I had listened to with such fascination. In *Bandit*, the pressure she felt of so much "inexactitude," and indeed ineptitude, sometimes elicits impatience and even anger. But it is by design a polemical book, and its author became known internationally as a moral watchdog against the trespasses of bad dog-watching. Perhaps she might have liked in this capacity to have been thought of as an Airedale.

Vicki Hearne died in August 2001, and could not write her own introduction to this reissue of *Bandit*. In her third book of poetry, *Parts of Light*, she concluded a somewhat prophetic poem called "All of My Beautiful Dogs Are Dying" with these lines, and I'll let her own lyric tone conclude this preface to a pointedly unlyrical book:

> …Without the beautiful dogs
>
> No one dares to attend to desire;
>
> The sky retreats, will intend nothing.
>
> Is a ceiling to rebuke the gaze,
>
> Mock the poetry of knowledge.
>
> My death is my last acquiescence;
>
> Theirs is the sky's renunciation,
>
> Proof that the world is a scattered shame
>
> Littering the heavens. The new dogs
>
> Start to arise, but the sky must go
>
> Deeply dark before the stars appear.

John Hollander
January 2002

Acknowledgments

THERE IS, oh, there is Plato, of course, because he records Socrates' remarks on the learning that constitutes a protective and stalwart hound's work, even though I feel sometimes that there is something inelegant about being grateful to Plato. There is also, momentously, Mark Twain, for making fun of the dogfighter's yarn.

And there are a few editors I owe, though they had nothing to do with the details of producing this book. One is Anne Freedgood, whose work on *Adam's Task* has earned her a permanent place in my heart even if she does keep going to the horse races (and never inviting me). And Michael Parrish, who, as editor of the *Los Angeles Times Sunday Magazine,* gave me invaluable backup on a number of projects. And there is Upton Brady, who had the idea, and even visited the kennel in order to expound upon the idea, that I should not only write this book but also write it down.

Above all there is Joy Johannessen, who has both reminded me and taught me—I needed some teaching—that editing is a noble calling. I welcomed edited copy when it appeared in FedEx packages, welcomed her blue pencil, because responding to her blue pencil was a true work of writing, as though blue were the muse's favorite color.

But editors get paid to do what they do, some of the time at least. Diana Cooper provided infinite inspiration *pro bono,* largely by inscribing in her manners and way of going that scheme (rather than collusion) of spirit and intellect that is the heart of all true writing. Diana, amazingly, locates circles by means of horses rather than the other way, a matter of some moment, and I have learned much from observing her do this. I could, I suppose, have learned this from Pascal or some other mathematician, had any mathematician lived long enough to discover horses by means of circles, but as it happens none of them did, and I didn't. I learned it from Diana Cooper and her writing.

There is a certain amount of dedication to the ways I think about some lawyers, especially Frank Cochran, because without Frank Cochran there would be no story to tell about the only dog to get off of death row in the pit bull wars, and without his sanely abrupt, feisty responses to various incoherent pieties uttered in the course of the case I would have found my way to fewer clarities, since some of the incoherent pieties were mine. Also, I learned from Frank Cochran what lawyers do when they go to heaven. (They lawyer.)

What I learned from George and Lillian Bernard is: what true cynicism in action can look like, how it comes about that the word "cynic" comes from the Greek for "dog," and what that has to do with Rin Tin Tin.

There were also the hundreds of people who sent me clippings, articles, recent and aged studies, and so on, and in particular the Endangered Breed Association, which paid a significant portion of Bandit's legal fees and, through the integrity of Linda Emmert, kept me supplied with information and backup of many sorts. As did Michael and Terry Walsh, Dick Koehler, and Donald McCaig.

The Yale Institution for Social and Policy Studies provided invaluable support.

This book is dedicated to Robert Tragesser. He went on countless errands to the library, bookstore, grocery store, and above all pharmacy, and walked Bandit while I brooded luxuriously on the problem of expressing exactly how wonderful it is to walk Bandit. That, however, is not why this book is dedicated to him. It is dedicated to him because he is the first philosopher of my ken to open a discussion of philosophical

. . . .

matters by acknowledging not only that there might be a dog in the fog, but also that if it is foggy our view of the dog might be obscured and thus that we don't always know what we are looking at or talking about, nor even what the murk is composed of. There are plenty of philosophers who *pretend* to be capable of knowing that it is foggy, but it takes enormous skill and insight actually to do this, especially if the newspaper is open to a story about a monstrous canine mutant on the loose and even more especially when it might turn out, as it so often does in human speculative enterprise, to be the fog of one's own breath on the windowpane that veils the landscape with ferocious shapes.

Author's Note

A FTER MUCH head scratching, I have decided
to follow an unusual convention for breed names—roughly, the
convention I would use in correspondence with a knowledgeable dog person. In the case of names used by official breed
registries, I have capitalized all words in the breed name. Hence
I write "American Staffordshire Terrier" instead of "American
Staffordshire terrier," or "Plott Hound" rather than the more
conventional "Plott hound." When giving a nickname for a
breed, such as "pit bull," or when referring to a type of breed,
I use lowercase, unless the nickname includes a proper noun or
nouns, as in "AmStaff" for "American Staffordshire Terrier."

Note that this means that "Bulldog" refers to a breed registered by the American Kennel Club, whereas "bulldog" is either
a type of breed or, more frequently, a nickname for the American Pit Bull Terrier. "Bull Terrier" is an AKC breed—the sort
now called "Spuds MacKenzie dogs," but "bull terrier" is a type
of breed that includes Bull Terriers, American Staffordshire
Terriers, Staffordshire Bull Terriers, American Pit Bull Terriers, and so on. If I write "Collie" I mean the breed registered by
the American Kennel Club, but "collie" is a type of dog.

I am unhappily aware that all of this is distracting and confusing, but it seemed better to achieve accuracy this way than
with repeated parenthetical explanations that would be at least as
annoying and messy as the capital letters that now litter my
pages.

All of the events I cite in this book are actual—true in the courtroom sense of true "to the best of my knowledge and belief." I hope that the book is also poetically and scientifically true, true, that is, not only to my knowledge and best beliefs but also true to, faithful to, the world. In a few cases, however, I have suppressed names and locations, for a variety of reasons. One is to avoid boring the reader, since legal events, I have been forced to notice, are interesting in their full actuality only to a very narrow audience. There are the lawyers, of course, and there are the parties and witnesses, for whom every detail is telling and rich with significance, but by and large hearings and trials and the events that lead up to and follow from them are like deeply satisfying or else profoundly difficult conversations—you had to be there.

But I tell my story peculiarly, I know. I tell it the way I hear so many like stories over the telephone, breathlessly, leaving the (legally) important bits almost for last, as afterthoughts. I do this for the same reason people start their stories in the middle over the telephone. It is one way to try for lucidity, to avoid falling into that exhaustive illegibility for which chronicles, economic records, and legal files are both scorned and treasured. For legibility's sake then, I sometimes look at the facts sideways or upside down, in order to avoid being baffled by the accurate and misleading details. If my book remains baffled by truth rather than data, then it has that much artistic honesty at least.

This book harbors no fugitives from justice, whether human or heavenly. However, I do not include all of the guilty details here, even the details of the guilt of those I think of as the enemies of my dog, largely because the details of our guilt, anyone's guilt, obscure the brilliance of the life of the soul, the particularities of that exquisite shine of dwelling and action to be found in everything that is, in the world's being and happening as it does, that make it keep turning out that we can't help but have a use for a term such as "soul" any more than we can help but have names for each other if we are to talk to each other at all.

If I cannot help but imply morals to various stories as I go along, I wish to be forgiven for that; all narratives are postlapsarian, which is why the moral to a story will jump out and ruin one's writing. I will not threaten any readers who desire a moral, but sometimes I wish that they wouldn't.

You may say that the only question I began with was wholly private—"What is a dog bite?" When I say that it was wholly private, I mean that it was not among the questions being asked in any public forum, not a question anyone wanted me to speak to; it was a philosophical question in that it was a question I could not find my way to.

I don't mean that I did not already know a lot—a *lot*—about dog bites, a lot about how to prevent or cause them, a lot about how deceptive the phenomenon of a bite is, as deceptive as words themselves, as friendly, too—close enough, that is, to break the skin, as words are inevitably that close to us, from the beginning. It turned out that in writing the book I had to do what philosophy I managed to do on a hit-and-run basis; this book leads into the real book, the one called *Animal Happiness*. (Philosophy and poetry both can be said to begin in the experience of feeling rebuffed in the pursuit of the various happinesses that are their birthrights.)

This book is not, of course, a song, but it is offered in praise.

Prolegomena

 BANDIT'S PROSPECTS were not good. He bit three people, said the rap sheet. Then the city attorney came up with a rumor about a fourth and said to the judge, "He's diseased, Your Honor. He's been hit on the head."

"He has *genes*. Genes is what these dogs have, and their training is part of their genetics, and it makes 'em mean," went one bit of light-headed expert testimony.

One police report quotes a neighbor as saying, "Dog could not be controlled to stop biting." This neighbor did not witness anything, but the humane police are not a skeptical, suspicious lot.

There was much testimony about the Jekyll-Hyde syndrome, about how all of 'em turn on you eventually.

Effie Powell said from her hospital bed, "I felt his teeth sinking into my flesh."

"Pit bulls are *vicious*. The data is all there, in *Sports Illustrated,*" shrilled dozens of callers, eager to convince me of my waywardness in defending Bandit. Impatient with learned arguments regarding illegal search and seizure and the Uniform Administrative Procedures Act, a prosecutor said, "This case has been due-processed to death, Your Honor. The dog should be destroyed!"

Pit bulls have double-jointed jaws so that they can "hold with the front while they chew away with the hind," says the literature of the Humane Society of the United States, and a taxi driver in New York said no, it's triple jaws, he saw a veterinarian say so on TV. Quite often, when you bring your beloved pit bull into a veterinarian's office, worried about her health, the veterinarian, instead of keeping his or her attention concentrated on the medical question at hand, will tell you how vicious your dog is or ask if you've been to any dogfights lately.

Calico Silver, in a brilliant if somewhat erratic essay about dogfighting yarns, in which he praised especially one Mark Twang, identifies poets and other writers in terms of their residence on a metaphysical place called Lookout Mountain. This essay appeared in one of the "underground" fighting rags I chanced to see in a tack store I stumbled on. These magazines are characterized by pseudonyms and a high degree of allegory and magical realism, a genre or style that I have come to associate with writers living under military regimes, police states, and the like. Lookout Mountain survives from the days of moonshine; it is the place from which you can see the revenooers from afar. I suspect Mark Twain himself would have no trouble understanding the idea that the spot from which you can see the revenooers coming is one location of visionary truth.

In these allegorical maps of America, New York City is a place way out past the foothills, in the cloudy mists of the valley. Calico Silver himself lives fairly close to the top of Lookout Mountain, so has learned a lot, though not everything, he says, about bulldogs and bulldog yarns.

It seems a fellow called him up one day and asked him if it was true he had fought a two-headed dog named Cerberus. He hadn't, of course, but he said this had a little truth in it, and wrote, "This story is called a Jive story. It is a way the writer has when the understanding of true stories is small."

It is this way for our species. This is not the only way it is for us, but this is one way it is—we are a lonesome and threatened tribe, and we tell jive stories. Calico Silver's jive story here is not, of course, the one about the two-headed dog, but the one about being *asked* if he had a two-headed dog. You need something like magical realism to say what it is like to have local representatives of humane organizations demanding that you admit that your own dog has double jaws or two heads or is a "time bomb."

The double jaws, the double heads, the dog-as-time-bomb—these stories have a little truth in them, not as much truth as the old Rin Tin Tin stories had, but some: the dogs are strong and quick and loyal. But "the understanding of true stories is small," because we all get distracted. For a brief bit, when my social conscience had carried me away from the true path, I was on talk shows and learned from that experience that signs of education in a letter or voice were signals that the writer or speaker was going to yammer on about pit bulls being bloodthirsty, and about dope dealers. A voice or letter that sounded or looked to be working-class would tend to predict someone wanting to tell me something sensible. I don't mean that they would necessarily know anything. They would usually say, "They aren't all bad," and then tell me a small story.

One that I recall in particular was told by a woman who sounded to be in her seventies. She said she had had a pug, and that her pug had gotten old and blind. And that a pit bull had lived next door.

"And that dog was so kind to my Jouncer. He played with him, kept him company, and when Jouncer started to get close to the street he would take him back into the yard."

There is a literary tradition of assigning common sense to the working classes.

In the course of my involvement with the Bandit case—or rather, the case's involvement with me (I did not go looking for it, it just pounced on me, out of nowhere; in fact, I was writing a book about horses and content to be doing so)—I realized that while quite often the impact of an actual pit bull, panting amiably, is powerful, we can't turn our backs on the Pandora's boxes we open when we trade in Pete the Pup for Cujo, even though Pete the Pup, of the old *Our Gang* comedy series, was real, and Cujo almost entirely an artifact of the special effects department of a Hollywood studio. Where you can leap to, wrote Stanley Cavell, depends on where you stand. In relationship to animals, we stand in a great tangle of words, hip deep even in the easy areas, so it is through words that we have to make our way back to the mainland of reality.

I have here written an entire book in an attempt to return to the ordinary insights and the ordinary virtues of my world as it was before the Bandit case.

ONE ···

Why I Did It

*Every word they say chagrins us and we do not know where to
begin to set them right.*

—EMERSON *"Self Reliance"*

THE BANDIT CASE, as of this writing, has been go-
ing on for three and a half years. For all but the first six months
of that time, Bandit has been my dog. In that time I have used
the services of five lawyers, have been threatened with jail and
other things that come of contempt of court charges, have heard
that some cops were out to get me, others out to protect me,
have entertained some very, very strange phone calls and mail,
have had my dog alluded to on the front page of the state
newspaper as Public Enemy Number One. I have all of that
time worried about someone killing my dog for what looked to
me like purely political reasons. Some people say that the motives in question aren't purely political, are more psychological,
but that is *really* scary, so I try to leave those contemplations
alone.

Still, I am not especially oppressed, as things go for animal
people nowadays, but that is because I have lucid intervals and
a really good lawyer, and because I learned to train dogs from
the best, and so I have a lot of backup. It doesn't hurt that I am
white, educated, and female, but these are troubled times and
you can't rely on the traditional bigotries the way you used to.

As I said, I have been threatened with jail. Now, this is very
peculiar, because I am an animal poet, and in a healthy society,
or so I always figured, the animal poet is a ninny, someone who
goes around at the edges of things fussing harmlessly and ob-
scurely over Kant's mistakes about wild animals and Socrates'
praise of dogs, tripping over her Airedale, not making as much

sense as her family and friends wish she would. At dinner parties, the animal poet inserts into the conversation unwanted information about the true life history of Toto, the Cairn Terrier in *The Wizard of Oz*, and is more or less gently tolerated for this.

At the university, especially in the philosophy department, everyone used to say, "Go away, little girl, we're busy," and while this was irksome, we cannot any of us have as much of heaven as we want, as the sheepdog Sirrah said posthumously to Donald McCaig. In those days the roof sometimes leaked, but there was so much intellectual freedom for me that I was able to write entire books without even knowing the names of any lawyers.

Nowadays, I let my lawyer see my manuscripts before I let my *agent* see them, not only to protect me but to protect my dogs, and while my lawyer, Frank Cochran, is proving to be a quite good, though somewhat expensive, creative writing teacher, it means something when an animal poet has to show manuscript to her lawyer. It means what the presence of lawyers usually presages, that there is a major topic slouching toward one to be born, and also that one will probably be unequal to the task. It is a bad sign when the dog story becomes a politically sensitive genre.

The topic in question is: Justice.

Not justice for poets. Like tiger trainers, poets are on their own as far as justice goes, and must make what they can of what comes their way. But the topic of justice assaults most people at some point or another in their lives; to be human is to be fated to such an assault. That is what makes justice such a big topic—not the fact that it is intrinsically all that interesting, but the fact that it is of general concern, like radon or cancer.

I personally do not find justice all that interesting, not nearly as interesting as, say, the pedigree of the pup I am on the point of acquiring, or Landrover Smith, a chimp I met recently, or the poetry of Wallace Stevens, or the prose of Mark Twain, and other things that journalists used to call "human interest," but the topic—justice—has assaulted me, and I have to do something about it, have to deal, as we say of other crime victims, with the psychological repercussions. I am singularly ill-suited for the task. Once I was going through some back issues of the London *Times,* looking for the answer to some questions about world peace, and came across a story about a man who was arrested for having a donkey in the passenger seat of his car. He said it was a very small donkey, and the cops said it didn't matter, donkeys had to be in the back. World peace went out of my head, and there I was looking for more donkey stories.

Now I have a dog story to tell.

At the time of this writing, many Americans believe that there is a breed of dog that is irredeemably, magically vicious. This is not the only reason the current era is going to go down in history as one of the most remarkably hysterical and super-stitious of all time, but it is a bigger reason than current spec-ulation allows for. The dog in question is said to be good at guarding dope dens, to suffer from something called the Jekyll-Hyde syndrome, to be an indiscriminate killer of tires, weeds, kittens, and people, to exert two thousand or sometimes twenty thousand pounds of pressure per square inch with its double- or triple-jointed jaws. There is a great deal else said about these dogs that is agonizingly ungrammatical, such as the expert view that they have "vicious genes" and "their training is part of their genetics." These dogs are popularly called "pit bulls." They don't exist, so I call them Voice of God dogs, to distinguish them from real breeds. The God these dogs are a Voice of does not exist, any more than the dogs do; this is not so much a God of vengeance as of grime and banal confusion, and is not to be mistaken for anything real in the way of divinities. What true theologian would be so rash as to suggest that the true God, Who is Owner of the World, or *kono shel olam* in Hebrew, would own a dog who is a horror largely of banalities and poor clichés? *Kono shel olam* might own a very terrible dog indeed, but not one that deals dope.

I started using the phrase "Voice of God dogs" one day when a district attorney in Rochester, New York, asked me what I

would say if a dog suddenly and out of nowhere attacked someone. The hypothetical bite situation he described was impossible, could not take place, so I asked if he meant, "Like the Voice
of God?" He said yes. From this and other events I take it that
there are people who believe in some God that the Voice of God
dogs represent, and that these dogs must be fought tooth and
nail by the district attorneys of the nation, for the sake of . . .
justice?

The unreal Voice of God dogs are to be distinguished from
the dogs of God in a wonderful fourteenth-century fresco by
Andrea da Firenze, in Florence, which shows the Dominicans
guarding the gates of heaven, and in the foreground a row of
dogs helping them. The title, *Dominicanni,* contains a pun on
"Dominican" and *domini canii,* or "dogs of God." At one end of
the fresco are, unmistakably, bulldogs—pit bulls. At the other
end are, unmistakably, hunting hounds of the greyhound/
staghound sort now classified as gazehounds. In between, the
dogs vary from each other in phenotype by virtually indiscrim-
inable degrees, so that the painting shows a visionary progression from the stocky and stalwart and therefore divine to the
slender and swift and therefore divine. It is very much as though
the artist were of a Platonic bent and wanted to picture all the
actual forms that conceal (or for him reveal) the ideal form Dog.
Da Firenze's dogs and da Firenze's God were not of course what
the DA was asking me about, and not what I mean by the phrase
"Voice of God dogs."

In the Rochester case, by the way, a man was on trial for
manslaughter, and I might as well tell you what I know about
it. A man named Mark and his dog, Pete, had gone on a Fourth
of July picnic. Present also were a man named Mike and his
brothers. Mike was throwing firecrackers at Pete. Eventually,
Pete bit him on the thigh and fled. Thereupon Mike's brothers
beat Mark up, and then took their brother to the hospital. Eleven
days later, Mike was released, or rather was scheduled to be
released that day, when he died suddenly of an embolism. There
was some attempt on the part of the defense to have entered into
evidence hospital records showing that anticoagulant medica-

tion, which is supposed to prevent embolisms in the case of thigh wounds, had not been administered, or had not been properly monitored. For some reason, the medical evidence was not deemed admissible.

Pete the dog was killed, of course. Perhaps the death of the dog made it turn out that the hospital was blameless, sort of the way victory in war makes the winning side turn out to be blameless, because once someone is dead they are no good to anyone, and then you can say, "They were no good."

Pete was eight years old, and in the habit, on walks, of waiting at street corners for his master to catch up, rather than skipping across heedlessly by himself. I thought that showed a sense of responsibility in the dog, and so testified, but try telling a district attorney whose eyes are wide and glowing with a vision of the Voice of the God of Doom that a given pit bull has a sense of responsibility.

The district attorney asked me if it wasn't true of Staffordshire Pit Bull Terriers that their genes have become vicious as a result of their being owned by unsupervised urban teenagers and dope dealers.

There is no such thing as a Staffordshire Pit Bull Terrier, I told the DA, so he asked me to testify about the breed "whatever."

Remember: Mark was on trial for manslaughter.

Once the dog was dead, my services as a witness were not called for. I heard that Mark had agreed to plead guilty to the lesser charge of assault. I spoke with him several times, trying to get him to accept help in the form of funds for a new lawyer, but he insisted he was too frightened, that it would be too dangerous: "They beat me up, they destroyed my car, they will beat me up again."

They beat him up royally in the local newspaper, which was up in arms about this viciousness. The defense had proposed that outside experts be brought in to evaluate Pete, and this idea was mocked with a cartoon showing a sort of dog on a psychiatrist's couch, the psychiatrist in tatters.

All that isn't why I did what I did, but before I say why I did it, I should say what I did to get the topic of justice slouching toward me.

What I did: I meddled in some court cases. I rescued a dog named Bandit, even knowing that dog rescue is one of the most corrupt of all human activities. It can do enormous damage, just like on television, where rescue adventures leave the landscape littered with bodies and create enormous temptations to feel righteous about the bodies. I used to think about television when I heard all those hymns about Emmanuel rescuing the people of God.

Bandit was said to be a pit bull, but he is not. He was said to be uncontrollably aggressive, but he is not, because random aggression requires pretty advanced intellectual capacities, the ability to live by abstract concepts and so on, and Bandit is not that bright. He was said to suffer from the Jekyll-Hyde syndrome, but you have to be human to suffer from the Jekyll-Hyde syndrome, and you have to be able to misread Robert Louis Stevenson, and Bandit can't read. He was said to be diseased, but he is not. He was said to be untrainable because five years old, but he is not. Untrainable, that is; he was at one point five years old. He was said to have genes, and for all I know he does.

He was said to be "a dog like *that!*" I do not know what "*that*" means.

The state of Connecticut wanted to dispose of him because of all of this, or at least that's roughly why they said they wanted to dispose of him. Perhaps they made better sense to themselves than to me. In any case, they did not get to dispose of him. They wanted to take him away from his owner, an old man, and they did succeed in that.

Bandit is, as near as I could discover, the only alleged pit bull to have gotten off death row in the pit bull wars. The reason no alleged pit bull gets off death row is that the arguments in court are about a hallucination—a Voice of the God of Doom dog— and it is simply impossible to get anything across to people who are hearing Voices.

Bandit is my dog now, has been since a very hot day in late July of 1988. He belonged to an old man in Stamford, Connecticut, an old black man, Mr. Lamon Redd. Mr. Redd went to bat for his dog. He built a six-foot-high chain link fence around his property when the local dog warden told him to, attempting to save Bandit's life, and he got a lawyer, and he stayed in the fight like a trouper, but I rescued Bandit, and the old man did not get his dog back, which is how and why it turns out that dog rescue is by and large such a corrupt activity.

I hadn't intended any of this, to get involved with justice and the theology of the Voice of God dogs, or any of the rest of it. What I intended to do in the spring of 1987 was finish my book on horses and stay out of the pit bull wars altogether. I had, it is true, written a piece a few years earlier about what nonsense the superstitious belief in the viciousness of pit bulls is, but it is one thing to write something and quite another to buy a sedate skirt and respectable shoes and go off to a courtroom and become an expert. An authority. To encourage one's jowls over the collar of one's tweed jacket under cross-examination and speak with forceful but pedantic impatience. All of this is implausible behavior for an animal poet, but that is what I did, and it is Dan Rather's doing. Not his fault, but his doing.

I do not have a television and rarely read newspapers, or even the magazines I sometimes write for, but my mother has a television and is one of the last of the news junkies. The quality of news these days is such that it is hard to keep the faith, but she does her best. Onto the screen of my mother's television in California there appeared, out of nowhere, like the Voice of Doom: Dan Rather, reporting solemnly that in Dayton, Ohio, a man had been innocently jogging down the road when out of nowhere two pit bulls appeared and attacked him and killed him.

This story I found incredible, because the account of the incident didn't sound like anything I have ever known a dog to do. It is quite difficult to get a dog to perform a full-fledged man-stopping attack off his own property, which is one reason police dog training is a matter that occupies intelligent people

for years and years. The picture I was offered, of the man jogging innocently by and the two dogs attacking and killing "out
of nowhere" and "for no reason," simply did not make sense. I
also found myself worried silly, because I have always suspected
that it is expensive getting a Dog Bites Man item on the desk of
a major newscaster, and I wondered who had paid for the crisis.

Various dark thoughts crossed my mind about the victim.
Especially, I wondered darkly what the good doctor had been
up to, because I had had occasion earlier in my life to look at and
reflect on some bite studies in which it turned out that boys are
bitten more often than girls, and because it was just all too
perfect, somehow. Like the opening of a horror movie. Innocent jogger, evil pit bulls coming out of nowhere. I am all in
favor of safety and have spent most of my life haranguing people for indulging their dogs in a way that creates the danger of
a bite, but that has to do with reality, and this story Dan Rather
was telling had little to do with reality.

I also assumed that in Ohio someone was mounting a statewide pit bull ban. I do not believe that politicians control the
media in the way they would like to—when I said that Bandit
had been slandered on the front page of the state newspaper, the
word "state" didn't mean what it means in the case of Tass—but
there are constraints on what a reporter can use as news that add
up to a picturesque *pas de deux* between the media and policy-
making activities. Hence it turns out that if you read the newspapers and watch TV you can make some fairly good guesses
about what the politicians are up to, especially if you don't read
or listen to what the politicians *say,* because they never have
anything to say . . .

And so I heard Dan Rather reporting on what sounded like
something out of a horror flick, and assumed that some senator
in Ohio was using pit bulls as a campaign issue, and this proved
to be the case. A few months after that broadcast, Ohio passed
what must be a singularly unconstitutional law, declaring that
any animal of the breed commonly known as pit bulldog was
prima facie vicious for purposes of that law, except dogs lawfully
engaged in hunting or being trained for hunting. Not that the

prima facie vicious dog banned in Ohio exists outside the court-rooms and the media and whatever credence we are willing to give to these venerable institutions. Also, there is no such thing as common knowledge of dogs. People get ideas in their heads, but that is not knowledge, common or otherwise. There was, therefore, no such dog as the one banned, no such animal as a dog "commonly known as pit bulldog," but that did not stop a judge from ordering an entire kennel of Shar Peis out of the state.

In my circle of acquaintance there are a lot of people who watch television. Some watch PBS and documentaries; others watch commercial television. I know very few persons of a perfect and pure cynicism, but I do not know anyone who believes in what they see on commercial television. By and large my friends of high and low station tend to read the paper and watch television in order to find out what other people—"the public"—believe. I know some editors who believe in this "public" they are preparing the news for, a public that sometimes goes by such names as "Joe Six-pack," and Joe Six-pack is supposed to be irredeemably narrow-minded, monosyllabic, and gullible. But my experience of watching people as they watch television and read newspapers has given me a different image of Joe Six-pack.

My image is of someone scoffing and saying, "People will believe anything." This person of my experience is close to monosyllabic, but what can you say about television? So it may be that the deep superstition here, the one worth understanding, the widespread and unquestioned belief that will make this century memorable for its superstitiousness, is the belief that there is someone out there believing what they see on television, and further, that believing what you see on television can even be a case of belief as philosophers analyze it. In my experience, when the crazy, sleazy ads with their sick images of people and animals and music come on, or when the nauseating sitcoms with their brain-damaged ideas of human interaction appear, Joe Six-pack shakes his head and says, "I know other people don't feel this way, but they hadn't ought to do that. Good taste matters."

I am older than I was, so most of my Six-pack friends have switched to Scotch and a reduced alcoholic intake, or else herbal tea, since their stomachs can't take the carbonation and their minds can't take the confusion as well as when they were younger, but they say the same sort of thing.

At one point, I had a fevered and malicious idea about what to do about one of mine enemies: Blackmail. My idea was to hire a detective and get something on one particularly trouble-some person and use it to stop him from killing dogs and mak-ing children and old men weep. I produced this idea, while in front of a television, in a whole room full of Six-packs, and they all said, "No, don't do that, there's no point in going down to his level."

My friend George Bernard, over at the kennel, does not care much for beer but switches channels even faster than *A Recent Study* said the Average Viewer does, which was once every thirteen seconds. *A Recent Study* said this was evidence that the attention span of Americans was in bad shape, and I guess it is, because George keeps saying, "I can't stand this crap." No at-tention span.

Understanding what goes on when people watch television became important to me for a while, because it was important to know Who Is Slandering Our Dogs. A lot of beleaguered dog owners thought it was The Media and Those Reporters, and there was a joke that went the rounds of the country for a while. Q: What's worse than a pit bull with AIDS? A: The reporter who gave it to him. But it wasn't the *media* feeding out solemn remarks about savage fighting dogs with double jaws who learn to kill human beings by practicing on dolls and declawed kit-tens; it wasn't and isn't the media lobbying for laws that would take away a dog owner's right to a hearing. So I made my own indelicate version of the joke. Q: How did the pit bull get AIDS? A: The humane society fucked him over.

Which humane society? There are thousands. It was persons whose names appear on the letterhead of the Humane Society of the United States (HSUS) who produced most of the expert testimony at first, especially one Dr. Randall Lockwood, Ph.D., though there were odd things coming from Drs. Clifford, Wright, Fox, and others. It took me a while to tumble to this, months of poring over clippings, wondering how Pete the Pup got replaced virtually overnight by a short-coated Cujo. As I said, there are thousands of humane societies and humane officials and humane experts, and their very ubiquity makes them anonymous, and even though they fight with each other as much as they do with you and me, they seem to be everywhere and nowhere, like locusts. In time, however, certain proper nouns began to emerge, and even I, who have no training in political epidemiology, noticed one name in particular, that of the HSUS, popping up in literally hundreds of clippings from all over the country intoning solemnly about the viciousness of pit bulls. I also have some of their literature, including a letter of August 14, 1987, from HSUS president John Hoyt, saying that the vicious dog situation created an urgent need for new felony and manslaughter prosecutions of owners. He asked for the reader's help "in funding this unexpected crisis. We have spent thousands of staff hours and thousands of dollars in extra expense on this project."

I read not only press clippings but as much historical material as was available in the languages I know, and I began to see that it is usually a humane society of one sort and another, in the last one hundred and fifty years, that is funding a crisis of horror. Sometimes it seems as though the horror story is the only one the major animal and child welfare organizations have to tell. The child or the animal is, in the material I have seen, either sweet and innocent and suffering or irredeemably vicious and dangerous; the babe at your breast becomes the dope fiend who steals from your purse and beats you, all because of some Bad Man or Bad Woman who breeds supernaturally vicious dogs or concocts magic potions in the cellar.

The very image of the mad, bad dog—Cujo, for example, the sweet family pet who becomes a fiend from hell—is in part the result of a campaign started by the Royal Society for the Prevention of Cruelty to Animals, as I learned from Harriet Ritvo's splendid social history *The Animal Estate: The English and Other Creatures in the Victorian Age*. According to Professor Ritvo, the RSPCA was casting about in the 1880s for an issue to gain popular and legislative support for its programs; like the HSUS in the 1980s, the RSPCA wanted help in funding a crisis. Fervor for the cause prompted someone to hit upon the idea of getting the public worried about rabies, and pretty soon there was widely believed to be a rabies epidemic, caused by canine sexual frustration, some said; others said, as they say now about the pit bull "epidemic," that it was caused by lack of proper education—dogs would not get rabies and bite people if only they were raised properly, with respect for the church and for their elders.

There is such a thing as education, of course, and it is worthwhile, but the term "education" in this context means various kinds of sympathetic magics, according to which the character of the parent or instructor is supposed to rub off on the pupil. It works on the principle of a radium treatment or the laying on of hands. On this view, teachers and parents are not so much to know how to do things and teach them as to be themselves morally sanitary, contagiously hygienic. Hence a quotation from an education expert I heard on a radio talk show who said that it is true that television programs are just about as godawful as everyone says they are, but they are good for children because they teach "values on society." He may have learned to say that from watching television. What he wanted was a clean society.

Social hygiene movements worry me. I think of purges, of the Salem witch trials and the Spanish Inquisition. I am not always all that brave, so I trembled in my boots when I heard Dan Rather's report on the pit bulls who killed the pillar of the Dayton community, which could be seen as a clever little allegory about how these evil and unsanitary dogs are contaminating everything upright and righteous.

Here and there it will seem to the reader that I am replacing one horror story with another, and there will be some justice in this. I am human, and I am telling a story about what seems to me to be a horror. The horror in question is the fact itself of horror stories, of for instance Dan Rather's tale about the dogs attacking "out of nowhere." This story, like the horror stories sometimes told about the viciousness of Jews or blacks or witches, has the effect of making both teller and listener feel very righteous about their assaults on Jews or blacks or witches. Images of outlandish viciousness—images given to us in the name of morality, of gentleness—are used to make everyone feel good when the bad guy gets got. Hence the Ayatollah sponsoring a manhunt for Salman Rushdie on the grounds that he is outlandishly, even hellishly, vicious, and the extraordinary fact, the fact that I do not know how to assimilate, that the person who is the *object* of the lethal assault is said to be the vicious one. It seems to me that the fact that there exist horror stories, that there exists *that* structure and fiction of interpretation, is one of the most anomalous facts about our species.

Wolves do not tell horror stories, whether gleefully or piously, and cougars do not, and field mice do not, and if, as I am not the first to suspect, the difference between people and other animals is a difference in a capacity for moral concepts—that is to say, we can get so outraged by something that we write books about it or round a lot of people up and torment them in the name of some kindness or piety—then the structure of the horror story is a clue about the nature of human morality. It is as though the knowledge of good and evil is given by the special effects department, or at least it is in general from the special effects department that we are willing to take that knowledge, perhaps because the idea that evil is banal is less tolerable than the idea of the fires of hell.

Once we have the knowledge of good and evil, once we start seeing monsters on every street corner, justice slouches toward us, a major topic hoping to be born, and justice is a very tricky topic, so beware of your language when it starts producing monsters.

I found out more about what had happened in Dayton. The victim may or may not have been jogging. He was an M.D., a pillar of the community, and the dogs were owned by a prostitute. The doctor had been at her house earlier in the evening, and she had sent him away, and he had eventually returned, breaking in. Actually breaking into the bedroom where the woman and the dogs were, said some reports. The DA asked for a manslaughter indictment on the dog's owner, but the grand jury refused to indict her, on the grounds that she had done nothing wrong, a fact that was not reported by Dan Rather.

A few months after the Dan Rather report a Dutch psychiatrist named Mark Vandenberg called me up. All I knew at first was that there was this rather precise Dutch voice coming over the transom, saying that it felt that someone should get hold of one of those bad dogs in the news and show that he is a good dog. I was nervous, because M.D.s and psychiatrists and such generally make me want to run like hell even when they don't earn their keep at the Mid-Hudson State Hospital for the Criminally Insane, but at least the man was not American, so he might not be bonkers in a way that would interfere too much with my own mental health.

Also, his proposal—it came like the Voice of an Angel, you see, saying, "Here, here is what you were promised. Here is your intellectual birthright."

Dr. Vandenberg could not have known that, and might have been more cautious if he had. Certainly I should have been more cautious, but I was not. What happened when he said, "Take one of these bad dogs and show he is a good dog," was that I remembered Hearne's Law. I formulated this law about a quarter of a century ago, when I first began to study the remarkably illusory nature of society and laws and institutions and Rome and New York and Eden. The law says that if you need a really good, sound, steady-hearted dog, the thing to do is to find a court case accompanied by a lot of hullabaloo in the press about a vicious dog, and get hold of that dog, and there is Rin Tin Tin.

I reasoned quite simply, as follows. When there is a stink about something in the papers, it means some politician or bureaucrat or charity head wants the stink. Some *Untier*. *Untier* is a German word for "monster" and is used somewhat the way we use the term "inhuman," except that it doesn't mean "inhuman" but "unanimal." *Tieren,* or animals, will take on any opponent—both the worthy and the unworthy—but *Untieren,* or humans, ennobled, some say, by the knowledge of good and evil, take care to preserve their pride of place in creation by never taking on a worthy opponent when they can avoid it, so they pick on a poor and unsophisticated family when they want to raise a stink about dogs. The name of the stink varies; nowadays it is called Protecting the Public and Preserving Society's Rights, or sometimes, Values on Society. The *Untieren* learn Values on Society from television and not from the Constitution, in which there is no mention of either the Public or Society. By *Untieren* I do not mean Joe Six-pack but rather people who have lost the moral candor of animals without achieving the moral consciousness appropriate to human beings.

If a given case continues in the news long enough to be a phenomenon, that means that the poor or working-class family is fighting back. Fighting back is expensive. It often turns out they are having to mortgage the family farm in order to do it, unless, as in at least one case in Santa Barbara, the owner is homeless and has nothing to mortgage.

It takes quite a dog to compel that kind of loyalty. In the case of Mr. Redd and Bandit, it took quite a dog to compel him to build the fence and get the lawyer and the rest of it.

I didn't know about Bandit at that point, but I told this odd person with the Dutch voice that his idea was interesting, and soon we were meeting and conspiring, and not too long after that I was on the telephone listening to Robert Bello, a lawyer in Stamford, discuss the Bandit case. Especially, I listened to Bello read the police reports, the rap sheet, as it were, and listened to a history of bites. *Serious* bites. Listened to a story of a ravening monster and said to Robert Bello, "That's a good dog!"

Bello does not care for dogs all that much, and said, "Uh, yes, well, ahem." He was doing this—doing it *pro bono,* I might add—because he liked the old man, not because he is an animal rights nut. It was later that he told me he doesn't like dogs all that much. All he said when I said, "That's a good dog!" was, "Uh, yes, well, ahem."

*   *   *

Here is what I learned from the conversation with Bello and
a subsequent visit to Mr. Redd's house.

On a hot evening in early July of 1987, Mr. Lamon Redd, in
his late seventies, was sitting on the front porch of his modest
house on Henry Street in Stamford, Connecticut. Bandit was
with him, as Bandit always was. There never was a better dog
for sitting on your porch on Henry Street than Bandit; everyone
in the neighborhood agrees about this. The world goes by, and
Bandit keeps watch, over Henry Street and over Mr. Redd, and
over the neighborhood generally. Neighbors and passersby
greet him enthusiastically: "Hey, Bandit!" The garbage man
stops for a chat, as does the mailman. "Hey, Bandit, how you
doin'? He lookin' good, Mr. Redd. He lookin' good."

Normally that is all that is required of a dog, keeping watch,
but on Henry Street crime is a personal matter and doesn't
happen over the telephone or through the courts and public
prints, but rather to yourself and your portable property. In
1974, an article in the *Bulletin of the New York Academy of Medicine* speculated that the rise in dog bites in New York City since
1965 was a result of people's fear of rising crime. My experience
suggests, however, that it is crime itself, not fear of crime, that
causes dog bites. If you break into someone's house, their dog
might just bite you. If you assault someone, the same thing
might happen. If you tease or torment a dog, the dog might bite
you even if you are under age.

And as Lily Mae McClean said, "You gotta be a little vicious
when someone comes in your house, wants to kill you. Bandit
is a good dog. We didn't worry about these kids breaking in
when Bandit was here."

A Little Vicious. That's what Valerie Humes, who came by
and made a documentary about some aspects of the case, called
her film.

Mr. Redd is black, is from Virginia, was a steelworker for
twenty-three years, is now retired. His daughter, Lily Mae Mc-
Clean, who works as a housekeeper at St. Joseph's Hospital,
lives with him. Lily Mae understands Mr. Redd a great deal
better than I do, knowing exactly when to call him Daddy and

when to chide him impatiently, saying, "Redd! Cut it out!" Mr. Redd owns the house at 189 Henry Street, parts of which he rents to boarders, and the house next door at 191 Henry Street, where there resided one Mr. Johnson.

People on Henry Street say "Mr." and "Mrs." and "Miss" to their neighbors, except when some other locution is to the point. Lily Mae McClean gently calls Mr. Johnson "that boy, yes, that boy, he helped my daddy," but she is a privileged person. Others say "Mr. Johnson."

In July of 1987, Bandit was as he is now a grand sort of dog, but he wasn't an obedience-trained dog, and taking him for a walk was a strenuous matter. He was no different in this regard from most dogs, but he is heavy and powerful, so when he pulls on the leash he takes most people along with him.

Bandit is not a pit bull, but he is one of the bull breeds, the kind of dog who takes with enthusiasm to weight-pulling contests and wins going away. They love to pull, do the bulldogs. And people in housing projects and other dens of iniquity do indeed often buy wide leather collars for their dogs, just as Dr. Clifford of the Medical College of Toledo, Ohio, writing for the *Journal of the American Veterinary Medical Association,* says they do. In his article, in the section on helping veterinarians to identify pit bulls, he writes, "The distinguishing characteristics of fighting dogs include short ear crops [and] wide leather or web collars with heavy rings may be worn." Now, that's science!

Pit bull owners buy wide leather collars because they don't want a narrow one hurting the dog's neck, and also because the wide leather collars are quite expensive and they want to do right by their dogs, like a Poodle owner buying a diamond collar or a jeweler's-link gold and silver collar for Fifi.

In the case of both pit bull and Poodle owners, this affectionate foolishness leads to trouble. Jeweler's link is an irritant to Fifi's skin, and since the smaller Poodles are quite often irritable enough without jewelry, it can increase Fifi's snappishness. For pit bulls, the trouble comes about because it is so much easier to pull on a wide leather collar, and remember that weight pulling is a game, a bliss, a delight, for the bull breeds. The resulting slathering from the dog has about as much to do with viciousness as the wide-open, bright red mouth of a Golden Retriever hot on the trail of a Frisbee.

Bandit liked to pull. So it was Mr. Johnson who would take Bandit for walks and often feed him for Mr. Redd. As a result, Mr. Johnson and Bandit were buddies, pals.

The houses at 189 and 191 Henry Street are separated by a walkway that is possibly six or eight feet wide. On July 9, 1987, Mr. Johnson had a quarrel with his girlfriend, who went home to or called Mama, whose name is Effie Powell. Effie Powell came over storming, with her husband. It came about that Effie Powell hit Mr. Johnson with a broom, which Mr. Johnson seems to have deserved. Mr. Johnson left 191 Henry Street by way of the walkway that separates it from 189, followed by Effie Powell wielding the broom.

Bandit brought the assault on his friend to a screeching halt, with his teeth.

This is neither a domestic farce nor a prelude to a Fido Award from Gaines, as it would be if the assailant and assailee were of different genders and races, and if Bandit were agreeably shaggy. Bandit was impounded, and Mr. Redd was ordered to build a six-foot chain link fence and a doghouse if he wanted his dog to live.

Half a year or more later, I told this part of the story to Ben, who was visiting the kennel. Shortly afterward, Ben's friend Billy came in to visit, and asked, as everyone asked, about the notorious dog.

"What did he do?"

"Oh, some guy was beating up on his girlfriend, and Bandit bit him," says Ben.

"Well, no wonder!" says Billy. "What do you expect?"

Other versions of this story sprang to people's minds. Bandit was defending a child. He was defending a white man against a black man. Most frequently he was defending a woman. It was hard for people to hear the story, respond as to a story about Rin Tin Tin—for they did, they kept seeing scenes from Rin Tin

Tin, when I told it at least—and keep in mind that it was a *woman* that Bandit bit. A *mother*. To be fair, I should say that most dog-bite victims are male, also that most assaulters are male. But people didn't hear me when I said Bandit had bitten in defense of a man, and especially not in defense of a black man. Righteousness and violence on behalf of a black male just don't go together in people's minds, so they would decide that Bandit was righteous and then they would make it a woman Bandit was defending, or a white man. Or at least make the bite victim turn out to be male.

About Bandit's motives: We know that Effie Powell was committing assault. But we also know that she was generally raising hell *on Bandit's property,* and that may have been more important than the assault. One thing I do know: Bandit had a reasonable motive.

Under a great many laws about dog bites, the dog is not to be held to be vicious, and the owner is not to be held liable, if the person bitten was teasing or provoking the dog or was committing a trespass or other tort at the time of the bite. And Mrs. Powell seems to have been committing two torts—trespass and assault. This is not to say that Bandit understands the Fifth and Fourteenth Amendments to the Constitution, only that there is here and there some overlap between a dog's map of the world and human systems that grant rights to the dog's owner.

It is difficult to know what, if anything, the laws that give a dog a right to bite express, but they often reflect an awareness of what dogs are actually like, and were probably lobbied for by people who knew something about dogs. They are property laws—laws, that is, that concern the dog's status as property—and are by and large analogous to laws about damage caused by one's inanimate property.

When dogs are given the right to self-defense and defense of their property, it is by virtue of their status as themselves property of people, just as some of our rights to defend our families are given by virtue of that's being *my* daughter the drunk was getting too friendly with. Is this an accidental benefit of a corrupt and exploitative relationship to animals? Or are the angles

of possession a clue to the angles of rights? Bandit is alive because Mr. Redd vigorously defended his property rights in the
dog.

But back to the action. Someone called the police, and Bandit
was impounded. The local dog warden said Mr. Redd could
have his dog back if he would surround his property with a
six-foot-high chain link fence and build a doghouse. I am not
sure how the doghouse was supposed to protect the public, but
there it was.

I mentioned that in many states the dog-bite statutes do not
count a dog vicious if the person bitten was committing a crime,
but Connecticut is different. The local dog wardens in Connecticut have the power to tell you to do whatever the hell they feel
like telling you to do. The statute in Connecticut about biting
dogs does say a few things about the circumstances of a bite, but
its language does not even define "biting dog," with the result
that a dog who so much as barks or looks at someone cross-eyed
can be deemed a biting dog. What the statute says is:

> SECTION 22-358, SUBSECTION (b):
> Quarantine of biting dogs. . . . the commissioner, the chief
> canine control officer, any canine control officer, any warden
> or regional canine control officer may make any order con-
> cerning the restraint or disposal of any biting dog as he deems
> necessary.

The rhythm here is distinctly unconstitutional to my ears. I
don't want to be an alarmist, but this statute gives a dog warden
more power than the cops have. And there are other statutes
that make a point of not requiring prospective dog wardens to
have any training. There is a little blue book the state puts out
that explains that dog wardens do not have to be trained in order
to be members of the police department. The confusions here
are enormous. Are dog wardens cops? If they are, why aren't
they answerable the way cops are? And why don't they have to
be trained if they are going to bear arms and have police powers?

Even if they had any training, when you appeal something a
humane cop has ordered in this state and others, you appeal it to

his boss, or to his boss's boss, instead of to a court, which is about like appealing to the precinct captain. You have to find something dramatic and compelling and unprecedented that will help or threaten some senator's or governor's campaign in order to go further than the chief humane cop.

And you have to have a lawyer who is so interested in justice and so intelligent that he or she can see that when someone takes your dog away from you your civil liberties are in question.

Mr. Redd built the fence. It goes around the whole of his front property, and it cost him four thousand dollars. Mr. Redd is a poor man. I assume the fence was duly inspected. While it was going up, Bandit did time in the pound. At least six weeks.

When Bandit returned, everything had changed. In particular, he was no longer as responsible for himself on the porch as he had been for the past four or five years. He always, for example, left the porch to go into the yard and pee, but now he peed on the porch. And Mr. Redd took a switch to him for this. Switched him quite a bit, apparently. And Bandit bit Mr. Redd in the arm.

Not without warning, for as Mr. Redd said to me, "He notified me, grrrr, grrrr, but I just kept on whupping him and they took him away, and that's why I fight so hard for him, because if they kill him it's my fault."

I believe Mr. Redd when he says Bandit never wet on the porch before, because this dog has a powerful sense, though not, obviously, an undamageable sense, of the proprieties. After six weeks in the pound, he peed on Mr. Redd's porch. After two weeks of training, he would wait to pee until I arrived at the kennel in the morning, in order to avoid fouling even the outside part of his living quarters.

Bandit came home in a sorry state, according to Mr. Redd and Lily Mae McClean and other residents of Henry Street with whom I talked. Lily Mae shook her head and said, "It's a shame, what they did to that dog, a shame." She was referring both to his behavior when he returned from the pound and to some wounds he had on his face and flank. These wounds left scars

that somewhat ruin his expression, giving him a sneering appearance if the light is right. There was speculation that in the
pound someone had decided to match Bandit against another
dog and see how that would go. I asked my vet if he thought the
scars were from fighting, and he said they looked more like
scars from a beating, though he said that off the record, and not
to accuse anyone of anything.

Lily Mae and Mr. Redd said that the wounds came about
during Bandit's first stay in the pound. The state in some person
or another has denied that the wounds got there when Bandit
was in the pound. In the TV footage of the second arrest of
Bandit, after he bit Mr. Redd, I cannot see, after many view-
ings, any fresh wounds or blood, which suggests that the
wounds were not the result of Mr. Redd's "whupping" him. I
have no idea how the wounds got there, nor for that matter how
there came to be a small hard lump in the skin of Bandit's neck,
which one veterinarian said might be a BB. On the one hand,
Mr. Redd had confessed to beating Bandit, but on the other
hand I saw the coverage of Bandit's second incarceration, and
. . . but I am getting ahead of myself.

Bandit wet on the porch, was whupped, and bit Mr. Redd.
At this point a neighbor called the police, Bandit was seized
again, and a disposal order was issued.

Mark Vandenberg came to know about this case and set himself to doing some matchmaking between me and Robert Bello
so that I could be, God help me, an expert witness. As I have
said, Robert Bello was taking the case *pro bono,* and it was rather
noble of him, I thought, because he not only doesn't like dogs
very much but was in fact scared of Bandit.

At the time Bello and I first spoke, Mr. Redd was appealing
the disposal order the local dog warden had issued. In Connecticut, Canine Control is a statewide organization that is part of
the Department of Agriculture, so that meant an administrative
hearing, which meant a kangaroo court. As I have said and must
repeat: Appealing a dog warden's destruction order is a little bit
like appealing on the grounds of wrongful arrest to the precinct

captain, because even though the dog warden can seize and destroy property there is no procedural machinery in place that gives the right of appeal outside Agriculture. A familiar and dreary kind of bureaucratic malaise—but don't get the idea that bureaucrats are faceless and merely frustrating and boring.

Kangaroo court or no, one wants to do one's own part properly, so I drove to the Stamford pound to take a look at Bandit. I brought with me a leash and collar. I also brought a nose thumper, I am ashamed to admit. The nose thumper was to have handy in case he attacked me.

This is evidence of how powerful *words* are. I knew, knew more surely than I know my proper name, that if the dog would let me take him out of the cage at all, he wouldn't be a problem to handle. Of course, I didn't then know that he was not a pit bull, but even if I had known, I had no reason to be afraid of him. His rap sheet told me that he was a dog who already knew what life was all about, a reasonable animal.

The only thing I had to worry about was whether or not he had been agitated in his cage. That was possible, but if it created a problem, the problem would be that he wouldn't let me in the cage to get the leash and collar on anyhow, and the nose thumper wouldn't do me any good without some backup, and the only backup I was willing to rely on was that of my training teacher and friend Dick Koehler, whose name is a household word in dog circles. Alas, Dick was in California, three thousand miles away, and blissfully unaware of his coming participation in the case.

But I hadn't trained any dogs or horses for a while at that point, except a little desultory work with my own dogs. I had been teaching in a university, spending all my time around people who believe what they read, mostly, and I suffer from the usual brain damage of my species, some problem in the wiring that causes me to be distracted from what I know by words. Words such as "vicious" and "uncontrollably aggressive" and so on.

It was a chilly day in late November, the kind of damp chill that Connecticut specializes in. My husband, Robert Tragesser, came with me, and we parked the Jeep in the parking lot by the pound. In that little corner of Stamford there must be a permanent low-pressure system, because it is always dank. Or so I figured, sitting in the car, trying to decide whether or not to take my weapon in with me, wondering what sort of heroine I was going to turn out to be. Not that I was thinking in literary terms just then. I wasn't thinking in *terms* at all; most of my knowledge of dogs is visual and kinesthetic, so what I was doing was cherishing my forearms and upper thighs and imagining this dog leaping at me, unstoppable, uncontrollably aggressive, and I hadn't handled a dangerous animal in years. And there had been a lot of doughnuts and cigarettes and Scotch and soft hours with the keyboard and in the library and even some witty conversation under the bridge since the last time I walked into a situation, all of that stuff wearing away the support system for the bridge. A suspension bridge.

"That's a good dog!" I had said to Bello, but I am as much a person of words as anyone else, even though I do not read newspapers or watch television. And the possibility that Bandit had been teased, agitated, was real.

I left my truncheon in the car, on the grounds that if I was wrong about dogs in general and about this dog in particular, it wasn't going to help in any case, although I gave a split second's thought to leaving the window down and the car unlocked, or to asking my husband to carry the truncheon, but that didn't seem right, since in order for Robert to be handy with the truncheon he had to be handy with his own body, too, and it wasn't his fault his wife hared around the countryside looking for vicious dogs to mess with instead of . . .

Instead of whatever it is wives do. So I left the truncheon in the car, and Robert and I walked into the front office, and there I met the dog warden, who seemed, I was interested to note, even more nervous than I was. Present also were Mr. Redd, Robert Bello, and a young man who was Mr. Redd's grandson, I believe.

Said howdy to the dog warden through recalcitrant lips. Dog warden jerks a thumb toward the door to the kennels and says,

"He's back there. Last cage on the left." So I pulled out of my pocket one of the leashes I had brought with me.

Here the dog warden got a little turbulent. He said I couldn't actually take Bandit out of his *cage,* and I demanded to know how I was supposed to evaluate him through chain link, and the dog warden said I had to sign a release, which I did. I don't know whether or not it made him feel any better, but it made me feel better, because it was such a defensive gesture on his part that a certain feeling rose in my breast, an at the time hard-to-identify feeling, a primitive, joyous feeling of contempt for the enemy. He wasn't playing it straight, wasn't in a position to play it straight, for whatever reason, and I was, and there is nothing like knowing that you can play it straight to cheer you up.

I *needed* cheering up at that point. I was the only person I knew, including Bandit's lawyer, who was even *trying* to say he was a rational dog, and I hadn't met him yet, and it was kind of tricky finding ways to continue to believe myself when it would be my own body—a poor thing, but mine own, you understand—that would be the proving ground.

I have written down "a joyous feeling of contempt," and I have written truly. My inward lip curled in a snarl of disdain for the dog warden. If there had been words to my loathing, I suppose they might have been something like "Poor little shivery-chinned bully. Despicable little pseudo-macho twerp."

Thus I bolstered my expertise and humane authority.

Later, and not very much later, I came to have more merciful feelings about Warden Winski, but that was later, and I am telling you now about the shining courage I took with me as I walked down the kennel aisle with my escorts, proposing to demonstrate that everyone was wrong about the most vicious dog east of the Rockies. I was afraid.

Like everyone else I was afraid, not of Bandit himself, but of a dog who had been constructed from paper and emotions and colored lights and costumes—the brand-new, neat brown costumes of dog wardens and Canine Control officers, for example—and when a human being is afraid of something made out of shabby words and papier-mâché, she is at her worst.

Contempt for the dog warden is not one of the cozier or more admirable feelings in my emotional repertoire, but it felt better than being afraid of a dog, and it was enough to make me walk down the aisle toward the cage. At least, it helped. I beat back the ferocious false dog of the ferocious false God with ferocious contempt, you might say, like St. Anthony managing to banish the demons by refusing to believe in them, only my work isn't as clean as St. Anthony's. My knowledge helped, for sometimes knowledge helps, like a silver cross against the devil. But knowledge isn't always enough, and the less reputable activities of the mind and heart, such as building one's contempt as one builds a fire against whatever shadows sicken one, have their place in adventures.

I *told* you that dog rescue is a nasty, corrupt business—and this is only the beginning.

TWO ···

Biting the Hand
That Feeds Him

*But, ah! presently comes a day, or it is only a half-hour, with
its angel-whispering—which discomfits the conclusions of
nations and of years!*

—EMERSON, "*Experience*"

I WAS ESCORTED down the aisle by the dog warden,
a dog trainer friend of his, and an assistant dog warden. It is not
my imagination that there was a certain amount of gender feeling in their swagger—at least, so Robert said later, and he would
know. The dog trainer's name was Tom Ponelli, and he and I
were at the head of the little procession that came to a halt by
Bandit's cage.

The cage was decorated with a vast red sign the details of
which I do not remember, except that it had the red word
"Dangerous" on it, also the exclamation "Pit Bull!"

I said nothing then, but this phrase calls out for scholarly
exegesis. The term that was on that sign, and related terms, are
used confusingly even when they are used correctly, so I think
I had better say something about terminology. You may skip
this section if you like.

First: In 1898, the United Kennel Club began registering a
breed of dog that was variously known in this country as bulldog, bull terrier, bull-and-terrier, American bull terrier, pit bull,
pit bull terrier, Yankee terrier, and Rebel terrier. There were
then as there are now relatives of this breed, to confuse matters.

As near as I can make out, no one was in any particular
agreement about what official name to give these dogs, and the
situation was complicated then as it is now by a reluctance on
the part of some to signal certain facts about the breed's history
too clearly to the world at large.

It was a fighting breed, also used to hunt boar, but used as the ultimate "pal" breed too. The idea that strength and loyalty and fighting ability and friendship are part of a single constellation of virtues has been variously symbolized, as by Teddy Roosevelt having a pit bull when he was in the White House, and by a famous poster of 1914 that represented the major participants in World War I in terms of national breeds. Germany is a Dachshund, France a French Bulldog, Russia a Borzoi, England an English Bulldog. America is a Pit Bull Terrier, wearing Old Glory around his neck.

In any case, the United Kennel Club, probably under the impression that it was clearing up confusion and behaving diplomatically, especially as regarded disagreements from opposite sides of the Mason-Dixon Line about whether to call the dogs Yankee terriers or Rebel terriers, decided in its infinite wisdom on the name "American (Pit) Bull Terrier." The "Pit" in parentheses may have been inserted in order to distinguish between true fighting dogs and other kinds of bull or bull-and-terrier breeds. The UKC standard for the APBT includes a scale of points to guide judges in the breed ring—so many for coat, tail set, head shape, and so on. The first item on that scale, and the one most heavily weighted, is "personality and obedience."

For quite a while, the important distinction to make in this country was between the American Pit Bull Terrier and the English breed called the Bull Terrier. In literature of the first part of this century the APBT is often called the American bull terrier, and the breed the American Kennel Club now calls the Bull Terrier is called the English bull terrier. ("None of your English bulls," says a character in Thurber's story about his beloved pit bull Rex.)

Things got more confusing in the thirties, when the American Kennel Club decided to recognize the pit bull as a breed but didn't want to call it a pit bull. The pit bull was becoming genteel, as the (old style) bulldog had in England in the middle of the nineteenth century. So to erase the taint of the dog's fighting origins, or so I read it, the AKC in turn in its infinite wisdom called pit bulls Staffordshire Terriers. Staffordshire is in

England, and this is an American dog, but it sounds better to say "Staffordshire," so people did.

Shortly thereafter, the AKC decided to recognize yet another bull breed, a genuinely English breed this time, called the Staffordshire Bull Terrier. This dog is generally somewhat smaller and squatter than the pit bull, though it is considerably more athletic than the (dog now called by the AKC the) bulldog. There being insufficient confusion created by this move, they then renamed the Staffordshire Terrier the American Staffordshire Terrier. The AmStaff breed club still calls itself the STCA, or Staffordshire Terrier Club of America.

So now we are looking at two official registries for the pit bull, and three official breed names by 1940: the UKC's American Pit Bull Terrier, and the AKC's Staffordshire Terrier and American Staffordshire Terrier. Meanwhile, there was a third registry, the American Dog Breeders Association. As near as I can make out, the ADBA came into existence in response to what some perceived as the UKC's wimping out on the subject of dogfighting sometime in the first or second decade of this century. The ADBA registers the American Pit Bull Terrier, as does the UKC. An AKC AmStaff can be cross-registered as a UKC APBT, and either can be registered as an APBT with the ADBA, but there are in fact differences that have developed in the types or lines of dogs associated with the different registries.

Adherents of the three registries argue lengthily and learnedly about whether these are the same breeds or not, and there are good arguments on all sides. The fact that many dogs are triple-registered irritates some of the godlier souls of dogdom no end. ADBA hard-liners say that UKC and AKC dogs have no right to claim kinship with true pit bulls, since the dogs have not been game-tested. ("Gameness"—a quality I will discuss at some length later—is itself endlessly controversial.) UKC and AKC hard-liners say that fifty or seventy years of separate lines means that all the lowlife nastiness has been bred out of their dogs. Before the dogcatchers started rounding up and outlawing so many dogs, however, many people were proud to say that the AmStaff and the APBT were the same breed.

There is said to be a kennel of pit bulls in Massachusetts. The story goes that the perimeters of the kennel are patrolled by three American Bulldogs because pit bulls are just not a guard breed: "They're so friendly anyone can come in and steal one."

But competing claims also surround the term "bulldog." Deep pit bull fanciers will often call their dogs "bulldogs." This means something like "true bulldog" or "real bulldog," and is a bit of polemic against the idea that the dog registered by the AKC as the Bulldog is a real bulldog. Also, before all the bureaucratization of breed names, your true dog man would be likely to use an expression such as "bull pup" to mean roughly the dog now known as the pit bull. Mark Twain, borrowing from contemporary tradition, calls the pit bull named Andrew Jackson in "The Celebrated Jumping Frog of Calaveras County" a "bull pup."

Hence my true colors show when I use an expression such as "the dog registered by the AKC as the Bulldog"; as far as the AKC is concerned, dogs that look like Handsome Dan, the mascot of the Yale football team, are instances of the Bulldog. As far as pit bull fanciers are concerned, the (true) bulldog is the American Pit Bull Terrier.

Not so far as Bulldog fanciers are concerned. Phyllis Helmar, who has been in (AKC) Bulldogs for forty years, insists that there is no more loyal or loving breed. It is certainly difficult to find a more affable, even Pickwickian dog, but her list of the breed's beauties might sound to someone else like a list of faults—she values them for the very expense and trouble involved in keeping them, because, as she puts it enthusiastically, "With Bulldogs you have to go that extra five yards." With any fancier it is hard to tell at a given moment whether they are listing a breed's advantages or disadvantages; many people have thought that when I was praising my own favorite breed (which happens to be the Airedale Terrier) I was committing slander.

Aware of the intricacies of breed questions, people who know what they are talking about reserve the term "pit bull" to mean a dog registered with either the UKC or the ADBA as an American Pit Bull Terrier. If they use the term, as I do, to refer to an AmStaff, they will quickly add, "An AKC dog."

Bandit is, oh, most assuredly, *not* an American Kennel Club dog. Nor is he a UKC dog. Neither the AKC nor the UKC would go near him with a ten-foot pole. The American Dog Breeders Association would and did, however. At one point I suggested to Kate Greenwood, who is president of the ADBA, that although Bandit is not a pit bull, he took the rap for the pit bulls, and could he be an honorary pit bull? She agreed most graciously and sent a form for single registration for Bandit. So now he has a full name, a registered name, and his registered name is "Definitely Bandit."

Kate Greenwood's action here, it must be noted, was unusually civilized, complexly gracious, because she not only accepted a dog of unknown background into a noble family, like accepting a bar sinister cousin, but she also trusted me not to breed him and then claim that his pups were purebred pit bulls. Bandit's status as an honorary pit bull is like someone's status as an honorary Ph.D.

So there was that vast red sign that said, with stunning bureaucratic ignorance, "Pit bull!" There was nothing civilized or complexly gracious about this designation. In the cage behind the sign was—well, not a pit bull, not what the sign said. Dog Warden Winski must be given credit for having said then and there that he thought Bandit might be an American Bulldog. At that point I wasn't sure what Bandit's breed was, only that he was not a pit bull. He has a distinctively "fiddle front," meaning that the legs bow out when the dog is seen head-on, and appear to bow in again toward the pasterns. This is not a conformation you see often on pit bulls. He has a slightly retroussé nose—the classic old bulldog nose, which I have seen hints of once in a while, but not so well defined, in a few pit bulls, and which is the trait, exaggerated beyond reason, that gives the modern English Bulldog so many breathing problems, though no problems of mind or heart. His back seems slightly long to someone whose eye is accustomed to classic terrier or pit bull builds, and somewhat odd in shape. Until I developed an understanding of his structure, or at least got used to it, it made him look like he was trying to be a mastiff and then suddenly decided, toward the loins, to be a hound, but not in time to pull it off.

Warden Winski's suggestion that he might be an American Bulldog sounded to me like one reasonable guess, but I knew that breed mostly from photographs—at the time a variety of bull breeds was starting to gain popularity, and you can't keep up with everything, a fact I wish the authorities would acknowledge about themselves. I contemplated other possibilities, all of which I duly noted in my report. He has more in the way of jowls than is usual in a pit bull. The jowliness makes him slightly subject to infections around the mouth, where the wrinkles are. I don't mean he is in any way deformed, in and out of the vet's every week like some breeds are.

Also, pit bulls are pit bull *terriers*. Even in the most bulldoggy individuals, there will be something—a sprightliness in the stance, some suggestion of the possibilities of tap dancing and vaudeville, some impish gleam in the eye—to suggest the terrier. It is a subtle thing, but it is often obvious when you put a pit bull next to a bulldog of any variety—you can see, faintly, the blackface, and hear the tambourines.

There was no terrier in this guy. He had stalwartness written all over him, but it was not terrier stalwartness; there were no angles of tap dance to it, at least no tap dance I was familiar with. He had a song, but I was not to learn that day what his song was. It was, among other things, the song of the draft animal, the pulling champion, not a song I had heard before. Once I heard it, once I realized that a dog is capable of living to pull the way some horses live to jump, or some Border Collies live to work sheep, I would come to reflect bitterly on the RSPCA's success in outlawing the use of cart dogs. Pulling is not the only subject of the verses of this song; there are other glories, which I will get to later.

He was beautiful. I did not see that day how his parts added up, since they did not add up to any of the breeds I know well, but I saw that they added up. I had Hearne's Law to guide me, of course, the law that said that everything I knew about the case indicated that this should turn out to be a good dog, but I really didn't expect him to be that beautiful, nor to give out such a powerful cogency.

His behavior in his cage was not such as to suggest cogency to the average onlooker, I am aware, and I am not claiming that my first sight of him wiped away my worries like the sun vanquishing clouds. It was still a cloudy day, and it was still a dank, clanky, unfriendly place, and I was being Hovered Over by Ponelli and Winski.

Bandit was stiff and a little growly about the various presences, especially the dog warden. When Winski approached to within two or three feet, Bandit threatened. When Winski backed off, Bandit calmed down. If Winski came up and stood quite close to the cage and refused to retreat, Bandit gave up trying to drive him away and ran to the back of the run, lowering his head and circling frantically, as if unable to find a place to hide. I would like to report that at this point my heart went out to Bandit, but it didn't. If you really want to help a dog, then letting your heart slip its lead is a luxury you cannot afford. You keep your heart close to yourself, just as in a dangerous situation you keep your dog close, to cooperate with your mind, figuring out what to do.

I asked both Winski and Ponelli to approach and back off several times, curious to know if it was just Winski. It was. Bandit growled perfunctorily at Ponelli, but it was Winski he had strong opinions about.

Someone—Ponelli, I believe—had the bright idea of putting his shoe up against Bandit's cage, which elicited barking and growling. That intrigued me, and I arranged for several shoes, including my own, to be placed against the cage wire. As far as persons approaching went, it was only Winski he worried about, but Bandit didn't want *anyone* sticking their feet out. You can read this more than one way. It is possible that Bandit had a kind of anti-foot fetish because his mother did strange things to him with shoes, and it is also possible, as I would later testify, that someone had, more than once, kicked his cage, agitated him. There is no proof of this.

"Agitation" is a term for a collection of techniques designed to elicit aggression from a dog. It can be done intelligently or stupidly. Most so-called attack dog training done by amateurs consists of agitation and not much else. It is, if you like, systematic, or not so systematic, teasing of a dog. A skilled agitator can get some dogs worked up without doing anything overtly hostile, just by going into "creep" mode—doing a little method acting, as it were. You invest your body and mind with sensations of cunning and fear and illegitimacy and approach the dog, and a "sharp" dog, with high aggression, will alert and in some cases attack.

A fair number of people, usually relatively young males, become interested in agitation for its own sake, and I have known of shelter personnel amusing themselves by agitating dogs.

I *hate* that. It is dumb, infantile, boringly mischievous. Mind you, I respect good police and protection dog training highly; in protection work you find some scuzzballs, but you also find people with the genius of integrity. Agitating a dog for the sheer hell of it, or in order to besmirch the dog's character—oh, I think of all dark and grimy subversions of what is meaningful. Graffiti on Titian's *Venus,* lies about history, the McCarthy era, rape instead of true sexual feeling, Mark Twain's books maligned, children encouraged to turn in their parents, parents encouraged to turn in their children. When you agitate a dog without also committing yourself to the dog by teaching him the rest of the work that makes the agitation something besides an occasion for rage, you are fucking around with Rin Tin Tin. I think of bureaucratic lies, not that I believe that bureaucrats can help themselves; deception is as natural to a bureaucrat as . . .

As stalwartness is to Bandit, but more of that later.

I did not particularly want to believe that anyone in an official position had been agitating Bandit, because things were already scuzzy enough, and this was only a few days into my involvement in the case. I didn't even want to *suspect* that anyone had been illicitly agitating Bandit, not only because it would be hard to prove, but because it meant that my job—recall that at this point in the story I haven't actually had any contact with Bandit without chain link between us—was that much dicier.

I respect and am not afraid of a police dog who knows his job, however serious a man-stopper he is, because if he knows his job his judgment has been developed. In the Times Square subway station and in Grand Central, there are frequently police dogs, and they cause me to turn nary a hair, not because they are harmless—they are *not* harmless—but because the ones I have seen plainly know their business, and their handlers aren't so bad either. (I do not mean that there are never what K-9 cops call "bad bites." I do not mean that the world is a fairy tale with a happy ending.)

A dog who has been agitated without any other kind of training is a different matter. Agitating a dog without also training the dog—that is cruelty to animals. As I said, I didn't want to suspect this, but Bandit was behaving in a way that cried for interpretation. He was very upset when Warden Winski approached his cage, and I was studying this, and by way of studying it I asked Winski to approach and back up several times.

And entertained dark suspicions in spite of myself, though suspicions is all they were.

Winski wasn't aware of my suspicions just then, I don't think. At least, that is the conclusion I drew from his willing cooperation.

Please note that another possible interpretation of Winski's willingness to cooperate with me is that he was innocent of agitating Bandit. Anyone who tells you differently should go to church more often. Anyone who claims that they can tell for sure from an animal's behavior that the animal has been abused or agitated is lying, or at least misguided, whether or not they have sufficient moral and intellectual development to know a lie when they tell one, or when one takes over a relationship.

Bandit's aggression in the cage is also subject to more than one interpretation. There is the barrier syndrome, for one thing—a lot of dogs who are perfectly agreeable otherwise will bark and menace from behind a fence or wall. But Bandit seemed to have a particular thing about the dog warden, and to be extremely distressed when Winski stood by his cage without moving. Ran to the back of the cage, circled, tried to hide. Also, as I have said, responded with menace to a foot—anyone's foot—placed near the wire.

Here are the possible interpretations:

1. Someone had teased the dog, possibly with a stick, possibly with a pressure hose. Agitated him, that is.

2. The dog simply was going stir-crazy from confinement. "Kennel stress syndrome" if you want a fancy name for it. Winski, being the person who had authority at the pound, would naturally be an object of aggravation even if he hadn't actively teased the dog.

3. Before Bandit was impounded he had had some agitation of some sort. Nothing very systematic, but enough to make him think that he had to guard his run for his own safety. Remember that Henry Street is a high-crime neighborhood, and living in a high-crime neighborhood is natural agitation— natural attack training, if you like, and if you keep in mind that I here use the term "training" somewhat ironically.

Any or all of the above are possible explanations for Bandit's responses to Winski. I do not know whether or not Dog Warden Winski is guilty of anything but irritating me with his macho swagger, which is not a crime in this society. Also, that day I sensed in him a real dog man struggling to emerge from the postures of authority. It is condescending of me to say so here, but it is true, and it is important to recall that the official lines of action in a court case are no map of the integrity of the various participants.

Winski is a Schutzhund enthusiast, I learned that day. "Schutzhund" means, literally, "protection dog" and is the name of a sport in which tracking, agility and obstacle work, protection or "bite" work, and obedience are tested—the skills needed by an all-around police dog. Winski has German Shepherds and spends time training his dogs in addition to working full-time. And he is young, too young to know much about the tangles that result when some true knowledge of dogs gets mixed up with something some state wants to do, whether the motives in question are pure or not.

If he has German Shepherds and works them in Schutzhund, he has to know something of how deep the heart of a dog can be. Another thing that follows from his enthusiasm for his Shepherds is this: The landscape of virtues that is a good German Shepherd is different from the landscape of virtues that is a good American Bulldog, and he might not have had the background to respond to Bandit's qualities. That is, he might not have known how to read him, and not knowing how to read a dog makes you afraid of a dog, and that can lead you to fail to do the things that make the relationship with the dog work out. He did say at one point that giving Bandit back to Mr. Redd would be like putting a loaded gun in someone's hands, which means his speech habits, like those of many Americans, are mechanomorphic. That is, he here attributes the traits of a machine, in particular a machine's unquestioning responsiveness and obedience, to an animal. To Bandit, who is not, unlike a gun, unquestioningly obedient.

Look. *I* was afraid of Bandit at that point, and I had Hearne's Law to sustain and comfort me. I have no access to Winski's thoughts and intentions, the shapes of his fears or his courage.

As I have said, Winski went along with whatever I asked him to do at first. Ponelli, however, seems to have suspected that maybe it wasn't just the dog I was evaluating, that I was curious about wrongdoings of the human sort, and he interrupted this stage of my investigations with a move that would have been admirable if it hadn't been too abrupt for grace. He brought my explorations of Bandit's responses to the employees of the state of Connecticut to a halt by hunkering down and holding out his hand, a gesture that elicited tail wagging and smiles from the monster.

"Well," he said with brisk authority, "the dog's okay. But we have some other problems."

Then he turned to me and repeated that the dog was fine. I was too busy looking at Bandit to look at him and Winski and see if any glances were being exchanged. I don't even know if he stopped my experiment deliberately or not, and if he did, whether he meant to help Winski by preventing any more speculation on my part, or to help me by suggesting I didn't have to take the powerful dog out. Or he may just have been expressing his own crisp, authoritative nature. These are all speculations of mine, and are presented only to give the reader an idea of my state of mind, which at that moment was distinctly uneasy, irritable, and intimidated. I have noticed with canines that a pushy, swaggering male will sometimes cause a female temporarily to back off and sigh, or even to display a little submission. Nonetheless, the males don't intimidate the females all that much, not the way human females are intimidated.

So, in the interests of fairness: I was intimidated, by the posturing of both Ponelli and Winski. And ashamed, because of not knowing any techniques for putting them in their places. I am easily bested in almost any battle of wits unless I am cornered, so am not of the stuff of nobility.

Because I didn't know whether Bandit would try to fence-fight, I didn't want to take him out with the other dogs lunging at the wire, so I asked to go around to the outside run. In this pound's setup, each dog's run is divided into two, with guillotine doors between. All the dogs were in the inside runs, so if we let Bandit into the outside run before taking him out, we would not have to deal with the distracting presence of the other dogs. Since dog aggression is not related to people aggression, and since my first concern was to determine whether Bandit was, as some say, "people-mean," and not whether he was scrappy with other dogs, there was no point in working him with all the other dogs jumping and barking their heads off.

Both Winski and Ponelli must be given this much credit: They didn't jeer and say, "So you're afraid of him!" They responded to my request like grown-up dog people, didn't hoot and mock. That may not sound so amazing to you if you do not know how stupid and malicious people can get in these situations, but I do, and I noted the absence of hooting at that point with a touch of gratitude.

I went into Bandit's run to put the leash on him. He was already, to my surprise, wearing a good-quality training collar of the sort I import from a training supply house in Greensburg, Illinois. I do not know where that collar, which I still have and use, came from; it is not the sort you find in pet stores and supermarkets. Mr. Redd kept testifying that he had paid some-one to train Bandit, so the collar may have come from that trainer, or from Winski, or from someone else at the pound who knew something about training. Probably the trainer Mr. Redd hired—in the video taken by Channel 12 the day Bandit was impounded, he is wearing a chain collar, of what quality I can-not tell. It wouldn't have been Mr. Redd himself who found and purchased the collar, because no humane society, for all the pious education they inflict on small children, ever tells anyone how to find a decent leash and collar, even when they know, and no one unfamiliar with training would have known what collar to get or where to order it, much less what to do with it. (This is not all I have to say about humane education.)

The collar has two rings at each end, and in addition a small ring in the middle that looks as though it once had a license or identification tag hanging from it. I haven't any idea where the tags might have gotten to; that, like the scars on Bandit's face and flank and the question about his behavior toward Winski, is just one of the uncertainties one must learn to live with.

I put the leash on Bandit.

And got injured. I was rattled, and Bandit was rambunctious, and I grabbed the collar to put the leash on very clumsily, unprofessionally, so my thumb was caught between two bits of collar, and Bandit—who pulled in those days like a steam engine—lunged against the collar. Squashed my thumb a bit out of shape, my right thumb, which is still a little wide. This was profoundly embarrassing, getting injured putting the leash on, because a pro isn't supposed to screw up like that, and I have kept mum about it until now and am revealing it for the sake of philosophy.

Once out of the run, Bandit was eager to *move*. He hadn't been out in months, and the effect of the recess bell on a third-grade class is nothing to the effect on him of the open cage door. He charged. And he is quite powerful, and I am not, and he is quite coordinated, and I am not, so I got dragged around quite a bit in my efforts to get him to walk my way instead of drag-ging me his way.

Somehow or another—the details of this struggle (in which

there was no suggestion of teeth, mind you, just world-class pulling) blur mercifully—I got him into a small grassy exercise area, accompanied of course by the troops.

About the magic of dog training. I had Bandit walking on a loose lead within five minutes. He wasn't *committed* to walking on a loose lead and no longer pulling me off my feet—you don't eliminate a lifetime of policy in five minutes—but he was no longer pulling. I accomplished this by longeing him.

That means: When he headed north, I dropped some slack in the lead and headed south. He would hit the end of the line and travel my way for a bit, and would then take off heading south, going by me. Now that he was heading south, I headed north, dropping the slack so that my momentum compensated for my relative frailty. Pretty quickly he realized that that was just the way I was going to be about it, and he adjusted his behavior accordingly.

I appealed to his conscious mind. So he did the reasonable thing and quit pulling.

He was alone in his reasonableness, or so it seemed to me. Ponelli started going through maneuvers of the sort that are meant to elicit a charge and/or a bite in the sport of Schutzhund. Bandit has a very low defense drive, and so regarded this odd behavior with little interest. Did not lunge for him. I nearly did, but Bandit didn't.

You see, when you have a monster dog around, all the Dog Trainers have to assemble and see whether or not the monster has read the same book they read about attack training.

So there were the macho dog trainers, Winski and Ponelli, who stood back when the plump middle-aged lady opened the cage to get the monster out. Now that the monster had spent around fifteen minutes not-biting the middle-aged lady, they got bolder. Heartened, Ponelli grabbed the leash from me, shortened it up in his left hand, and began yanking on Bandit, saying, "Heel, heel, heel," and "Sit, sit, sit." Bandit promptly reverted to his steam-engine imitation, and Ponelli's arm got tired, so I had the dog back pretty soon. Ponelli announced with great authority, "He hasn't had any training," I suppose because Bandit wouldn't mind him.

When Ponelli started his "agitation" moves as part of what I supposed was deemed some sort of evaluative activity, I thought, "If this dog goes for him, I don't know if I can hold him." Later I wondered whether the image I had, of Bandit lunging for Ponelli and the leash being ripped from my hands, may have been a case of wish fulfillment, since by then I knew that Ponelli's antics weren't likely to impress Bandit, and that my original estimate of him, based on the police report, was confirmed in spades. This dog cares for nothing but reality, does not acknowledge anything but reality, and Ponelli on that particular day did not have all of his reality with him.

Dick Koehler says that if you have too many macho dog trainers standing around chatting, that can be agitation enough in some situations, a remark I report in my own defense. Still, if it was wish fulfillment that prompted me to worry about Ponelli's health, if it was the same thing I see reported in the papers, wives having these moments when they imagine their husbands dead, then it may be that the psychologists who assert that there is nothing wrong with such fantasies have been living in the world of theory for too long. Here, that is, is more of that toxin and corruption I keep telling you constitutes dog rescue. You will go wrong if you get the idea that my character is particularly weak in these situations—I have observed many dog rescues, and the tainted pattern of uproar is pretty constant in all of them. People get agitated.

Bandit's failure. Very low on aggression. High on drive, high on self-esteem, hard as granite, but low on aggression. So he didn't lunge, and except for my thumb there were no casualties. He simply regarded Ponelli curiously and turned down, rather politely, I thought, what he saw as an invitation to play.

So for his own reasons, Ponelli said that Bandit hadn't had any training. But he had, as I did not find out that day. Not enough training, and maybe not of the right sort, but he had had some, and plainly he had liked it.

We walked around to the front office, where Mr. Redd sat in state. Bandit leaped for his master and nearly enveloped the old man with his embraces. Someone proposed at this point taking the leash off, a move that was vetoed by Robert Bello, who said, "Uh, I don't care that much for dogs."

Lawyers don't have to approve of their clients, of course. Not that Bandit was the client—Mr. Redd was, and I think that Bello liked Mr. Redd, though not as much as Bandit does. Bello expressed amazement that I had been able to handle Bandit so easily, and I just nodded over the roar of my thumb.

One of the assistant dog wardens present was a woman who had stood with my husband and Mr. Redd and his grandson, watching me do about-turns with the dog, dumping him by running the other way before he could dump me. Bandit was quite good-natured about this, though it must have been surprising to him to find that the only way to stay on his feet was to keep an eye on me and go where I went. Mr. Redd's grandson wanted to know what cruel things I was doing to their dog! The dog warden, the woman, said, "It's called 'training.' She's on your side." And so I was. It can be, I must say, tempting to believe in the reasonableness of women, but this is not always wise.

What I learned about the dog was that he was fundamentally sound. Not my favorite sort of dog—I don't care for that particular bullheadedness routine. But I admired him, and didn't think he deserved to die, or to be in the pound.

A few days later, at the first hearing on the disposal order, there was entered into evidence a video of Bandit jumping and barking in his cage in the pound. The video showed a fellow in a Canine Control uniform eliciting the jumping and barking. And here I have to insert some more general information about canine behavior. The bull breeds are on the whole pretty quiet in kennel situations. If you walk into a kennel building that has forty dogs in it, thirteen of them pit bulls, chances are good that the thirteen pit bulls, if they haven't been there long enough to develop stress symptoms, will be the only ones not jumping and barking. Bandit is no exception. When I first got custody of him, I boarded him at George and Lillian Bernard's kennel, Silver Trails. During his first three months there, he showed *no cage aggression at all*. He did retreat and circle when approached, but that behavior disappeared within the first week without any special attention to it on my part or anyone else's.

So you have to work at it to get this dog jumping and barking. The video was, for me, further evidence that he could have been—only *could* have been—agitated in the pound, as I testified. So was the rapidity with which the stressed behaviors disappeared at Silver Trails. But none of that is proof of anything except the childish courtroom behavior of Canine Control, and anyone who says otherwise is wrong.

This first hearing was on December 10, 1987, shortly after I evaluated Bandit at the Stamford pound. There were several newspapers and several TV stations at the hearing, so it was hard to find room for the participants. I don't know why there were all those TV cameras there; I certainly wouldn't want my behavior recorded if I were going to behave as badly as people behaved at that hearing, but I have subsequently been told that I don't know how to use the media.

That is where I met Frank Intino, chief Canine Control officer of the state of Connecticut, in the State Office Building in Hartford. Present also was Warden Winski, who testified that Mr. Redd didn't have what it took to handle this dog, to be a "pack leader." Everybody except me testified that Bandit was a pit bull, or a "Staffordshire Terrier."

I testified that he was—look, devils get into me in these situations. So I testified as follows:

> He may be an American Pit Bull Terrier, but is also possibly an Argentinian Dogo, a Swinford Bandog, an Olde Bulldogge, a Dogue de Bordeaux, an American Bulldog, or an American Pit Bull Dog. (This latter breed is distinct from the American Pit Bull Terrier.) In any case, the mastiff blood in him is more evident than is usually the case with the American Pit Bull Terrier.

I also testified that he weighed as much as one hundred pounds. He doesn't. He weighs seventy-five pounds. But is so much more powerful than most seventy-five-pound dogs that my mind just found itself thinking: One Hundred Pounds!

I was impressed with this dog. Everyone was impressed with this dog.

Testimony against Bandit was given in terms I have mentioned, terms that were to haunt and harass my mind for some time to come:

"These dogs are killers. They have vicious genes and their training is part of their genetics."

Predictably, there was also testimony about the Jekyll-Hyde syndrome. I don't know who thought that one up, but it was a stroke of depraved genius. The idea is that some dogs can go around being sweet house pets for years, and then something snaps in them and they "turn on their masters." The nice thing about the Jekyll-Hyde syndrome is that reasonable behavior on an animal's part doesn't come anywhere near amounting to a rebuttal of the claim that he has the Jekyll-Hyde syndrome. If anything, when a dog behaves in a friendly way, that strengthens the argument that the dread syndrome is present.

The claim about the Jekyll-Hyde syndrome is, like all the popular ideas about pit bulls, baloney. There is no such thing as the dog discussed in the press and in the courtrooms, and I am not the kind of writer who would lie to you about a thing like that. There exist dangerous dogs. There exist dogs who are not wrapped tight. In particular, there exist fear biters. And there exist a few, a very very very few, dogs who will go for just about anyone. I knew one dog—one dog—who liked to bite people and who didn't straighten out after the owner put a lot of effort into training him, using the Koehler method. That dog, Liberty was his name, was definitely bad news. He was a Malamute.

My husband was at that hearing, and he said a melodramatic thing afterward. He said, "So that's what the Brown Shirts were like!" He meant various representatives of Canine Control. "Brown Shirts" may be a little strong, one might even say emotional, but there was certainly a lot of strenuous social hygiene in that room.

*   *   *

Mr. Lamon Redd, black and frail and elderly, with the ramrod bearing of a Virginia gentleman, and wearing a gray wool three-piece suit, rises to defend his dog.

Is *allowed* to rise and defend his dog. I suppose that if you now asked the participants why he was allowed to rise they would say they felt sorry for the confused old man. But his defense of Bandit was not all that confused. It was ineffective, but not confused. Defense given in these terms:

"I spent a lot of money on his training and on that fence.

"Bandit a good dog. Everybody in the neighborhood like him. The ladies always come by to talk to him.

"All the ladies in the neighborhood like him. Not just the colored ladies. The white ladies like him, too."

In the middle of the righteous accusations, the noise and the importance, the talk of Jekyll-Hyde syndromes and vicious genes and pack leaders, was this voice saying, "The white ladies like him, too."

Later a reporter who had covered the hearing would astonish me by saying that I seemed calm to her, unlike everyone else. I was not calm. I was too shocked by what I had heard and seen to speak, but speechless is not calm. I staggered out of there. I *fled,* ignominiously.

Fled to Mark Twain's house, which is nearby, and a joyously gaudy business it is, too, to use Huckleberry Finn's favorite word of approbation. It is not a term of approbation in Hartford. The tour guide made it plain that the good citizens of Hartford were still unhappy about the presence in the neighborhood of this gaudy person who smoked cigars and *drank.*

Mark Twain lived next door to Harriet Beecher Stowe, a real lady, a good housekeeper, who did not drink, although her son did, quite a lot. I walked through the two houses, with Mr. Redd's voice echoing in my heart, in my stomach. "The white ladies like him, too."

Mr. Redd was making a mistake, but not all that big a mistake as these things go, about the forces that had ordered him to build a doghouse and a fence that he could not afford, and that were now testifying about the irredeemable viciousness of his dog. Nor, I suspect, was he making a mistake about the likelihood of his speech melting anyone's heart, but one says what one can. I subsequently visited his neighborhood, as I think I have indicated, and the picture he created in the passage in which the appeal to the finer feelings of white ladies occurs was accurate.

And at bottom Mr. Redd was right in his perception of the forces at work. The pit bull "hysteria," as it is called, is one of the cleverest pieces of racist propaganda I have ever come across, and I used to study history and grew up in the South, and have a daughter who is a veteran of the Israeli army, so have had more than one occasion to brood about racism. But this was Connecticut, not Virginia. Mr. Redd is from Virginia, where the racism is fairly straightforward. When you have straightforward racism, then the fact that the white ladies like the dog is straightforwardly evidence in the dog's favor. Not so in Connecticut, where there are no niggers, only bad neighborhoods. So Mr. Redd's plea didn't work, but his was the only fully relevant remark anyone made at that hearing. "The white ladies like him, too."

I remember Martin Luther King, and being young and thinking that the world would change, that there would come a time when "The white ladies like him, too" would no longer be an imaginable or relevant defense of anyone, dog or human. I was wrong about that, racism is now chic again, so I fled and took a tour of the houses of two figures, Stowe and Twain, who came up with energetic responses to slavery. I didn't know what I was going to do about the pain I was feeling.

The pain was from an old injury. In Lake Charles, Louisiana, it came about at one point that I was seven years old and saw Niggertown for the first time. A vision visited me, a kind of Marxist vision, I suppose, for in my vision it came to me that Niggertown was necessary in order to support the fine, wealthy houses at the other end of Lake Street, and that the scars on the residents of Niggertown were necessary to make meaningful the fine-grained complexions at the other end. I am no economist and don't know if that was true, but it is what the vision said, and it made me weep. I wept so hard I did myself an injury, and that injury acts up now and again and is my social conscience.

So I went to the houses of Stowe and Twain, looking for inspiration. I didn't get any in Stowe's house, because I there learned that in order to emulate her I would have to do something that involved housekeeping, and I am no housekeeper.

"The white ladies like him, too." What was I going to do about that? What did Mark Twain, who seems also to have had some old injuries that would flare up on him from time to time, do about it?

Well, he wrote *Huckleberry Finn*. Thus becoming an even harder act to follow than Harriet Beecher Stowe in some ways, but at least *Huckleberry Finn* wasn't housekeeping.

There is, by the way, literary controversy about the ending of *Huckleberry Finn*. When Tom Sawyer comes on the scene with all his adventurous fantasies and starts "rescuing" Nigger Jim, thereby creating considerable hazards to Jim's health and peace of mind, the book, say the critics, goes downhill. Becomes silly, empty.

Tom Sawyer in that book is the perfect figure of a humaniac, dead-set on rescuing Jim at whatever cost to Jim's health and self-respect. Tom Sawyer in that book is, I suspect, Mark Twain's portrait of Harriet Beecher Stowe, great lady and author of *Uncle Tom's Cabin*. It was perhaps silly and vain of Twain to insist on naming his humaniac "Tom," but a poor boy from the South—"That's all he was," said my guide, "a poor boy from the South"—a poor boy from the South, living in Hartford, can get some impolite ideas, and even without impolite ideas, even hewing faithfully to the politest ideas he can manage, he is open to the charge that he is dangerous, even vicious, full of vices.

Henry Street, for instance, was a dangerous neighborhood when Bandit lived there, but it wasn't *vicious*. It was a light-hearted, innocent place, according to a hard-bitten reporter of my acquaintance, and this is the important detail, although "lighthearted and innocent" may seem an odd way to describe a high-crime urban neighborhood.

I was going to explain this one day to the assistant attorney general in a hearing about a different case, involving a pit bull named Cookie. I am fond of saying that there is no such thing as a vicious dog, and word of this must have gotten to the AAG, because under cross-examination she asked me if I believed that there was such a thing as a dangerous dog.

I said, Why, of course there is, who have you been talking to? And I was going to help her out of the trouble she got herself in and explain that it was viciousness that you never get in dogs, because they lack the intellectual faculties required for viciousness. I was actually feeling a little sorry for her, because she had pounced out with that question with such joy, thinking that I would say I didn't believe any dogs were vicious, but she forgot herself and said "dangerous," and I had to answer her honestly. I started to explain about vicious, but she wasn't having it, and moved right along to her next question, which was about Staffordshire Pit Bulldogs, and that question was unanswerable since there is no such breed.

That hearing was more enjoyable than the first one in the Bandit case, because the rules of evidence were followed, which meant that I got to bullyrag the prosecution around a little and encourage in my breast ignoble feelings of triumph. These ignoble feelings were, as I have already said, inevitable, because I was there to rescue a dog, and this rescue business is corrupt as all get out. The more successful it is, the more corrupt it becomes.

The hearing on December 10, 1987, was not slowed by any niceties about the rules of evidence. It became a shouting match, and the hearing officer, Vincent Majchier, then deputy commissioner of agriculture, lost control of it. The state's case was presented by Frank Intino, chief Canine Control officer.

I remember being asked by Mr. Redd's lawyer, Bello, what I thought of the video Intino entered into evidence. The video had taken me a bit aback, actually, because it showed a Canine Control officer getting Bandit roused up, so I thought it ought to be evidence for our side, but it wasn't. I started to reply that I saw a dog being excited by . . .

And that is where all the shouting really got going. Intino said that was ridiculous, a dog being excited, and he went on for a while about Bandit barking at the man who fed him, leaving out the opportunity to point out that when Bandit bit Mr. Redd he bit the hand that fed him, and then Vincent Majchier precipitately declared the hearing adjourned. I later began to have the impression that adjourning whatever was going on was his principal survival technique, since that is mostly what I saw him do, adjourn hearings just as one thought one was going to get a word in edgewise, but I don't really know Majchier, and he may just have been having a bad day. I know I was.

Majchier upheld the disposal order. Bello then appealed the case to superior court, specifically, to Stamford Superior Court, where Judge Harold Dean presided. That hearing was held on February 8, 1988, and there were expert witnesses galore against Bandit. At least, there were a lot of people there in uniform. (As Lily Mae later said to Mr. Redd when he asked when he was going to get his dog back, "We don't know, Daddy. Some people's got a lot against Bandit.") Also present were Mr. Redd, Effie Powell, and Mr. Johnson. Warden Winski was there, and an Officer Simon, and a police chief, mind you, and Assistant Attorney General Robert Teitleman and City Attorney James Minor, and the *New York Times* and the *Stamford Advocate* and the *Hartford Courant* and TV stations and I don't know what-all.

And me. And Dr. Mark Vandenberg. I had bought some hair rollers and curled my hair in an attempt to look organized at this hearing, and I remember that Mark thought this was funny, because the result was not all that organized. I remember also that Mark predicted that the judge would go our way—or at least, he claimed later to have so predicted—because the judge kept giggling, and also because of his tie, a tartan tie, I believe.

I gave testimony. The judge asked me if the dog would be kept where he couldn't hurt anyone, and I said, "Absolutely, Your Honor," and the judge asked would I keep him in a licensed kennel, and I said, "Absolutely, Your Honor." Opposing attorneys complained that the judge had not heard the evidence, and here were all these experts brought at great expense, and the judge said he *had* heard the evidence, he had talked to "the dog lady." This was to be the first and the last time that a word from me was sufficient, so I record the moment. The upshot was that the judge said I could have the dog for training. I think he did this because it seemed to him to be a way to get the case out of his courtroom so more serious matters such as rape and murder could be gone into. I thought that was a reasonable way to think myself, since the idea that dogs are my business and not that of the courts or the state is one that comes naturally to me.

So, at a word from Judge Dean, I had Bandit in training, but his prospects were still not all that good. The air was thick with jive stories, no one knew what was going on, except that instead of the state killing the dog that afternoon, Vicki Hearne put him in her Jeep and drove him to Silver Trails, The Animal Inn.

Bandit doesn't happen to be a pit bull, I kept saying with what was, in the context, excessive pedantry. Bandit, that is, is not a dog of the breed judges are directed to evaluate first for personality and obedience, as in the UKC standard.

"What breed *are* we talking about?" asked a cameraman from Channel 30. "When we talk about pit bulls, what breed are we talking about?"

We are not talking about *anything*. It is a solitary feeling to have nothing to say, so we console ourselves with words, and with intellect, and with newspapers. We have replaced dogs with ragged, ungrammatical words, traded awareness for an autistic, crippled, resentful, and violent language.

Bertrand Russell knew that the price of intellect is ignorance of the world immediately before our eyes, but he seems to imagine that to know what is before us is to be "wild," despite the fact that what we call atrocity is necessarily and always buttressed by civilized intellect. In *Our Knowledge of the External World,* Russell writes:

Intellect, in civilized man, like artistic capacity, has occasionally been developed beyond the point where it is useful to the individual; intuition, on the other hand, seems on the whole to diminish as civilization increases. Speaking broadly, it is greater in children than in adults, in the uneducated than the educated. Probably in dogs it exceeds anything to be found in human beings.

This is not written in admiration of dogs or intuition, or in despair of civilization, though I don't know why not. Russell says as plainly as he can that the more civilized people are, the less likely they are to know what is going on in front of their noses, but counts the world well lost, despite his acknowledgment that intellect can be "developed beyond the point where it is useful to the individual." The implication is that there is some other world besides the one before us, the "world" we have in mind when we speak of the world of the imagination, or the life of the mind, or the front page of the *Times*. There is something to this. Some people can endure prison with the aid of philosophy—not philosophy's truths, but its absentmindedness. This doesn't make prison good.

In any case, for Bandit it is iron bars that a prison make. Cement and chain link, actually.

As of this writing, Bandit lies at my feet, the first dog in the memory of anyone I know to survive a disposal order, per an administrative ruling of July 29, 1988, in the State Office Building in Hartford, Connecticut. The legal story is not over, but Bandit is for the nonce safe.

He is resting but has arranged himself in such a fashion that he can instantly survey all possible approaches to me, as he always does. His breakfast is nearby, and he is hungry, but when I put his bowl down for him a few minutes ago my young Plott Hound, who is a quarter his size, flirted her head at him and said, with her usual sauce, that she wanted it, so he sighed and lay down. He will not eat until later, when the puppy has finished and is napping. My (real) pit bull bitch Annie lies across the room, content to have at last some help in the trying business of bringing up the young hound.

The story of Bandit is, in part, the story of how the true

knowledge of dogs remains hidden, a better-kept secret than any in the Pentagon. Russell's word for what distracts us so that we lose the world is "intellect," perhaps because that was the name for what his life was most profoundly promised to. If I am promised to anything, it is to language, so "language" is my word for what steals the knowledge of dogs away from us together with the rest of all that is sweet and fluent and real in our *mundo*. This does not mean that I have a love-hate relationship with language—I do not know what the terms of such a relationship would be; but the fact that it was language that created the false dogs and false dangers on which so much money was spent, and also language that created in the same motions and dismissals real and brutal dangers for many dogs and many human hearts, is something that has my attention.

A human being is, terrifyingly, a creature who can have before him or her a real dog tenderly greeting his friend and fellow countryman Patrick the Cat, and see flying above them a flag depicting a snarling two-headed monster devouring kittens, with a slogan on it reading "Kill All Pit Bulls" or "Defend the Faith," and believe in the monster more readily than in the dog. Ours is the species that developed or else received the fullest gifts of language and thus the capacity to be brainwashed, the capacity for paranoia, for autism, and for making the world safe for democracy, or for Communism, or for two-car garages, or for the Aryan ideal.

We have traded awareness for language. It is our fate, then, to have to return to awareness through language, or at least to make the attempt, to have to deal with speaking or not speaking, writing or refraining from writing, all our lives long, whether in our individual selves and moods we take the destruction of the Tower of Babel to have been complete and permanent, or not.

THREE $\cdots\cdots\cdots\cdots\cdots\cdots\cdots\cdots\cdots\cdots\cdots\cdots$

Bandit Himself

". . . What is that little animal you are so tender of?"
"He is my dog, Toto," answered Dorothy.
"Is he made of tin, or stuffed?" asked the Lion.
"Neither. He's a—a—a meat dog," said the girl.

—L. FRANK BAUM, *The Wizard of Oz*

FIRST OF ALL Bandit, because without Bandit himself the meaning of the politics—Bandit's politics and the various politics of his friends and enemies—cannot be given any more than the meaning of a word can be given apart from the life of the sentences spoken for or against the word. Like the meaning of a judge's sentence, which cannot be given without the people and files activated by the judge's words.

One of the judge's words in this case was "Bandit." However, in the course of the bureaucratic and political idiocy that led to Bandit being on the front page of the *Hartford Courant* as a vicious dog, no one with a political stake in his ferociousness has managed to *refer* to Bandit, to mean, when they say or write "Bandit," the dog who is right now teaching my husband to throw Cheetos for him to catch. To the extent that one has a political or rhetorical stake in using the name of a dog, to that extent one becomes incompetent in the use of the dog's name; this is a fact given, not by the generalities of political corruption, but by some hard logic inherent in the ease with which we use names in the third person, by contrast with a dog's incomplete mastery of the third person—or, as Buber would perhaps have it, by contrast with a dog's mastery of the second person.

Bandit was sentenced to death, in the garish language of the newspapers. Bandit does not know what a disposal order is. That pinnacle of abstraction and intellect is reserved for our species. Enthusiasm for the trope of anthropomorphism should not be allowed to obscure the blessed limits to a dog's understanding, which limits also mark the places where a dog's understanding is more acute than ours, but I will get to that later.

Anthropomorphism is a relatively young word, according to the *OED*, which gives an entry of 1753 that uses the word to refer to a theological error—attributing human traits to the deity. It seems to be slightly past the middle of the nineteenth century that the word comes to name an injunction against attributing human traits to animals, which would of course have been about the time that intellectuals became comfortable with the substitution of a scientific catechism for a theological one. (Not that it matters much whether you say "genes" or "devils"— the confusion and the corpses smell the same when you are done.) I have spent a great deal of time winning for myself an understanding of how and when anthropomorphic terms are accurate, but it was accuracy and not a commitment to any particular figure of speech or figure of salvation that prompted that dialogue with my own skepticism. Nowadays in some circles anthropomorphism has become a cherished mode, but I am as queasy now as I ever was about received doctrine, articles of faith—this is, if you like, a perversity, an illness of temper or temperament—and I do not think you can execute someone who does not know what an execution is, only what killing is. You can kill them and *call* it an execution, of course.

The commissioner and the governor and the law recognize disposal orders, may even be said to cherish them, but Bandit does not, cannot, which is one reason it is so hard to embarrass him; he has no fear of socially organized violence.

However, he does recognize and cherish obstacles. A pile of boulders or a truck bed or a stone wall interests him the way tossed balls interest retrievers, or the way the opportunity to run interests hounds. The way lions and bears interest Airedales, or the way sheep and cows interest Border Collies and Corgis. The way new formal possibilities interest musicians, poets, mathematicians, logicians. Say that "singable" is how the sacred objects in some composers' worlds can be roughly identified, so you can think of "surmountable" in order to know whether a given object is sacred in Bandit's world. I do not mean "sacred" and therefore to be worshiped or protected from heresy, but simply sacred and therefore sacred, a Thou Shalt uttered in a language that has no Thou Shalt Not in it. The heart of a horse-woman sings for horses, by way of horses. The heart of a philosopher, if it sings, sings for and by way of problems, the heart of a soprano for and by way of songs, the heart of Man o' War for and by way of running. The heart of an educated Blood-hound sings for and by way of tracking.

Bandit's heart sings for and by way of boulders and all else that is, most gloriously and aptly and splendidly, negotiable, vaultable, climbable, scalable. So Bandit's first trick, his first piece of fancy work, consisted of his jumping onto an indicated object at the command "Bandit, Up!" and off at the command "Off!"

The first such object was not especially glamorous. It was a fiberglass grooming tub, a bit over two feet high, that was overturned and waiting behind the kennel for installation. Because it was molded fiberglass, it was somewhat slippery to jump onto and wait on, and also, when not in its ordained place in the grooming room but rather among the leaves and trees, it wobbled a bit, but this did not trouble Bandit—indeed, it encouraged him, because he is a very brave dog about anything that presents itself thus to him. This is his fountain of virtue.

My friend Diana Cooper basely demanded to know the practical application of "Up!" and "Off!" So I told her sternly that this was Bandit's idea, that he had said, "Ma'am"—we didn't know each other very well then, and he was still rather formal— "Ma'am, I could get up on that thing and down again quite grandly if you liked." So I stood in front of it with Bandit sitting at my side, bent over and picked him up and put him on the tub, at the same time saying, "Bandit, Up!" I had him wait up there for a few seconds, and then said, "Off!" while tugging a bit on the leash. He returned to heel with zest and power. I "placed" him through the exercise one more time, and the third time simply tugged on the leash as I gave the command. The fourth time, I gave the command without any other aids, and he jumped up and swung himself around with exalted precision, and sat like a heraldic statue waiting for the cue to jump back down.

A liking for granite grandeurs runs in the bull breeds, which is no doubt why they are the heraldic dogs of Western painting tradition. One day, wanting a suitably unusual photograph for some purpose or another, I went with my dog Annie and a photographer to the local game preserve, where there is a large lawn in the middle of which is a rough wall, three to four feet high and four to five feet wide, made of boulders. In order to get Annie in the air, leaping in gladly triumphant relation to the stone, I placed a dumbbell on one of the boulders, on the side opposite to the one she approached in her run.

Annie is not an especially enthusiastic retriever, but she is a proper bulldog, and for her as for Bandit surmounting the boulders activated something deep and willing in her. She was not in top physical condition, since it was winter and I don't always work out how to exercise my dogs in the winter, so she fairly quickly got tired. I would set her up about twenty-five feet from the wall on a Sit-stay, and then go back to stand by the wall and arrange myself in whatever pose the photographer wanted this time, and when the photographer gave the signal, I sent her: "Annie, Fetch!"

Fetch she did. Off lead, mind you, and with a joy that would break your heart if you allowed yourself to brood about how many forces are arrayed against a dog's achieving mastery and exhilaration. Over two rolls of film, thirty-six frames per roll, were filled with her jumping, and the photographer missed her a few times. She charged the wall and jumped, every time. Her feet must have gotten sore on the rocks, and since she had been living a sedentary life, jumping nearly a hundred times onto anything would have been taxing. Also, these boulders, like the grooming tub of Bandit's introduction to agility, rocked and wobbled, causing her to lose her footing sometimes. This encouraged her, literally filled her with heart, stirred her imagination, and the imagination of a dog is something worth understanding.

Annie is not especially pliable or sporting about discomfort. The other day Robert took her and his Plott Hound, Lucy Belle, into the game preserve for a relaxing ramble. It began to rain a bit, no more than a drizzle, really, and Annie wouldn't have it, insisted on being taken back into the warm, dry house. Her imagination was not at all stirred by the idea of a woodsy walk in the rain.

One day I was visiting my friend Georgiana, whose grounds include a small hill leading up to a pasture and a stone wall. In front of the wall are two levels of decorative boulders, with the result that there is a kind of three-level obstacle several times my height and quite steep, mostly at a slant sharper than forty-five degrees—an interesting agility problem, so I set Bandit to working it. That is to say, I put him on a Sit-stay and pointed out the boulders-and-high-stone-wall arrangement, and sent him off to work this new version of King of the Mountain, with the command to retrieve a dumbbell I had tossed on top.

Now, when Bandit is seriously playing King of the Mountain, the effect is rather powerful. Literally breathtaking. A greyhound takes possession of the landscape with her grace and speed, a bloodhound with his intent focus on finding, a German Shepherd with moral courage, a Poodle with gaiety and exquisite courtesy. Bandit does so with his power and spring; that is how he calls to, commands, the sacred.

Afterward, in Georgiana's kitchen, she said, "That was quite an eye-opener. The way he did that, how much he wants to do it for you." She was right—when he works like that it is a literal eye-opener; people's pupils widen with interest when they watch. She was also right that he wants to do these things for me. But he wants to do them for Bandit more deeply than for me. Also, he is put together in such a fashion that doing things for me is doing them for himself, since commanding admiration and respect from me (rather than love and approval) is a way to be in command. He wants to live for himself, and this is his honesty. I have read a book by a psychiatrist who came to believe that some of his patients were possessed by evil, and one such patient was a young woman who cried out, "But I want to live for myself!" This was the clincher for Dr. Peck, the devil was making her do it. So in these terms, the terms of one corner of American psychiatry, it is the devil making Bandit do it. Or, in the language of the press and of the solemn experts on the evils of Bandit, it is his genes that are to blame.

Bandit is also loyal to me, and relies on me to appreciate him properly, to be pleased, but to be pleased with exactly what he is doing and not with something else. So you can say that he wants to please, and specifically to please me, but this has to do with his confidence that I am competent at being pleased by who he is, how he commands himself, and not an idiot who thinks that just because I do some of the planning and scheduling of retrieves and surmountings, the work therefore belongs to me. The difference between commanding a dog to sit and commanding him to retrieve or negotiate obstacles is like the difference between requiring mannerly behavior in a classroom and commanding the students to draw a picture or write a poem. The picture or the poem belongs to the artist no matter who commissioned it, and some dogs are more insistent on this aspect of things than others. I do not command Bandit's joy, and the emotionally dishonest desire to be able to command a dog's competence and joy, instead of his obedience, is the violent sentimentality that stops some people and dogs from achieving real work in retrieving. (The sentimentality in question is not, by the way, something I am immune to. I have met some people who seem to be immune to it, but I am not one of them.)

It is a violence, our desire that dogs should work for our pleasure, and people who cannot imagine any other motive in dogs than to give their joy and competence over to the handler imagine that is what all training is like, and turn violently, either against the dogs who refuse their blandishments, or against trainers, or both. One day a trainer friend of mine said, "What is this "wants to please' business? Why don't these people just go into pornography and have done with it?" Well, in a way, some of them have, or so I find myself feeling when I read certain slathering descriptions of the ferocity of pit bulls.

Perhaps, though, perhaps we are discovering the devil when we discover that Bandit's intelligence has various shapes, including the shapes and textures of stone walls, mountains, boulders, heraldry. You might even say that mountains are what this dog has the ability to prophesy, for when he suggested, barely two weeks into my acquaintance with him, that he could surmount the overturned grooming tub, he had known nothing of hills or boulders or mountains, having been a city dog, having never seen a boulder or for that matter a cow. He had my responsiveness to him, the knowledge that this particular kind of responsiveness existed, and he saw the grooming tub that afternoon in, shall we say, a new light, and he looked at it and prophesied great boulders and mountains. Accurately.

Bandit is an American breed, specifically an American Bulldog. America is not the only land of prophets, but it is one of them—one of the things "America" means is: the landscape that could resonate for Whitman, Twain, Emerson, Thoreau. Thoreau, who wrote, "It is not that we love to be alone, but that we love to soar, and when we do soar, the company grows thinner and thinner till there is none at all." Bandit is gregarious enough in the absence of boulders; it is not that he loves to be alone, but that he loves summits.

It can be spiritual and political tragedy when the wrong sort of control is attempted over a dog's or a person's or a nation's capacity for prophecy. It is hard, it is nearly impossible, in fact, successfully to disapprove of a Pointer's capacity to prophesy birds, or a bulldog's to prophesy boulders. To succeed in this is like succeeding in disapproving of the birth from its smooth oval of a winged dragon all of iridescences and courage and sharp vision; it is within our power to control the imagination by killing the dog, but not by disapproving of the dog.

Of course, it is through control that the imagination learns to use its wings. A ballet dancer spends hours and hours and hours at the barre. Many plodding hours on more mundane retrieves preceded Annie's stone wall mastery. "Control" is a tricky word—it is not a compliment to say that so-and-so is "into control," but it is a compliment to say that a violinist has control. My sense of what kind of control is not only good but enjoined on me by my knowledge of the transcendence of dogs is simple: With Bandit, I exerted strict control over only one thing at a time, and only over things I could control, things that were not problematic. (I cannot—no one can—force him to love boulders.) Hence I forbade certain actions—chasing cats, say— but not thoughts. Bandit makes certain sorts of sadism very hard, if not impossible. He will neither work nor frolic for anyone in response to flattery, for example, cannot be distracted from himself in that way, which is part of what it is about him that adds up to the temperament trait of *hardness*. He does not respond to phoniness or to coaxing, largely because he is, as photographer Enrico Ferorelli once noted, always on duty. And in training him I made no attempt to improve his disposition or his attitude.

It may be that for America political tragedy is signaled by a promise to improve America's disposition, to make a landscape of summits serve as a backdrop for the muted manners of the genteel and contained spirit. I have heard a rumor about Whitman, that he sent President Lincoln a copy of *Leaves of Grass* and that evermore when he was down he would say to himself, "Well, the President understands me if no one else does," and that this comforted and sustained him somewhat. What a grandiose idea! Delusions of grandeur, one might say, except that the grandeur of *Leaves of Grass* is no delusion. More power to him.

I am talking about giants. So was Bandit's former owner, Mr. Redd, who built at the order of the dogcatcher a large fence so that he could continue to house Bandit, and Mr. Redd knew that to house Bandit is to house a giant. In Valerie Humes's documentary, *A Little Vicious,* which is all about how very much like a dog Bandit is, how superlatively a dog, you can see and hear Mr. Redd describing the day Bandit bit him. Bandit, you recall, had returned from the pound with his manners somewhat eroded, no longer wholly intact, and he had peed— copiously, I assume, because he always does—on the porch. And Mr. Redd had struck him for this: "He notified me, grrrr, grrrr, but I kept whupping him so he grabbed me. That's why I fight so hard for him, because if they kill that dog it's my fault."

That reminded Robert of these lines from Emily Dickinson, and he kept quoting them, so did I:

> If you would house a giant,
> Give a giant room

But this isn't how the lines go, as it turns out, not how Emily Dickinson's lines go at all. The lines actually read:

> The power to contain
>
> Is always as the contents
> But give a Giant room
> And you will lodge a Giant
> And not a smaller man

That about sums it up about temperament. I once heard someone say that no one has managed to inherit Emily Dickinson, and this may be true, but it may also be that through an alchemy of what is literally sublime that giant of hers continued for a while to be a poetic property, or just a fact, the fact of Wallace Stevens's "giant, on the horizon, glistening . . . And in bright excellence adorned." "It is," writes Stevens, who lived in Hartford, the town in which various snippings of Bandit were proposed, "a giant, always, that is evolved, / To be in scale, unless virtue cuts him, snips / Both size and solitude or thinks it does . . ."

And here is something interesting, that while I refuse to be the priestess of anthropomorphism, or for that matter of Bandit, no damage is done to Stevens's poem if you find in the literal leap and elongation of the power of a bulldog the knowledge that to be talented is to have a housing problem, as it were, for one says of dogs, "But where are you going to keep him?"

Bandit is an American Bulldog, and a good one, so a literal giant, the sculptor of vatic lines, sculptor in a way only, of course, and the vatic lines are only lines in a way, lines of his desire and lineaments of leap, and when I read Diana Cooper the part about her basely demanding to know the practical application of "Up!" and "Off!" she denied it hotly, laughing like a fool all the while, for she knows something of giving a giant room, of standing out of the way of dogs and horses who care only for a real version of themselves, their own kindness and their vast, swift, sharp iridescences.

In my country's heart, I like to think, are many dragons, even if the academy is somewhat absent about where it laid down Dickinson's poems sometimes. Whitman. Williams, too, oh yes, Williams, and Stevens, and Mark Twain, and the story of Paul Bunyan is fetched from afar in the reaches of this country.

When I speak of Bandit's heart singing for boulders I am speaking of his "temperament," as trainers say. In some cases temperament is a matter of the sublime. This is not necessarily reassuring, but it is worth living for. I mean that it is temperament and not training, nor what is usually meant by "goodness," that would send a dog like Bandit, if we were in a different time and place, over not just one set of boulders but hundreds of them, over the mountains of Joshua Tree National Monument on a search, pads bleeding, legs swollen, running a fever, cactus or no cactus. Stories about artists are often stories about suffering—Michelangelo sweating on the scaffold under the ceiling of the Sistine Chapel, for example—but the focus on suffering obscures the glorious and terrifying facts of temperament that kept him up there.

The idea of temperament degenerates rapidly into the idea of "personality," just as discussions of great artists tend to decay into gossipy discussions of psychology. Or as the idea of obedience degenerates into the idea of dogs wanting to please people, or as the idea of virtue degenerates into the idea of meekness and submission. There used to be a notion of virtue as expressed in the old word *virtù*: what is brave, shining, manly. In the work of Shakespeare, the translators of the King James Version of the Bible, and others, a virtuous person was not a reassuring person, but was in fact dangerous, especially to those who lacked virtue and were therefore vicious. We still have our virtuous heroes—Mr. T on "The A-Team," for example, who is certainly not a reassuring person. Nor is he even a mentally healthy person in the usual sense—his compatriots have to drug him in about half the episodes I have seen because he is afraid of flying.

It is just that he is—well, if he were a dog I would say, "That's a lot of dog!"

There is a tradition of thinking of the domestic virtues and *virtù* as opposed to each other. And in the American tradition the figure of large temperament, or *virtù*, is usually male and has no domestic life. If the figure of *virtù* is a woman, she can have an admirer who asks her to marry him in each episode, but she turns him down.

But domesticity is actually a matter of courage and imagination, which is why it cannot be legislated any more than the terms of art can be, why prescribing the forms and manners of sexuality, kitchen habits, and so on always leads to tyranny. Each case of achieved domesticity transcends the forms of domesticity the participants inherit, whether they work from them or against them. We show our awareness of that kind of transcendence when we speak of the loyalty and courage of the dog, or of the achievements of certain architects. However, we have reconceived the domestic virtues somewhat basely, which is one reason no one wanted to be a housewife for a while there. Some people have said that there are no American novels about adult love, nothing to compare with, say, Goethe's *Elective Affinities*, a novel that acknowledges some of the vast forces operating at a house party. This is not entirely true, but sometimes it is hard to find in America any virtue but *virtù*, which may be why some people cannot conceive of a dog's power as anything but viciousness.

A curious turn indeed, when strength is conceived as viciousness! As though vices were powers of the soul.

Bandit's and Annie's *virtù*, their power, is a power of the hearth as well as the boulder. The American Bulldog, the Plott Hound who will take on a boar or a bear should one come up, the American Pit Bull Terrier—all of these fighting, surmounting, and long-striding dogs of the sublime are literal, unlike Mr. T and unlike the holograms of themselves politicians project onto television screens. The reason the suburban dog owner is so often disappointed when the cute puppy grows up to be a constant nuisance rather than a contented creature of the hearth is that dogs who have no work cannot know the contentments of the hearth, and a dog who has no command of her own work is never meaningfully responsive to her human partner's commands. People are like this, too, which is why there are so many tales in Western tradition of the knight who has to fight dragons before he wins the fair lady. Since the fair lady is given, at best, tatting and knitting to do while he is gone, some feminists have said that fighting dragons is to be abjured, but the demands of the sublime for both Annie and Bandit are as beyond social and political correctness now as they ever were.

Virtue is necessary for a meaningful life of the hearth, but some of the virtues of the hearth are grounded in the virtues of the quest—for, say, ever larger and grander boulders—just as some of the virtues of the quest are grounded in the virtues of the hearth, and none of this is easy, none of it is bloodless.

I cannot go into the sublime as expressed in the dogfighter's yarn in much detail, because Bandit is not a pit bull and that is another book, but I would like to note that the dogfighter's yarn is an American yarn, one letter of the sublime, as Mark Twain knew early on when, in "The Celebrated Jumping Frog of Calaveras Country," he gave us, by way of mocking us for our grand ideas, also by way of admiring them, the story of Andrew Jackson, a bull pup who would get hold of a hind leg, and that was it for the other dog, and no matter how he was ragged around Andrew Jackson never let on but that it was a picnic for him. We are told that Andrew Jackson would have been a great dog, too, except that one day he was matched against a dog who had no hind legs, and thus Andrew Jackson lost, was lost forever.

This is the problem of the American sublime, neatly stated. It prophesies boulders, but for what?

There is more—I hurry to say this—there is more to Bandit's grandeur than mountains, and he has more than one hold on me. He is a very formal sort of dog—he belongs, Diana says, to an earlier age; his style is black tie. Or at least he does not have Yankee manners, meaning, north of the Mason-Dixon Line. His accent is normally gentle, like Carson McCullers's or Eudora Welty's. If, for example, he wants to go outside and I am preoccupied with my computer, he sits nearby, his posture quite formal, a stipulation of his reluctance to disturb me: "Excuse me, but when you are free, if you could render me a little assistance." This is very different from Annie's manners. She is the leader, not as Eisenhower was a leader but more the way— well, more the way a mare or a bitch is. If her first request is ignored, she leaps into the middle of the keyboard or barks imperiously: "*Will* you attend to your responsibilities?" You don't keep a lady waiting. Nor do you keep her out in the rain. And she has the right and the duty to bring this to your attention if need be.

I learn things about dogs that other people don't because I train them, so that they know how to say, through the tokens of training, what has not been said before, and I also neglect them, because when I am writing I become unconscious of my surroundings. So my dogs are in a way like wild animals in that they are more complexly educated than most domestic animals are, and my absentmindedness places demands on their ingenuity. This is especially evident in Bandit's case, since reasoning about the setup is generally his first response when things go awry.

"That dog reasons!" said George one day, and so he does. "I swear he reasons!" said George. "You can *see* him reasoning." This is true; it is one of Bandit's minor weaknesses that you can, indeed, see him reasoning—he does not have a perfect poker face. He gets lost in thought, and you can tell that he is Thinking Something.

One day Robert addressed me, got my attention. Bandit had—and I think I was vaguely aware of this—asked me to take him outside. Since he had been out not too long before to relieve himself, I ignored him and also ignored what he had to say, all of which had to do with my having been on a trip, leaving Bandit behind, and in the three days since I had been back I hadn't done anything with Bandit, having a deadline. Recall that Bandit's manners forbade him to leap into the middle of my work or otherwise make a pill of himself.

So, according to Robert's report, he had given up on me and

gone upstairs to ask Robert to take him out, using just that posture that means, "Excuse me, so sorry, but it is a matter of some urgency." Robert left his work, came downstairs, and took out Bandit's leash, whereupon Bandit refused to go with him and instead led him to me, now sitting with his chest facing me, looking sometimes at me, sometimes back over his shoulder at Robert.

Robert said, "I'm sorry, Vicki, but you're going to have to take him out. He wants to go out with you—I won't do at all." So I took him out. And he didn't so much as lift a leg, ignored his favorite trees, leaf piles, the stone wall, and even the life-sized cement statue of a German Shepherd on the front lawn. He indicated quite plainly, by heeling with enormous precision whenever I moved off toward another tree, still thinking he needed to pee or something, that he wanted to work. Not to play. Not to relieve himself, but to work.

There is a clue here, in Bandit's expansion of the meaning of the formal posture of sitting, that points to differences between animals and machines. Human beings do not do well when required to come up with words that have one and only one meaning, because for us the primary mode of forming a class or a category is through trope, figures of speech. As Stanley Cavell has shown in a marvelous passage in *The Claim of Reason*— though I do not know if what I am now thinking of was uppermost in his mind—there is a large variety of worlds we learn to inhabit by learning a vocabulary. This is not a matter of inventing worlds, as one might do with a board game or a computer, but of discovering through imagining, in Wittgenstein's terms, or discovering, uncovering, a world by means of mastery of the ways a new vocabulary interlocks with the new world. The new world is not necessarily a richer one, though there is a tradition of thinking of all learning optimistically that makes us suppose that "new" and "more elaborate" are synonyms when they modify "world," even though people who master the vocabularies by means of which one learns to survive in a cage (prison, hospital, boarding school, concentration camp) quite unmistakably report learning impoverishment.

Frost's cold line about what to make of a diminished thing chills because Frost knows that there is diminishment.

Diminishment is a thing that can be learned, a thing dogs can learn in relationship to people, and learn it as we do through new vocabulary words when the new words displace instead of learning to dance with the old ones, or the old versions of themselves. When you teach a dog to sit through dominance, or through so-called positive rewards, such as biscuits, you diminish his world by reducing the complex of meanings that the family of gestures we call "sitting" can have to the impoverished meanings, referents, and emotions at work in phony (human) games of "pack leader," or worse, far worse, you strip the gesture of any possible referent beyond "dog biscuit." A well-bred German Shepherd puppy at eight weeks will follow a human being from room to room in the house and will sit when the human being stops moving. This sitting of the good Shepherd is full of many eloquences: "I heard that sound too!" or "Here we are together, what next?" or "Here we two, with our different forms of balance at the halt, shape the world of this room." Continual treat reinforcement of the puppy's sitting discourages the puppy from trying to mean anything but a treat. The same thing can happen to people: Truth becomes a dog biscuit, an M&M, a sitcom, or cocaine, through the dominance displays that human beings call "positive reinforcement" or "reassurance" or "pack leader," whether or not the human beings know that in the process they and the dog have lost a language and thus a world.

Bandit cannot be dominated, so even if I had tried to dominate him with dog biscuits and threat displays, he would have continued to be himself, which is how it came about that he eventually had the registered name "Definitely Bandit."

Cavell's discussion of a child learning to say "kitty" is not a discussion of impoverishment. He traces a natural history of the literal that begins with something that might be called metaphorical. The child in his example is able to point at a fur piece and say "kitty" before she learns that a fur piece isn't, say, literally or actually a kitty. Say literally rather than actually, because the child who learns that the family companion named Snowdrop is "kitty" and who subsequently and spontaneously points at a fur piece and says "kitty" is not losing touch with actuality. But there are things about the actuality of the word "kitty" that she does not know until she can point to a domestic shorthair, an Abyssinian, a Siamese, a Himalayan, and say, with no trace of metaphorical spark and vault, "kitty." She will know even more when she can look at the kitties in the *Encyclopedia of Cats* and see a photograph as literally a kitty. From there, intellectual advancement may take the form of a teacher—perhaps a philosophy teacher or a law teacher or just some English teacher—teaching her and her classmates that a photograph of a kitty, or an account of one in the newspaper, is not literally a kitty, so don't believe everything you see or read in the newspaper.

Dogs, like humans, learn terms in three and four dimensions rather than on a linear model or from ostensive definitions. A dog in formal training is to learn that "Joe, Sit!" means this:

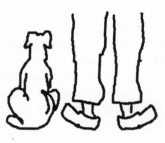

Now, this picture I have drawn is not meaningful to Bandit, not so much because marks on a piece of paper cannot be meaningful to a dog but because a dog cannot learn something this simple.

Learning the complex of motions and transfers of intention that we, mysteriously, can picture in this way takes a dog a while, not because dogs are dumber than people, but because a dog, like a human being, learns by means of the activity of projecting the term into new contexts. Say the dog is a kennel dog named Ashley. It used to be, before we had worked so much on "Sit!," that she greeted me by jumping against the gate, warbling, and tossing her food dish around. Suddenly one morning she greets me by sitting, very formal and square, and lifting her muzzle up into the posture that makes it easy for me to put her collar on. If I accept this greeting in any way at all—by, say, crinkling my eyes pleasurably—"Sit" will now mean "I'm glad to see you, and I, too, am ready to work." (And by the inscription "Sit," of course, I do not mean my utterance, but the posture, the gesture, the dog has made.) I have not asked the dog to mean "I'm ready for work," but the dog has projected the gesture so that it now does. That capacity on the dog's part to project terms through complex parabolas of trope explains how, in the case of an obedience-trained dog, the formal posture of sitting at your side, prepared for the next command, comes to mean, "I'm ready to go," or "I don't know what that noise is, boss, but I don't think it's gunfire," or "That man isn't drunk, he's dead," or "There's a lost person in this thicket," and because language is at least four-dimensional and of the essence of connectedness, the posture in formal work may also come to have the not entirely candid meaning "I don't know how that garbage got in the hallway!"

Formal training is in part a matter of keeping those hovering meanings under control. In an obedience trial you don't want your dog to woolgather, experimenting with new meanings of "Sit." It may seem that, say, mathematics is different from this, that in mathematics definitions and meanings hold still better than they do with dogs and children. But consider the following *bête noire* for philosophers of mathematics. A circle consists of "all of the points equidistant from a given point." Yet that definition can be used to make a square in Taxicab Geometry. In a city laid out in squares rather than rectangles, a cab driver who took passengers to all the intersections that are exactly three blocks from the corner of East Third Street and Jefferson Avenue would describe a figure that is, by the definition given above, a circle.

When a conceptual disturbance like this shows up, one first impulse is to say, "But that isn't what we mean by 'circle'!" or, "That's sure not how *I'd* use the word 'circle'!" It's exasperating, since what has happened is that "dis- tance" has been defined as something you measure only in horizontal and vertical direc-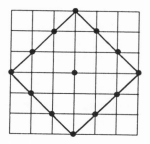

tions, and even if you make the grid infinitely fine, you still get a square this way, using "the definition of a circle." It's a different geometry, one in which the friendly and familiar formulas we learned in school fail. Taxicab Geometry shows that even in the purest of realms, mathematics, definitions and axioms are not the sturdy foundation blocks they seem to be. Some people find this merely annoying, but it is the sort of wobble in language and logic that Wittgenstein was prompted to honor deeply, among other things by remarking that meaning is use, thus pointing to the idea that the life of a concept is not to be discovered in a definition or a logical or grammatical rule, but rather in the interlocking precisions between the Word and the world. Hence, attempts to "teach" dogs the meanings of terms fail when they depend on, say, pointing at something and giving its name.

The life of a concept cannot be given to a dog arbitrarily, the way it can be to a computer. A computer is not restless with intelligence, and so is quite happy for a given "word"—the command key plus "v"—to continue meaning one and only one operation until the end of time. Not until the end of time like love, and not until the end of time like a physical law, but until the end of time like a computer.

Bandit, though, Bandit is not like this. He has a mind, and as Stevens said, "It is never satisfied, the mind, ever." No dog is like a computer, because for dogs as for people the literal use of the term "Sit" comes only after a period in which it invokes too much and is, some say, metaphorical. Means, perhaps, "Sitting here on the grass on an autumn afternoon just as the leaves start to fall and an hour before suppertime," and not what is represented in the drawing above, which isolates features of posture in no landscape at all. Computers never get to landscapes; dogs start in them. So long as the mechanical parts do not deteriorate, for example, being ready to go does not change in meaning for my Macintosh or my typewriter whether I write every day from 6:30 to 10:00 a.m. or neglect the whole business for a few weeks. I cannot accidentally or deliberately invoke a computer's sense of loyalty, duty, and community when I "ask" it to "search," but I cannot help but do so with a dog, cannot help but invoke a dog's entire world when I move with the dog into the postures of sitting or finding. The formal beginning of training with an adult dog comes when the trainer gives a meaning to a word, but what starts it is not the trainer's but the dog's contributions to the conversation.

There is, that is, in the case of a domestic dog, in the case of Bandit, inescapably the capacity for friendship, a capacity at once invoked, named, incarnated, and steadied into a grammar of exchange when the dog sits beside me. It takes time for a dog or a child to isolate the features of "kitty" or "Sit" that carry it into the aery, abstract condition we call the literal. Not the actual, but the literal. The actual is always and already given for a dog, especially the actuality of friendship, of that form of accepting the contingency that is one life's relationship to another. Our name for a political system that acknowledges friendship as the fundamental political mode is democracy.

And for Bandit himself, the posture "Sit," the posture called "Heel," the other postures that are the grids of the meanings of our work, are all things expressed in time, and by means of time, which is why I am prompted to say that they have a syntax before they have meaning. That for a dog, syntax is prior to semantics, but for a computer it is the other way about, say there is any syntax or time at all for a computer. And these postures are matters of loyalty the way marble is a matter of sculpture and the way sculpture is a matter of marble, melody is a matter of notes. By "matter" I mean both "concern" or "affair" and also "material." Loyalty is one of the materials meaning is built of; meaning is one of the materials loyalty is built of. Meaning is something that fails, as is loyalty—that is in their nature—but to say that is not to say that they do not exist; hence the logical absurdity of the idea that life is absurd.

Here is something else to note: Once "Sit" is in Bandit's world, then friendship cannot be given without it any more than Mozart's Quartet in D Major can be given without F-sharp. Not G-flat, but F-sharp, even though both are, from the point of view of an instrument measuring the sound of the note alone, the "same sound" (especially on the clavier), just as from an uninstructed viewpoint Bandit sitting when there is nothing better to do is the "same posture" as Bandit sitting next to me in response to a sudden change, perhaps the appearance of a stranger in the woods. It matters that we know this, even if G-flat and F-sharp sound the same to the deafness of a pitch-measuring device, and it matters what we call a dog's rights, even if all sits and all bites look the same to the zealousness of someone who is busy setting the blind mechanisms of judgment and pity in motion. Judgment and pity are effective, like a laser, and blind, like a laser.

By "judgment," by the way, I don't just mean the sort a judge performs, but judgments about whether or not this or that is the case. Like pity, judgment is something we do *to* the world, and to dogs; training is something you do *with* the world.

Because Bandit desires friendship and desires the power to choose friendship, he desires his work—in his own bullheaded way; he is not destined to win the Gaines Superdog Classic with his fastidious heeling. There are of course the climbing of boulders and other forms of accomplishment for their own sakes, but there is also work as the working out of the mandates of loyalty and commitment. A true obedience routine performed by a true working dog is signifier and thing signified in one motion, and not through the tricks of abstraction that give our species the ability to produce self-reflexive objects such as the liar's paradox or sentences that read "This sentence is false."

To go to Robert, to get Robert's attention and lead him to the leash and to the door and then to show a turn, a warp that swings everything around toward "Get Vicki's attention for me"—that is a work, and also a learning, because he learns in part through his own intention and in part through Robert's response that this is what one version of "Sit" now means. It now means something that I have not taught him to say but that is a projection of something I taught him about "Sit," which was, "I want you to keep up your half of the bargain, I want you to come work with me, let me show you how I want it." To belabor the point: When a leap such as Bandit performed with Robert is not acknowledged, the nascent meaning the dog is imagining rather than merely inventing will subside, vanish. And now things are not the way they were before he did this, because the imagination, unlike a computer, can subside into the muddle and murk of disappointment at the failure of meaning that is one expression, for us at least, of what we misleadingly call the fear of death. There are people who get paid to call the muddles and murks "depression" or "schizophrenia" or "paranoia," and while these words are not perhaps invariably meaningless, they are incompletely intended in the mouth of anyone who does not know that the failures of syntax are not primarily failures of a rule-governed sequence, but rather of response.

I will go on with this. There was a moment when I had taught Bandit that "Sit!" meant, "Whenever I say, 'Bandit, Sit!' you have to assume this formal posture. If you sit crookedly, or ahead of me, or only after a few moments of continuing to study the robin, that is ungrammatical."

I could not do this without also displaying in my responses a cogent grammar—if Bandit sits not only "properly" but with an extra fillip of display that means, "I am mastering this! I am what I am, Bandit who sits in majesty, ignoring robins and squirrels the way Mt. Everest ignores fleas," then I have to be able to say, "Yes, I read you." An unread (unreadable) message is not quite a message yet, which is how it comes about that syntax is prior to semantics.

Having done all of this, I have, whether or not I meant to, taught Bandit the possibility of such a grammar, the grammar of projections of terms through response. Of course, this grammar fails us all the time, and one of the things sanity is is imagining what to do when grammar falls apart, just as one of the things democracy is is an honoring of the importance of that grammar, the grammar that can be emptied as in "empty social forms," the grammar that can be abused by, say, inappropriate puns or what some psychiatrists call blocking, redefining, and reframing—it is usually ungrammatical to respond to the question "Who did this?" with "It happened before dinner," to respond to the question "Who?" with the answer to the question "When?" This is one route to schizophrenia.

In courtrooms the effort is made to prevent such bad grammars, so one synonym for opposing counsel's cry "Objection, Your Honor" is "That is irrelevant," but another is "That is ungrammatical." Despair at grammar's failures can take the form of cynicism, schizophrenia, the paranoid's capacity for hearing in what is said everything but what is said: Syntax is on the surface.

And dogs honor grammar, the surface, the syntactical implications of an exchange more readily than people do, which is their form of honesty. Their readiness is not, however, their helplessness, or their powerlessness—responsiveness is a power. Wittgenstein invites us to understand that a dog's sincerity is not something chosen, that a dog can be neither sincere nor insincere, but he is wrong, for there is: Bandit, oh, Bandit!

This is a dog who is honest on purpose, resolute in his sincerity, able to imagine an honesty beyond what I give and to call back into being my honesty when my commitment to it fails. To imagine more of friendship than I have taught him, to imagine what I could not about myself.

He is a bulldog, bullheaded, so the tone and ground and key of his imagination is resolve. Resolve is of a weightiness, of course, though it is not something that droops, but rather, in Bandit's case, as I opened by saying, the foundation of a surmounting. Given something sufficiently towering to surmount, a bulldog can discover the upper airs, come close enough to brush against the stars.

Meaning, semantics, cannot be given without grammar any more than marriage can be given without two. Friendship, love, loyalty—these are not the names of feelings, they are the names of various species of syntax. The politics Aristotle elevated, the *polis* he desired to be able to cherish—these are, like relations in a well-run wolf society, syntactical constructions.

FOUR ··

Bandit Himself:
What He Is Not

"And ain't it natural and right for a cat and a cow to talk different from us?"

—TWAIN, *The Adventures of Huckleberry Finn*

BANDIT IS NOT A WOLF. No dog is a wolf. I am not denying this at random, any more than I have denied that pit bulls have triple jaws at random, in the way a madman might suddenly deny that trees are bureaucrats, though the impulse to deny that you or your friends and family are wolves or in some way inhuman can lead to a certain sort of madness. I am denying that Bandit is a wolf because I have heard so often, from so many otherwise rational persons, that pit bulls and other breeds are like wolves, are derived from wolves. And I must deny it by talking about what wolves are like in my experience of them.

I suppose that you could, if you went at it long enough and lived long enough, derive a pit bull from a wolf, because all things are infinite and contain the universe in them, as Leibniz says in his correspondence with De Volder:

> In my opinion there never arises a natural organic mechanism that is new, because it always possesses infinite organs, so that it may express the whole universe in its way; indeed, it always involves all past and present time. This is the most certain nature of every substance. And we know that what is expressed in the soul is also expressed in the body; hence the soul as well as the machine animated by it, and the animal itself, are as indestructible as the very universe. It is for this reason that such a machine cannot be put together, any more than it can be destroyed, by any mechanical process. . . . my opinions on this score are not derived from our ignorance.

But deriving a pit bull from a wolf, like deriving gold from lead, would be such a wasteful and expensive affair that I believe that no one, including Mother Nature, has ever been so obsessed or sick with the fascination of cleverness as to do it. In particular, pit bulls brag to people and wolves never do, and I do not know how you make something so extraordinary as pride out of nothing. Also, if Leibniz is right that not only the soul but the animal is immortal, that "the animal together with its soul persists forever," then you would have to dismantle some other piece of the universe in order to make your bulldog out of a pack of wolves—no, it would take more than a single pack, it would take the whole universe of wolves, which is to say the whole universe—and I cannot see Nature doing anything so futile. Animals are not Lego toys, made up of parts of each other scattered on the nursery floor of time, and Nature does not violate Nature. (Though Nature violates happiness, often, which is why there is so much study of modes of survival—that is to say, of the various ways animals live in opposition to Nature.)

If you listen closely you can hear in this the beginnings of doubt that the theory of evolution is finicky enough to be true. Darwin was a man of towering, overwhelming insights, I believe, but some of his unexamined metaphors of relation are misleading; for example, the idea that wolves and dogs are "close relatives." This is in some ways a good insight; wolves and dogs can interbreed and produce fertile offspring. But so entranced are we with zygotes that we do not look to the conscious end of an animal in order to contemplate the notion of "relatives" and "closeness." Zygotes or no zygotes, there is no way in the world that you can derive a pit bull from a wolf, any more than you can derive a wolf from a pit bull. It doesn't help to replace pit bulls in your evolutionary equation with German Shepherds or something else popularly supposed to be "wolf-like." Pit bulls have short single coats, and wolves and German Shepherds have double coats, but so do bag ladies, and that doesn't get the theorist any further with the idea that a German Shepherd is more like a wolf than a pit bull is, because the mind of a German Shepherd is so radically different from the mind of a wolf as to present much bigger problems in accounting for how the one became the other than any physical difference could.

It is not a matter of a difference in IQ, and it is not a matter of the dog being kept in a state of arrested development. Bandit is as smart as any wolf, and as adult; no one looking at *him* has ever supposed that he is in a permanent state of puppyhood. Still, people say this sort of thing. Sometimes it takes the form of an idea that a dog is a debased wolf, a wolf made unnaturally submissive to our pleasures and whims and commands, a wolf brought down from a nobler condition. Sometimes people who say this sort of thing back up their opinion by neutering or euthanizing any dog who fails to live up to the expectation of eternal puppyhood. I have in mind followers of the line promulgated by People for the Ethical Treatment of Animals, or PETA. PETA's cofounder, Ingrid Newkirk, proposes spaying and neutering all dogs, and I have correspondence from PETA urging the humane destruction of pit bulls and other allegedly ferocious breeds on the grounds that they are unnatural products of human perversity and that it is cruel to allow them to live. There's a Catch-22 here; dogs that are not submissive, that are indomitable, are presumably less "debased" and therefore less exploited than submissive ones, but it is the presumably less submissive ones that are to be killed rather than at least allowed to live with their gonads rendered inoperative.

Apart from the dubious ethics of spaying and neutering and euthanizing an entire species, there is a terrible confusion here about what "submissive" is. Dogs who fail to be submissive enough for certain people's fantasies about what dogs are like, whether or not the fantasy is offered in praise or disparagement of the entire dog-human project, are *not* therefore more wolf-like, they are more doglike. The more a dog resembles Bandit in his indomitableness, the less that dog is like a wolf.

The problem with training wolves and coyotes and hybrids is that these animals are, in a training relationship, too submissive—and in their excessive submission is their distrust of us. Wolves are too submissive to *Homo sapiens*. Not: too aggressive, too dominant, too violent, too ferocious. They do not put up a fight such as Jack London describes in *The Call of the Wild,* where a dog dealer has to club a dog a dozen times to discourage the dog from tearing the dealer's throat out.

There is an idea of training and handling that owes most of its popularity, I suspect, to Konrad Lorenz. There was an insight in it at one point, namely that canine responsiveness to people is a matter of a human being taking the place of the "pack leader," or "Alpha wolf," and that a household in which there is a dog can be described in terms of a dominance-submission hierarchy. There is something to this idea, but it has gotten out of hand, and in the course of getting out of hand it has shown, once again, that dogs are kind of miraculous, because some of them, some of them, will work with you even if you draw mystical diagrams on the floor and invoke the spirit of the Alpha wolf, asking Him to inhabit your soul while you intone in the dog's direction, thus: "Look at me! Look at me! Watch me!" Ivaar Lovaas, who performs miracles with autistic children, teaches them to "Look at me!" But neither dogs nor wolves are pathological versions of human beings, and yet they will put up with our diagrams and insults, some of them. Others are freaked out by the intonings and bizarre ritual behaviors and shrink back, and then the other sacred intonation is uttered: "She was abused!"

Some dogs really *are* abused, but very few behavior problems can be linked to abuse, at least not if abuse is a matter of beatings. Beatings will of course adversely affect a dog's social confidence, but many dogs are simply shy and/or spooky, either in general or in response to particular situations. I have known dogs I am certain no one ever raised a hand to who tended to hit the panic button about all kinds of things, or one or two things, and other dogs who had in fact been beaten and neglected but showed no behavioral signs. Sometimes both temperament types will show up in the same litter, and you can pick them out at five weeks.

Most behavior problems are a function of some set of innate

temperament traits in the dog in volatile combination with behavior traits in the handler. For instance: The dog is innately
shy. The dog, out of innate shyness, spooks at a broom being
brought out of the closet, or at some helium-filled party bal-
loons. The handler leaps to reassure the dog. The reassurance
entails hovering over the dog, which causes a shy dog to crouch
even more and to be convinced that the initial worried reaction
was the right one. The hovering causes further shrinking and
spooking, and the kind words reinforce the idea that the spooky
thing is spooky. The dog gets worse, or at least never gets
better, and the handler shakes his head and says, "Someone beat
her."

Since a shy dog is often also a fear biter, the reassurance may
land the dog in the pound and the handler in court. Failing to
understand that *feeling* kindly is not at all the same thing as
responding in kind, or coherently, everyone then agrees that the
dog bit "because he was abused," as in Bandit's case, which
doesn't help other dogs any more than it helped Bandit, whether
with legal or spiritual problems.

Sometimes, of course, reassurance is the correct response, but
in a properly managed training situation it is not often necessary. In training, you teach the dog to reassure herself by increasing her sense of control over her handler and the world.
Because even the shyest dog has a certain amount of emotional
courage in relationship to our species, training *done properly* is
almost invariably effective.

Wolves, however, don't even have the emotional stamina of
a cautious, shy dog in relationship to human beings. The submission of a wolf can be grotesque, even hideous, but that is
because a wolf in the house usually has no choice but to be a
debased version of a dog, and not because dogs are debased
versions of wolves—if you must have your metaphor of height
and depth, of hierarchy.

Take Keesha, for example. She is a wolf hybrid—part tim-
berwolf, part Australian Shepherd, they say. She belongs to
some perfectly reasonable people in Virginia who contacted me
about training her because they were desperate to stop living

behind barricades, and desperate for Keesha to stay alive, which she was unlikely to do as things stood because she kept wanting to slip off, and the handiest place for her to slip off to was the sights of the shotgun the neighbor was likely to have out to protect his calves.

The barricades—that is to say, the elaborate series of rules in the house about how people were to go in and out of doors— had nothing to do with Keesha's being dangerous, for she is not dangerous, but rather with her inability to regard the house as home, as safe harbor.

So her owners paid me a fair amount of money to straighten the problem out for them. It was quite a problem.

I realize that there is a body of thought that would see death as a kinder alternative than training for Keesha, but that is an advanced form of kindness, and Keesha's owners are somewhat behind the times. Indeed, so is Keesha. A hybrid won't tell you very much about what she is thinking, but you can get an answer from almost any animal, even a bear, to the question "Would you rather get trained or be dead?"

Keesha's answer to the question was, resoundingly, "Trained. I'd rather be trained." You can count on the thumbs of one hand the varieties of animal mind and mood that will give the other answer—"I'd rather be dead"—to that question. In-deed, once she got the hang of it, she enjoyed training, because I insisted that she assume the postures of confidence, and Aris-totle was not wrong about everything. One of the things he was right about was that if you get the posture correct, the pertinent sensations and understandings will follow, which is how it came about that Keesha came to leap out of her run, wriggling with joy and going, "Woooo! Wooooo! Woowoowoo!!"

She would leap, specifically, out of her run and into position at my side. So even for a wolf training is not a fate worse than death—this must be understood. Nor is it a fate worse than living in a nice large cage, however well provisioned, if the behavior of trained animals is any guide, and if you take into account the limited conversation available to animals whose benefactors cage them nicely and think training is cruel. Such animals, especially if they are wild animals, often mock and caricature their rescuers, like small boys mocking their Sunday school teacher. Thus do many dogs behave, mockingly. If the owner of an animal who has the guts to mock the pieties of the owner imagines that the animal has been successfully *rescued,* then the owner will say, when the press is around, "Naughty, naughty," as the banana (or worse) hits him in the face.

I have seen, for example, a tape of Wallace Swett, a chimp rescuer, shaking his finger at some rescued chimps and saying, "Naughty, naughty!" I also watched him look sadly at one chimp, Tyrone—into whose cage he did not dare go, Tyrone being quite dangerous—watched him look at Tyrone sadly and point to his own head and say, "Tyrone has some problems." That is, I watched him attribute the chimp's natural aggression, the chimp's God-given ability to refuse to accept the terms of a cuddle/naughty-naughty relationship, to his being abused, to his having *psychological problems.*

Now, there is evidence that Tyrone had been teased, by someone other than Wallace Swett, in order to induce him to charge around his cage and roar. I do know that the chimps into whose cages it was safe for Wallace Swett to walk, the chimps who did not charge about and roar, had been worked by allegedly cruel Hollywood trainers, unlike Tyrone.

It is a fact that people do things to animals they ought not to do. Much more importantly, though, they leave undone things they ought to do.

I do not know whether Tyrone is still alive in San Antonio, Texas. Nor do I know what should be done with, to, or about him. I would be very, very surprised to learn that he was helped by the man who said sadly, "Tyrone has some problems." I would also be profoundly astonished to learn that Tyrone's patrons there at Primarily Primates tried the idea of learning how to train chimps as a way of helping them either to find meaningful lives in captivity or to return to the wild. This would astonish me because Wallace Swett received a fair amount of money from Bob Barker of "The Price Is Right" fame, who has been quite noisy in his insistence that the chimp trainers on the film *Project X* are cruel to chimps, and those trainers are among the few people around who might possibly know what to do about Tyrone. Bob Barker hosted the Miss America Pageant for many years, which means from my point of view that he hosted the celebration of travesties of human beauty for many years; I suppose it is natural that he should be as confused about the true beauty and power of animals as he seems to be about the beauty and power of women.

Here it is important to remember that there are many training techniques, and that the differences between them are not to be captured by the idea that some are more "humane" than others. "Cruel" and "humane" are not informative adjectives in front of "training technique." If someone tells me that a certain trainer is "cruel" or "humane," I am not enlightened, know no more about that trainer's way of thinking and working than if my informant had said "green" or "red plaid."

There are only two relevant questions about any training method. One is: Does it work? The other is: Does it lead to work at liberty?

This is where in-house trainers' quarrels begin. I, for example, believe that when the great dressage horse Ahlerich and his rider Klimke work, and Ahlerich steps out in that powerful, high, light-floating way, doing extensions at trot or passage, then Ahlerich is working at liberty, because it is impulsion—the horse's educated desire—that makes such movement possible, and not the rider's control. The rider is in physical contact with the horse, through the tack, but the tack is insufficient to force such movement, which belongs to the horse, is the *horse's* enlightened expression of his own talent; the tack is for communication, not coercion. Others prefer to reserve the term "at liberty" for work in which there is no physical contact between animal and handler and the animal is free to flee, as when Hubert Wells works lions at liberty in the Serengeti, on location with a movie crew.

In light of Keesha, consider the following bit of disagreement from one small area of animal training.

I have mentioned the idea that the trainer is the "pack leader," or "Alpha wolf," and that in order to train an animal you have to establish "dominance." In the case of dogs, some trainers will say of a given dog that he is "untrainable" or "crazy" because "he can't be dominated." Some of the maneuvers that go under the heading "dominance" are pretty strange, the sort of thing that only a grammar-maddened *Homo sapiens* could imagine had anything to do with how animals actually behave, with real "political" struggles among animals. You may be advised, for example, to flip the dog over on his back and hold him there while shaking him by the loose skin of the neck and/or jowls, or even be told to "mount" the dog. If the dog is small, that means carrying him around between your legs.

These postures are supposed to have a subliminal effect, like advertising. But animals do not have the wiring necessary for a subliminal effect to take place, which is why you have never seen a dog in a grocery store picking out Alpo rather than Kal Kan on the basis of the design on the label. It is human beings who need all that help distinguishing one food from another, except for very great cooks, who have learned to have an intently conscious focus on the food itself rather than its packaging, just as your dog does.

Further—I am giving my side of this argument—some of the best working animals can't be "dominated," and that is what makes them great, the fact that they have very little in the way of submissive impulses, but have instead powerful drives toward cooperation and accomplishment.

Bandit is such a dog. The talk about how vicious and uncontrollably aggressive he is amounted to a weak and corrupt allegory for this truth about him, that dominating him doesn't work. There were along the way one or two dominance battles, of course, or at least battles that were something like dominance battles. He and I had, not a disagreement, but a fight, about whether or not he was going to get to tear into Charlie's cows, and at its grimmest—this fight is on film in *A Little Vicious*—it came down to me hanging on to the leash and jerking, and bopping Bandit on the nose with a nose bopper, and Bandit being apparently about as phased by this as by a flea.

The fight went on for around half an hour. There are things to note about it. One is that Bandit was hell-bent on the idea that he was going to do in one of those cows, and I was hell-bent on the idea that he was going to obey the "Stay!" command I had given him, about five feet from the cows, some time before the fight started. Further, it was spring, and a cow with a calf is no dog lover, so from the other side of the fence were coming insults and instructions and dire warnings, especially from Clovis, who is not fond of dogs even when she doesn't have a calf to protect, so Bandit's sense of the urgency of Doing Something to Tame That Maniacal, Murderous Bovine was deep and sincere.

That is, the subject of our disagreement was not kindness to dumb animals, but whether or not he had to hold the Stay when something as glorious and meaningful and momentous as putting the blasted cows in their place presented itself to him. The cows were not placid, and might well have gotten tough with me as well as Bandit, so there was great provocation, not just in the fact of the cows, but in what they were saying about me and Bandit, and in the tone of voice they were using and the mayhem they were threatening.

Note: I did not take a green dog up to the cows and have it out with him—if you can, you avoid having any issues out with a dog who has no foundation for a decision to trust your judgment. We were already far enough along in training so that it wasn't a mindless struggle, but a very specific disagreement about whether I was going to get to mean it when I said "Stay!" The struggle was tiring and intense, but it was not a matter of "conditioning," as it would be, for example, if I were to set things up so that cows were associated with electric shock. Some people think that conditioning and behavior modification techniques are *kinder* than an all-out, direct battle with a dog about an obedience command. I don't think they are, because without a training relationship and the commitments it implies they don't work.

Also, it takes a good three to four weeks to extinguish a behavior using aversives, whereas it took less than an hour to have the fight with Bandit about the cows. Of course, he had to have some training first, but training pays off in a way behavior modification does not, since it teaches linguistic possibilities. Bandit learned something, and made a decision about, *me* that day, not the cows.

The next day, I took Bandit back up to the cow pasture, and he assumed, when he saw the cows, a benign expression, even when Clovis hurled insults at him over the cattle guard (which he could cross easily and she could not, as she knew perfectly well, by the way).

The message was not: If you menace the stock you will feel physical pain. That is a message to the dog's subconscious mind, and Bandit has very little in the way of a subconscious mind.

The message was: Here are the terms of working with me. And Bandit, being an honest sportsman, accepted the terms, did not try to block or redefine what I was saying—did not bite me, that is, because what was happening here was different from what was happening when he was whupped, different from what may or may not have happened to him in the pound. When something that is merely painful but not otherwise meaningful to him is the problem, he assaults the source of the pain when he can, as many dogs do. If you use a power hose on a dog of this sort, or kick his cage, or otherwise offend his dignity, he will simply assault you, because there the only term of argument is whether or not the person gets to hurt Bandit. If you capture a dog and use assault long enough when he can't get to you, and if the dog has no choice but to endure, then you can end up, even if the dog is Bandit, with a rather unhappy, messed-up dog.

You can even end up with a dog who circles autistically when you approach his cage, or tries to bite your foot through the chain link. I am not saying that anyone did that to Bandit, only that it can happen.

With a dog like Bandit, you gotta have respect. Pointing your finger at your own head and saying sadly, "The dog has problems," would not be a case of respect, no matter how it came about that his manners were less than perfect, no matter whether something you might want to call abuse was part of his history.

Bandit put everything he had into the project of Getting Those Damned Cows. Everything he had. It was glorious.

He did not once try to bite me, and he did not even try to take the nose thumper away from me.

If I had taken him up to the cows, waited for him to decide to go for them, and then pounded on him with some idea of "aversives" or "reward and punishment" or "dominance and submission" in mind, I might well be a dead woman, because you don't mess around with a good dog that way.

Love makes mistakes about this with animals. Love whispers at people like the very devil. Whispers as follows: "If he loved you he would leave the cows alone." Love can sometimes go on to say things such as, "And since you are so lovable, he would love you if he hadn't been abused," as though the dog's behavior or misbehavior belonged to the handler instead of the dog. Love is both irresponsible and wrong when it talks that way. It wasn't Bandit's love for me, nor his impulse to submit to me, that caused him to decide—consciously, with focus and deliberation and balance aforethought—to hold a Stay rather than go for the cows. It was his capacity to recognize the Stay command as part of our work, part of what we were in together. That is why he did not try to bite me—I was not saying, "I can hurt you if I want to," but rather, "*This* is how it has to be in the work." Since biting was not the topic of conversation, since Bandit is an honest fellow who addresses the topic you ask him to, biting did not come up.

When he decided to leave off harassing the cows, he decided it with a mental gesture akin to the thought a mountain might have about staying in one place. The next day, when I said, "Bandit, Stay!" he put everything he had into transforming himself into a symmetry and a rock-stillness, a decisiveness of immobility.

Bandit is indomitable. Wolves are another matter. Early in Keesha's work it quite often came about that I was asking her to sit at a time and in a place she felt it improper to do so. Her spine was curved in an S shape, her head was lowered and tilted, her feet were splayed, and her lips were pulled back in a classic wolf "grin" of submission.

This is the kind of posture that inspires human beings to demonstrate their dominance. The lower back hollows, the elbows come out, the hands are raised above the level of the elbows, the spine twists so that the human head is hovering over the animal's air space, the chin is either tucked into the chest so that the forehead becomes more imposing, or else the chin juts out, and the human being says . . .

A variety of things. Sometimes the human being says, "I said to SIT!" This will work in a feeble way with some dogs, although a human being who relies on dominance finds out that the dog will run off when the human gets more than fifty feet away—out of dominance range—which is why in some parts of the country there are baby gates around obedience rings.

And sometimes the human being, holding the same tense posture, says, "Easy now, baby, it's all right, Poppa is here."

From the animal's point of view, it doesn't matter which words are coming out of the mouth, because dominance is dominance, as dogs and wolves know perfectly well. Dominance can provide thrills and occasion healthy outdoor exercise, but it is not training.

Hence, I treated Keesha's submission displays—and a submission display is only one *tour jeté* of a threat dance—as disobedience, because the twisted, defensive, threatening postures of submission have nothing to do with working postures. I had asked for a Sit, not for an Abused and Oppressed Wolf-Wimp performance, I said. Said, quickly, emphatically: *Submission is not acceptable to me!*

Keesha got this, though not as rapidly as a dog would. Along the way, it turned out that I had to do something about a fair number of asymmetries and imbalances that had crept into my own postures. I had for a year or two been working only pit bulls and an Airedale—indomitable dogs—so it didn't matter to those dogs that my trunk twisted and tilted a quarter of an inch. If you are working with an indomitable dog, you can get away with allowing incoherences to creep into your posture, because

Homo sapiens and other primate display behaviors don't upset such a dog. I don't mean they are pleasing, but a little asymmetry is okay.

In practice, in training classes, many dogs end up trained despite the dominance displays that creep into the handlers' work. Since dogs have the ability to remain themselves in the face of our hovering, in a way that is well nigh impossible for wolves and other wild animals, they can learn what we have to teach despite the ethical incoherence of our teaching. Their many ways of doing this are articulations of their capacity for forgiveness.

Keesha would give me her submission display if I tilted half an inch off the true, into her "lane," as it were. I would correct her, and there was some progress, but not much until I realized that I was lying to her by being off balance. It was a while before I figured this out, so for a few days I began to wonder if I hadn't met my Waterloo in this critter. Worried, that is, that in continually evoking submission from her I was failing to train her—and I was. Her extreme sensitivity to anything remotely resembling a dominance display made her very hard to train.

Well, I got rid of the Oppressed Wolf stuff. With a dog, once you get rid of the Oppressed Baby routine, you generally have some nobility to work with. The form the nobility takes varies—it's a witty nobility in an Airedale, a dutiful nobility in a German Shepherd, a stalwart nobility in Bandit, a swift, fire-arrow nobility in many bird dog breeds, and so on—but it's all nobility.

With a wolf, once you get rid of the phony submission—I call it phony because submission is so often a reference to a bite—all you have is circus and vaudeville, and not the kind of circus and vaudeville that makes you catch your breath and realize how wonderful and various are the forms of art as ethical insight, either. All you have is the trickster part of the clown, and not the part where the clown is gentle with your self-esteem after he draws you, all unwitting, into the act.

The Indians of the Southwest have legends about Coyote. These are not legends about the noble wild canine slipping through the noble dark and mystery of the noble wild forest or desert. Coyote is a joker. He is not like villains in the Western tradition, animal or human, tricking people and animals for the sake of some gain—he just likes to trick you. It is a pure form of being. Secretariat liked to run, Bandit likes to surmount, poets like to poet, painters like to paint, Coyote likes to trick. I used to read the stories of Coyote in a bemused frame of mind, wondering what in the world it was about the world and its people and places that prompted the Indian tale-tellers to come up with these crazy stories, and finally I realized that it was not something primarily psychological or metaphysical, it was just what coyotes are like. I don't mean that wild canids have no *virtù*—if you think that Coyote is not a distillation of *virtù*, then your Renaissance lit prof did an insufficient pedagogical job.

Keesha's owner, the husband in the family, said, "She's a professional animal," and so there is admiration and respect at the bottom of that relationship, although the fact that Keesha continues to give him the bent eye outside of work troubles his soul. But she is a pro, has to be, for living in a house is no job for an amateur wolf, though in dogs the amateur tradition here is strong and worthy of celebration.

It takes courage for a dog to obey. Home is courage for a working dog. For a wolf, too. Home is courage for a wolf, but wolves are not at home with us. You can think of this in terms of "territory" if you like a more modern-sounding word. Dogs have varyingly strong senses of territory. Many guard and herding breeds have strong senses of territory, as do many terriers. Bandit, for example, spent hours on the porch with Mr. Redd, and when I say there never was such a dog for that job, sitting on the porch, I am indicating among other things that Bandit has a strong, close sense of territory, and that the old man was part of it. This is the sort of dog it is ridiculously easy to do "boundary breaking" with, that is, to teach the dog to respect property lines, not to wander.

Other dogs, whose imaginations are founded in a different kind of work, have weak senses of territory. Good hound men know this, know that if you want to keep hounds it is best if you also own your own county, because it takes about a county to give a hound room to stretch out a little, reasonable enough in a dog who is supposed to run that fox or rabbit or bear all day and all the long night long. Nordics—the Samoyeds, the Malamutes, the Elkhounds, and such—also tend to wander, as though for them home were travel, as it is for nomads.

However, as attenuated as a hound's or a Nordic's sense of territory may be, that sense will consist of a fundamental idea of landscape as something that has human beings in the center of it. Most training then entails, among other things, formalizing that picture of landscape, making a more precise dance of home.

Wolves are not like this; it doesn't matter how loose or tight a given wolf's sense of territory may be, since whatever it is it doesn't have you in it. A wolf in the house is always in alien territory, never really at home, and you never find out much about what home looks like to a wolf—they don't discuss that with you. So, even though the moves (when I do it) for training a wolf or a wolf hybrid are identical to the ones I use with dogs, what is going on is different. A wolf always feels shy, unfamiliar. If you have ever found yourself at a party and just wanted to melt into the woodwork or suddenly remember that you left the stove on or that your mother is dying and needs you and you really must go home right now, without apologies, you know something of how a wolf feels, I suspect.

In practice, the popular image of the wolf is so far from the reality that either the popular image or the animal herself might as well be a creature from another planet, and I never understood the idea that Rome was founded by a wolf.

Recently, I learned that Rome wasn't founded by a wolf at all, but by a pit bull, or a lady as near to a pit bull as anything twenty-five or more centuries old can be, one of Bandit's ancestors. But more of this later.

FIVE ··

"This Isn't an Animal Rights Case, Professor Wizner"

"Then [the wise man] will not willingly take part in politics."
"Yes, by the dog," said I, "in his own city he certainly will. . . ."

—PLATO, *Republic*

FIRST OF ALL BANDIT, but now I must digress.

"Why are cops so cynical?" asks the aristocrat curiously one day.

"Well, it goes with the territory," says I. "It's a kind of literary birthright."

Other remarks occurred to me, such as, For the same reason you are. A cop isn't middle-class, and so has no faith. Cops close ranks as any genuine elite does—or what is an elite for?—against what animal trainers call by the technical term idiocy and what religious leaders and prophets call illusion, or in some traditions Karma, the confusions that bind the soul to the temporal. In the course of doing so, elites of all sorts end up creating more confusions for the soul, closing ranks against truth and life itself. Sealing a crown or a homicide file is not, for example, immediately lethal, but it can be a mistake, an unforseeable mistake; our century has produced in crime fiction wonderful allegories in which sealing the file amounts to sealing off the soul of the writer of the file, just as the king's seal in earlier tradition becomes an emblem of the sealing off of the wearer of the crown, and confusion between the crown or the file and the king or the cop can be fatal.

"What happens to cops?" I asked George over at the kennel

95

one day. George being an ex-cop and now proprietor of Silver Trails, The Animal Inn. "What makes cops so cynical?"

"They sign on, full of high hopes, and then they find out that nobody likes them, and then, what really bitches them up is, they find out that they can't help anybody." Thus George, in one mood.

But another time George answered the same question, the one posed by the aristocrat, in a growl: "Constant abuse."

The TV was on, and he paused to catch some action on "The A-Team," one of the few programs he watches all the way through, without driving everyone nuts by flipping through the stations on the remote control. George really likes "The A-Team" because nobody ever gets hurt. He keeps saying, "I love it! See, nobody gets hurt!" After some plastique had blown everybody in this episode sky-high and they had landed on their feet, like cats, like gods, George said, "What'd I tell you? Look at them!" Then he added absentmindedly, "But there are some really crazy-mean cops out there." He went back to watching nobody get hurt.

But cops! I wanted to say, did say, to the aristocrat, I said: Cops! They are so goddamn dumb it would make you weep. Some of them, that is. Some of them are so goddamn dumb. I know a guy who's being retired early because he's going deaf. Reason he's going deaf is they didn't used to use ear protectors on the firing range, and everybody had to go practice. Do not think we are talking here about workmen's compensation, by the way, because we are not. So now he's deaf, and he is being forced to retire early, ten years after the onset of the deafness, because he's deaf. Unfit for duty. This comes up, miraculously, just short of the thirty years that would give him his full pension.

And cops are so unbelievably dumb that, knowing all of this and more, much, much more, they will go in and get a guy out of a burning car. Everyone will say, "You asshole! That thing's going to explode!"

You know what the cop says? He says, "Yeah, I know, but I can't just leave him there. I'm a cop."

He gets the guy out. The car explodes. He is not unscathed.
"Duh, I gotta help him because I'm a cop."
Who was that?
Oh, some cop.

I was not, by the way, brought up to understand that the
policeman is your friend. Not in Calcasieu Parish in Louisiana in
the fifties, no way. Huey Long's nephew was sheriff. It was
illegal for a black to ride in the front seat of a car with a white,
as my mother discovered one day while driving the colored
maid home. We said "colored" then, or "Negro," if we wanted
to flag that we were not racists.

It still does not occur to me to think that the policeman is
your friend, but I have known cops to do some pretty stupid
things. *Dutiful* things. I was once guarded half the night by a
cop, I never quite caught his name, a chocolate-colored cop
who . . . Uh, I can't tell that story. Gotta protect the guilty.
Also, myself.

The thing about police forces is that like universities, they
have mottos of grandeur and elegance: To Protect and to Serve.
Lux et veritas. And you find, starting especially, I am told, at the
rank of lieutenant, or else associate professor, a lot of clay feet.
People who haven't the foggiest idea what it would be to live
the life of the mind, keep the intellectual faith, on the one hand,
or to live that other good Aristotle was well-nigh obsessed with,
the good of the *polis.* Quite a bit of both Aristotle and Plato is
hidden behind those badges that say "Police." Quite a bit, too,
obscured by all that Latin and Greek and Hebrew inscribed on
and around university libraries. Socrates, I recall, was particularly voluble for a while in the *Republic* about the extraordinary,
nay, paradoxical, combination of virtues required for the guardians of the just city. Which is not to deny but rather to affirm
what George said: There are some crazy-mean cops out there.
Because Justice has fled the world, leaving behind a whole mess
of mortality, and no just city to guard. Spenser notes this in his
poem, in which there is of course no Justice though there is a
mortal, Artegall, who is the Knight of Justice, a dull fellow
beside some of the others—the first cop, the first dumb cop,

centuries before Sir Robert Peel instituted his "bobbies," or "peelers," in London. There are other mortal knights in *The Faerie Queene,* including some crazy-mean ones who lie, steal, flatter, rape, take graft. Cut up *babies.*

How do you guard the just city when there is no just city to guard? Socrates doesn't say, so I followed some mounted cops around for a while, looking every morning at the duty roster to see which cop-and-horse unit was to be patrolling where the next morning. Cops are actually not assigned to guard the just city, of course—justice isn't one of the locations on the duty roster. They are assigned to the beach or the wino neighborhood or the town green. There is no justice on the duty roster, but cops are supposed to go out and guard the just city anyway. How do they find it? How do you guard what you *know* isn't there even though the mayor keeps rattling on about it?

Well, you can make something up, imagine that you are in your own person the untarnished badge of justice instead of realizing that you wear a tin badge, which is crazy but not necessarily crazy-mean. You can give up on the whole enterprise, which is where you get your burnt-out-cop syndrome. You can become crazy-mean. Or of course you can just start out crazy-mean, even though some attempt is made to screen out sociopaths, some of whom are attracted to police work for the same reason that they are attracted to politics or law or medicine.

Consider what Joseph Wambaugh, the cops' poet, has to say about his going to bat as an expert witness for other writers who are being sued, about his refusing to settle when *he* is sued: "I'm one of the few writers who can afford to fight these things. So I feel an obligation to do it."

See what I mean about dumb cops? Obligation. Protecting and serving, and Wambaugh is rich, real rich. But still a dumb cop. There are these several kinds of cops. There are the rookies and the dumb cops and the corrupt cops and the crazy cops and the crazy-mean cops.

Wambaugh has things to say about illusion. The context is the suit brought against a writer for saying in his book that convicted child-and-wife-murderer Jeffrey McDonald was guilty of the crimes he was convicted of. The book was one of your usual pieces of emotion-(not soul-)baring disguised as investigative journalism, not my favorite book, but it is important that bad books flourish, I think, as the poet John Milton said, and as Socrates did not say. Of course, when Milton wrote about the matter he was talking about the actual world, and Socrates was talking about the ideal city, so their views differ. Having read both Milton and Socrates, I was interested in the fact that Wambaugh, whose books are often pretty good, appeared as an expert witness for that writer whose book I thought was terrible, and reports: "The jurors . . . didn't like us. They liked that sociopath who slaughtered his family. They didn't believe that he did it. They looked at that handsome, articulate Princeton physician, and they said, 'How can anybody who looks like that slaughter his own little children?'

"Because the average person just does not have any conception of what a sociopath is. None. They can't conceive that a human being who's educated and articulate can have no conscience. It's too tough a concept."

The concepts a cop needs for ordinary survival are "too tough." "Tough" here means both "intellectually intricate and difficult," like mathematics, and "dangerous," the way war is. Which is why and how so many cops are crazy-mean, or else, like Wambaugh here, so goddamn dumb it would make you weep, because if you know what Wambaugh knows—that juries are no more going to get it straight about writers than they are about cops or sociopaths or dogs, and thus that there is no just city—since he knows all of this, what the hell is Wambaugh doing out there on his white horse?

Anyway, that is all speculation. On February 8, 1988, you will recall, Judge Harold Dean of the Stamford Superior Court allowed me to take Bandit for training. I hadn't expected the judge to grant this petition, but I wasn't driving all the way to Stamford just to go through the motions, so a few days before the hearing I rang up Silver Trails, The Animal Inn. In the extremely unlikely event that I got custody of this notorious vicious pit bull, could I board him at Silver Trails?

"Sure," says Lillian Bernard. "Why not? We've got plenty of

room." So there was room for Bandit at The Animal Inn. Other kennel operators were refusing to board pit bulls, sometimes out of fear of the dogs, but more often out of a desire to protect their businesses—because what if it got out that you kept pit bulls and your other customers decided not to bring their decent, law-abiding pets to you while they went to Florida? Some kennel owners had a mistaken belief that pit bulls were banned in Connecticut, a belief that wasn't all that mistaken, at least not in spirit, but that belief did not match the letter of the law. Pit bulls are not as of this writing *legally* illegal in Connecticut, except in Wethersfield, which has a pit bull ban; they are just *de facto* illegal, like blacks in so many municipalities.

There was room for Bandit at The Animal Inn, but do not get confused at this crucial stage in the narrative and imagine that Bandit is the gentle savior of mankind, nor that George and Lillian were kindly host and hostess to said savior. For one thing, George is, as I said, an ex-cop and therefore dumb and/or crazy and/or crazy-mean and/or corrupt and/or burnt out. And Lillian is the wife to any or all of the above, so these are not the kind of people to give refuge to wandering Jews (though perhaps to their donkey), even if or especially if Mrs. Wandering Jew is about to give birth, possibly messily and noisily, to the savior of the world. Also, the expensively maintained president of your local charity is not going to take in dirty, vicious, wandering Jews either. In fact, no one takes in the savior of the world and his mom, which is how come the savior of the world grows up so hard to take, perhaps. But look: In the Jesus story there was no room at the inn, and in the Bandit story there was plenty of room at the Inn, so do not muddy up my story, please, with saints and angels and the like.

Say there were a savior of the world. It wouldn't be Bandit, because when Bandit first got acquainted with the not so placid beasts of the field, in the form of the white-faced Herefords, or polled Herefords, that Charlie takes care of over at the kennel, he wanted to have them for his own instead of just admiring their beauty. Figuring it out about the cows was a moment of self-discovery for Bandit. Several days of self-discovery, actually, because he was a city dog and at first didn't know about cows and such with their gentle lowing. He said, "What in the name of heaven is this?" After a while the answer came to him, as in a vision: "Those, why those are Cows! Cattle! Sons and daughters of Bulls! And I, Bandit, I am a bulldog! I have a heritage and a responsibility here." I didn't have to teach him this, you see—he just knew it, the way a prophet knows God. I did have to teach him to transcend the circumstances of his birth, and he learned that lesson pretty well. But no way was Bandit just at first going to lay his head down peacefully in a manger, not one in an already occupied stable, which is why he was not lodged in the barn but in a very nice double run in D building at Silver Trails, The Animal Inn.

Bandit has come to the defense a few times. You might even say he has saved people, but always in ambiguous circumstances with something a bit embarrassing about them, nothing proven in court, and please remember that he is a dangerous dog.

He *bites* people!

I do not love him for his bites, having learned the hard way that you can puncture yourself on a figure of speech, but there are plenty of people who hate him for his bites. Others hated his owner, liberally, for his bites. This, of course, is a figure of speech, too. To say that one hates the owner for the dog's bites is to mention the owner when you mean the dog. Killing dogs while saying that it is the owners who are bad is one traditional activity of humane societies everywhere. But while it is true that things were done to Bandit, many things also were done to Mr. Redd, who unlike Bandit has Fifth and Fourteenth Amendment rights. They are spelled out.

So Bandit's case is not an animal rights case, I kept saying to Steve Wizner, William O. Douglas Professor of Law and director of the Program in Clinical Law at Yale, when he would say, "I don't know anything about animal rights law."

I would say, "The reason you don't is because there isn't any such thing, but it doesn't matter because this is not an animal rights case."

Steve would say, "You keep saying that, but I don't get it."

So I would say, "Well, just listen."

He would say, "I always listen," and this is true, more or less. Professor Wizner thinks that listening to people's troubles and responding is part of the practice of law. He has *said* that to me! He said it to me when I told him, over a year later, that I was impressed that first day in his office that he had listened to me, and I asked him why he had done that. He replied that I "talk funny," and that interested him, and added also that I had mentioned *Bleak House,* a novel he likes enormously, plus I had pushed the buttons when I had mentioned that Mr. Redd was old, poor, and black. And I had told him, "Yes, I know that everybody believes that pit bulls are vicious, but it isn't so," which appealed because he likes knowing that something everybody believes isn't so. This, perhaps, is your clever-lawyer syndrome, but there are also dumb lawyers who will have you believe that the only reason to be interested in the law is because you are interested in justice, in seeing justice done. And Steve Wizner would say, "Listening. That's law, too." Do you believe that?

More sophisticated people hold that law is poetry, but Steve thinks it isn't anything, or else it is listening to people's problems and responding, or so he said one day, and only he knows whether or not he has earned the right to talk that way.

These conversations with Steve Wizner were not the only location of my sudden need in the middle of this case to figure out what the law is, meaning: that which is under discussion in the *Yale Law Journal,* for example, which has a vague relationship to laws, statutes, and ordinances of the sort often to be found in the files and on the desks of persons actively engaged in trying to keep a dog alive or a person safe, or the other way about.

I began investigating 𝕿𝖍𝖊 𝕷𝖆𝖜 itself in case it came up somewhere, because you never can tell. It hasn't come up so far except in casual conversation, as when someone expostulates, "But that's unconstitutional!" Still, it might, since there is so much testifying and trying and pronouncing of judgment going on.

The first question is, of course, "What is the Law?"
Or, "Why is there the Law and not something else?"

Steve Wizner says it isn't anything, as I have indicated, and cites in support of this view the fact that Japanese-Americans were shoved into prison camps during World War II perfectly legally. So nothing comes from nothing. In support of Steve's idea of "perfectly legal" it can be added that most of the atrocities in the history of our species have been perfectly legal, or as near as makes no nevermind, and maybe *that's* what distinguishes us from other animals, because moose and chipmunks just go ahead and do things, whereas people derive some inexplicable consolation and encouragement when they pass or interpret a law making whatever atrocity they want to commit a matter of Law.

Other thinkers, Mark Twain, for example, have said that what we do is make it *religious* to do something awful to someone else, but I would like to remind everyone that courts used to be ecclesiastical. I will someday develop a glossary of terms that includes an explanation of how "genes" and "devils" or "society" and "God" and other interesting synonyms work.

But to return: Steve's example of Japanese in concentration camps and many others make it clear that law is justice—is, that is, the justification of violent acts. So we are the animal that desires justification, or, briefly, justice. As when someone succeeds in getting approval for the practice of stopping people without cause and searching them, checking to see if they happen to be committing a crime, because what is desired is justice, a higher justice, higher than the Constitution.

Higher Justice—I am not sure of this, but I *think* that Higher Justice means when it is the *idea* of the thing rather than the thing itself that inspires you. Like when it is the *idea* of Bandit— an idea of a ravening monster with three jaws and no respect and holdings in Colombia and an appetite for human flesh—rather than Bandit himself that inspires prosecution.

Bandit himself makes prosecution difficult. In a journal called *American Jurisprudence: Trials,* there is an article advising lawyers who are prosecuting pit bull cases not to allow the defense to bring the dogs into court because "these dogs can be trained to act docile, and mislead the jury into believing that this is, indeed, man's best friend." You may think that this is a little bit like the problem of the handsome, articulate murderer on the stand misleading the jury into thinking he is the children's friend, but I don't think it is, not because I know all that much about psychopaths—I am no cop—but because dogs cannot be "trained to act docile." Human beings can be, but not dogs. Dogs can be trained to *be* gentle, say, and thoughtful and courteous and mild-mannered, but they can't be trained to *act* that way except in extremely limited circumstances, and certainly not in the trying conditions of a hearing room. The dog's true nature will come out, as a general rule, after a couple of hours of testimony, when he starts wanting to go outside to pee.

In a gloomy frame of mind, I showed that article to Frank Cochran, and he responded with élan, overcome by lawyerly *joie de vivre,* full of a vision. Bandit, he said happily, would be present at the next hearing so that he could mislead onlookers into thinking that he was man's best friend. This meant also arranging for one of his partners, Linda Francois, to be present at the hearing so that there would be one lawyer upstairs arguing learnedly about the No Dogs rule at the State Office Building, and another downstairs preventing me and Bandit from getting arrested and/or impounded for being there about to violate the rule.

Why was I doing all of this? Why was Cochran doing it? It is hard to say, especially as I do not dare speak for Frank Cochran—he speaks for me, not the other way—but it is possible that we were doing it because in our various ways we all desired justice. Me and Cochran and George and Lillian Bernard and Dick Koehler and Steve Wizner and Linda Francois and, yes, Frank Intino, and other characters, all gathered in the State Office Building because we desired justice. Human beings gather in hearing rooms because they desire justice. A hearing room is a funny place to look for it, but that is not to refute the fact of the desire, only to note that, as Socrates says in the *Euthyphro,* justice is a tricky thing, a tricky thing founded in desire.

Justice isn't all that we desire, but it is hard to deny that as a species we do desire justice. If you are willing to do some violence to the history of the word "kindness," as it appears both in Scripture and in the wonderful poem of Donald Davie's that serves as the epigraph of this book, or if you are willing at least to allow me to do this violence, then we may go on to observe, in the words of Proverbs 19:22, that "the desire of a man is his kindness." Things have changed: kindness is no longer something that belongs to people, only to lords or to societies, like justice, and justice is now the kindness of many of us, which means that concentration camps are an instance of the kindness of our species, of the ways it pays its dues, of the distorted forms of intimacy we buttress with our solemnity and piety. As when Jews were sent to concentration camps in the thirties in Germany, propelled there in part by arguments produced by the head of the major German humane society of the period, the Tierschutzverein. Hermann Göring by name.

Let me say that more slowly. One of the striking things about the memories of my friends who lived through the 1930s in Germany is that in some cases it was not until *Kristallnacht,* in 1938, that they had any sense that Hitler meant anyone "real" harm. What people were aware of when they thought of Hitler and the Nazis were words, words such as "purity," "nobility." There were ideals everywhere, according to the memories of my friends, and the ideals included kindness to animals. Hence there was not much stir when Göring went on the radio to urge the incarceration of "cruel" scientists of blood "alien to our nation" and to reassure his audience that true Germans were kind to animals. In a radio broadcast on August 28, 1933, he announced, "In order that animal torturing shall not continue, I have now stepped in . . . and will commit to concentration camps those who still think that they can continue to treat animals as inanimate property." This speech was specifically concerned with vivisection and the religious use of animals, and unless you were offended by its anti-Semitism or had some awareness of what the lack of restraints on the power of the Tierschutzverein signified—for Jewish scientists, say—it probably sounded reasonable enough. It emphasized the use of anesthetics, noting that "necessary" animal experiments, especially on rats, which are "not as susceptible to pain as our domestic pets and [are] most certainly not worthy of our sympathy," would be acceptable.

The important fact about Göring and you and me is that we are human. Hannah Arendt's essay of 1945, "Collective Guilt and Universal Responsibility," notes that understanding the horror of the Reich is "not aided by speculations about German history and the so-called German national character. [The murder machine] relies entirely upon the normality of jobholders and family-men." This normality consisted in *decencies*—care for the security of one's family, compassion for animals. Thus, for all that I am here in the middle of a book in which there are figures who are from my point of view villains, I keep returning to the discovery that if I want to understand human villainy, one place to look—not the only place, but one place—is into myself, and not to look there for my hatreds, but rather for my loves and my loyalties. The fate of popular ideas of the bulldog breeds, which are sometimes viciousness incarnate and sometimes decency incarnate, may be a clue to the fate of any human moral trait. Not the *idea* of the trait, but the trait itself, as though there were something to the idea that for us virtue cannot be innocent.

But I have gotten too general here, which is what tends to happen to discourse when the big issues come up, and I shall lose my balance if I do not return to some details. I am told that in Germany in the early thirties Dobies were held to be vicious because, like the Jews, they were of impure blood. Our own horror stories about people and dogs are usually horror stories about blood that is "too pure," as it were. Strange, vicious mountain people, or pit bulls, or ghetto dwellers, are imagined to be tainted because "inbred."

Viciousness is a real trait in the fantasies of those who propose injustices against those who are believed to be vicious, whether the "vicious" ones are pit bulls, novelists, Jews, blacks, witches, or people who smell because they have no place to take a bath. Quite often the viciousness is a "tragedy" that causes mental distress to those who must stamp it out. Quite often, as in the case of a piece of correspondence I have from a PETA representative, the euthanasia of the vicious is held to be a "sad necessity." At other times vengeance is openly expressed, as in the case of states that have what are called "paraphernalia" laws, which make it a felony to own "dogfighting equipment or literature." (I suppose that since I own the works of James Thurber and Mark Twain, both of whom wrote stories about dogfights, I own "dogfighting literature." I doubt that there is a library in the nation that does not harbor material on dogfighting.) In any case, vengeance and anger may be openly expressed, or everyone may look very sad as they pass laws requiring that dogs and cats endure major surgery in the name of kindness. (There is as of this writing a law that forbids any breeding of dogs or cats in San Mateo County, California, and that requires you to have a breeding license in order to own an unaltered animal. Spaying and neutering are supposed to have no effect on a dog's general well-being, but there are special dog foods for altered animals, and spayed and neutered animals are not as strong, not as determined, not as joyful in their work as intact ones.)

The thing that seems constant in the case of the class of historical horror that is on my mind is that it is buttressed by talk of kindness. If "the desire of a man is his kindness," and if kindness prompts me to vengeful feelings, then vengeance is what I desire, and that is my kindness. People have a tendency to say "justice" when vengeance is what they desire, but it need not follow that we will inevitably get justice and injustice confused. The two depend on each other, like one half of the earth on the other half, and not, say, like the bits that make up a house of cards. You can know that one half of the earth depends on the other half without being specific about where one half leaves off and the other begins, and the same applies to that particular domain of justice and injustice which goes to make up the Law.

There was once a man named Robert Cover, who wrote in the *Yale Law Journal* in 1986:

We begin, then, not with what the judges say, but with what they do.
The judges deal pain and death.

That is not all they do. Perhaps that is not what they usually do. But they *do* deal death, and pain. From John Winthrop through Warren Burger they have sat atop a pyramid of violence, dealing. . . .

In this they are different from poets, from critics, from artists. It will not do to insist on the violence of strong poetry, and strong poets. Even the violence of weak judges is utterly real—a naïve but immediate reality, in need of no interpretation, no critic to reveal it. . . .

Between the idea and the reality of common meaning falls the shadow of the violence of law, itself.

Cover's article, "Violence and the Word," talks about how the radically different nature of the experience of a violent legal decision for various persons—the perpetrators of the violence (the judges), the imposers of it (jailers and the like), and the victims of it (the incarcerated or executed)—destroys the possibility of the law's having a common meaning, and I hear also an implied question about the possibility of common meaning at all.

Cover, I think, was on to something, and it is a melancholy comment on anyone's hopes for the future of human intelligence that he is dead. (Couple of years ago, at forty-three, heart attack.) I cite him, however, not to weep for him but to urge embattled readers to notice the significance of the fact that the term "Bandit" cannot come to have, no matter how well I write and no matter how sympathetically and knowledgeably you read, the same meaning for you as for me, because in this book I cannot use his name in the second person, only in the third person. I use his name to call him with, and there are created through various uses of the second person small clearings, arenas of clarity of response and thus of justice. Mr. Redd used his name to call him, too, but Mr. Redd knew things that I do not know and does not know things that I do know about dogs— evidence of this given in the fact that Bandit once bit Mr. Redd to make a point, and has never bitten me—and that means that the term "Bandit" cannot mean the same thing even for me and

Mr. Redd, even though we both learned its second-person grammar intimately.

All testimony about Bandit, including mine, must be given in the third person, so I cannot "share" what "Bandit" means, what that term refers to, not even with Frank Cochran or a hearing officer, suppose that one were miraculously to come into being, who was totally "on Bandit's side." This would be true even of a hearing officer who knew enough to get Bandit's breed straight, and I am talking about corridors full of people who didn't even know that much, didn't even pause to wonder if it mattered that he is neither a pit bull nor an "American Staffordshire Pit Bull Terrier," or that there is no such breed as "American Staffordshire Pit Bull Terrier."

Of course, language fails us, or we fail it, continually and utterly, and we and the world fail each other too. Alertness to this possibility is the foundation of skepticism, but skepticism can have both modest and immodest forms, as can speech. It is possible to use the name "Bandit," and even refer to Bandit, with or without his name, without knowing much at all. There probably is no such thing as full reference, even in a great poem, but we can be competent speakers when we are not lying or maddened by politics or some forms of intellect gone amok, or by ambitious yearnings to be inhumanly loving or kindly. Someone in the kennel might say, "When did that black and white dog in Run 63 come in? It must have been after I left last night," or "Do you want Bandit to have Kal Kan?" or "Whose dog is that?" or even "What kind of dog is that?" These would all be cases of competent referring, so long as the ambitions of the speaker did not outstrip patience and knowledge. If "What kind of dog is Bandit?" is a question thrown at me by an AAG bent on upholding a destruction order, on winning a case, rather than on finding something out, then reference goes awry.

The disposal order issued by the state of Connecticut doesn't even manage to meet minimal requirements for competent reference—because what is it when a dog of a nonexistent breed is disposed of, or ordered to be disposed of? And yet, sadly for our species, this and thousands of other cases are cases of something like reference, since the pseudolinguistic activities in question can be used to seize, tattoo, and destroy real dogs (and people when the terms in question are "witch" or "Jew" or "traitor").

Both language and pseudolinguistic behaviors sometimes sound like noise even to native speakers of the tongue in question. When the language is technical and competent—the shop-talk of honest mechanics or philosophers or lawyers or poets—it can sound like noise, sometimes insane noise, to an outsider, to someone who does not know the terms, the form of life, in question. When the language is incompetent, even if very clever, it will sound like insane noise to insiders, to people who really know how to use it. Some people have a higher tolerance for noise than others, and different responses to the noise. One possible response to an excess of pseudolinguistic noise is insanity, or the temptation just to relax and believe that the noise has meaning. This possibility is given in a passage from C. S. Lewis's *That Hideous Strength*. The hero, Ransom, is a figure of the truly religious man in a falsely religious world. He has been captured by some Ultimately Bad People, and is both tormented and tempted by being put in a room full of beautiful religious paintings. The paintings are powerful, splendid—but not quite right. Each one is a bit off somehow, and contemplation of the paintings nearly destroys the hero. Ray Monk's biography of Wittgenstein, *The Duty of Genius,* shows elaborately what other accounts of Wittgenstein have suggested, that he was, as it were, a man who could not tolerate noise, and that clearing up the noise was his motive for philosophy. Some modern work— I'm thinking of some of the results of neurolinguistic programming, also of Bateson's discussion of what he calls the "schizophrenic double bind"—suggests that at least some forms of what we call madness are cases not of language gone wrong so much as of people who cannot tolerate language gone wrong and do not have the resources to do anything about it. And we say of historical periods in which the noise of pseudolanguage is loudest, and is backed up with spears or machine guns, that the period itself is "mad."

Great poetry and philosophy are among the ways human beings have learned to respond to noise, to the confusing pseudolinguistic activities that in secular terms are a kind of by-product of our awesome linguistic capacities. (In religious terms, noise is confusion of the form: the separation from God.) Wittgenstein, unable to tolerate noise yet at great personal cost able to keep working toward clarity and to keep realizing that the noise was going to keep coming, managed philosophy in response. Wallace Stevens managed great poetry that was about both the noise and the possibility of clarity. Over the years he wrote much advice to himself about what to do about the noise, and wrote, of the clarity he achieved, that it was a "poem that took the place of a mountain," and said of his poem, "The vivid transparence that you bring is peace."

Robert Cover notes that one difference between poetry and the law is that "even the violence of weak judges is utterly real." Another is that the violence of the law is one of the engines that escalate noise and confusion into a not only deafening but deadening crescendo.

Like virtually everyone else I know in the pit bull wars, I found the noise of the babble about dogs intolerable at times, and madness seemed at some points like an almost comforting possibility. (What I mostly did was to tell everyone I knew more than they ever wanted to know about the bull breeds—a kind of social incompetence, also a form of madness.) The thing to keep in mind is that chaste speech is possible. We live in a world in which people incompetent to use our names can nonetheless refer to us and our dogs and children and friends and neighbors successfully; real people and dogs can be impounded, licensed, transported, and killed by, among other things, the more or less intellectual capacity that enables us to refer to real objects with contaminated language.

We have traded awareness for language. This does not mean that we have the option of turning our backs on language. Someone said to me recently, when I was claiming that a certain argument about animal rights would not hold water, "What does it matter whether or not you call it rights? That is just

words." I expostulated—the person was an English professor!—
that carelessness about words kills people. We do not have the
choice between language and the kind of awareness animals
have. The most thoroughly studied cases of people without
language—autism—are *not* cases of animals who look like people. An autistic human being is not merely without words, but
is also lacking in world, unlike a dog, who has world aplenty.

Hence it wouldn't matter if Bandit were indeed an American
Pit Bull Terrier and thus entitled to the nickname "pit bull,"
because the people who failed to know that he is an American
Bulldog also failed to know that there was something to know
in the first place, and are thereby disqualified as competent in the
use of the term "pit bull" anyhow. They are right once in a
while, of course, in a way, even though they do not know how
to mean the term "pit bull." They are right by mistake, though,
like my being right about where to put a symbol in a linear
equation, and not by accident, like a stopped clock being "right"
twice a day—there is something off about it.

Which means that there is something off about language, for
we learn language through both accident and mistake, and this,
too, is how we learn the world, as John Milton suggests we do,
through our errors, by our errors—he writes that error must not
be prohibited, for "the knowledge and survey of vice is in this
world so necessary to the constituting of human virtue, and the
scanning of error to the confirmation of truth, [that the safest
way of knowing the truth is] by reading all manner of tractates
and hearing all manner of reasons. . . . And this is the benefit
which may be had of books promiscuously read." And words
promiscuously uttered, I might add—which means that if I am
glad for anything in these mortal coils, what I am glad for
includes the false claim that Bandit is a pit bull, or an "American
Staffordshire Pit Bull Terrier," since I would not have known as
well as I do now how to use the term "pit bull" properly, what
the true referent for it is, were it not for the instructive activity
of calming myself down in the face of the tangles and confusions
of the courtroom.

What is "just" is "true," "accurate," and even "good"—a

carpenter must make a just, which is to say, true angle, for example, a "just" line is a straight line, the justification of a margin is the straightening out of that margin, and I was driven by the errors of the hearing room to a juster knowledge of dogs, as a carpenter is driven by a bad join to make a juster angle. It was an expensive, roundabout ride toward truth, but it got me there, briefly, so it may be not only that when all of us gathered at the State Office Building we were there in pursuit of justice, but also that we hadn't gotten all that lost, no more lost than one must of logical necessity be when justice is not, as I have said, a location on the duty roster. Nor on the docket. When you walk into a courthouse you don't find that "justice" is on any of the dockets, but rather Redd v. Department of Agriculture, or The People v. Charles Manson, or Smith v. Smith. And it may be that only in a hurly-burly of displaced persons and proper nouns such as you find in a courthouse will you discover enough error to make room for truth, enough unjustice from which some justice can emerge.

I suspect that my lawyer would scoff at this account of things, but that would be hypocritical of him, for he is into justice in this case.

There were two American Pit Bull Terriers at a hearing concerning a proposed breed ban in New York City. Like most pit bulls, these neighborly dogs read as their affable selves to most of the assembly. I do not know how they read to Dr. Kehoe, veterinarian to the Department of Health, but he kept asking if people had seen an Actual Pit Bull Attack. Witness after witness said, "Of course not," because the more pit bulls you know personally the less likely you are to have any significant experience of dog attacks. The question, though, seemed to give the questioner much satisfaction when he asked it, so I suppose that the affable dogs in the hearing room read to him as killers and therefore killable, and this is far from being the only detail that has caused the term "pit bull" to cease to be potentially of the stuff of common meaning.

I do not here mean to blink at the observations and discoveries of Wittgenstein and others about the public nature of language, nor to deny that by and large—only by and large—meaning must be or must be becoming shared, common, in order to be meaning at all, but some very peculiar things have happened to this term "pit bull," and to words such as "dog," and to images given by public objects such as movies and stories about boys and dogs, just as peculiar things have happened to words such as "Jew" and "black." I have been trying to lay out here at tedious length what Flannery O'Connor accomplished with deft and sagacious speed in her story "The Artificial Nigger," in which a boy learns to recognize niggers where before he had only seen people, just as in the eighties Americans learned to recognize pit bulls where before they had only seen dogs.

The term "pit bull" now has several kinds of meaning which, even though they are different meanings, aren't clearly different meanings in the sense the *OED* gives terms. One is private in that only a few people know how to use the term accurately to tell someone else what sort of dog is under discussion. As it happens, for example, there are only one or two persons in New York City whom I know to be competent in the use of the term. That is a pretty private sort of detail, not as private as a private language, perhaps, a language with no possible common reference, since I can say with some success to those of my friends who do not know how to use the term "pit bull," "That is not what I mean by the term," and they will respect that. Then there is this public, official, administrative, legal, and press use of the term "pit bulls," the thingumwackers that are artifacts of lies, hallucinations, and other whazzits from that collection of pseudolinguistic phenomena found on TV, radio, and in the public prints—artificial pit bulls in the worst sense of artificial.

Robert Cover's remarks must be put next to a great deal of Wittgenstein, and we must learn to understand that the fact that language is a public, shared phenomenon is not necessarily good news for stability of meaning and reference.

The same considerations apply, of course, to terms such as "kindness" or "person" or "crime" or "child" or "justice" or "America" or "poem." (As to whether or not the law is poetry:

I have noticed that flowery language can get out of hand in legal situations, but this is the sort of thing poetry cures, not the sort of thing it causes. Poetry is not opinion, judicial or otherwise, but Truth. Poetry is not true the way the testimony of a witness who does not perjure himself is true, but the way a dog is true to his own nature and to his master.)

It was pleasantly distracting, worrying about what the Law is, and why there is the Law and not something else, and these contemplations led me inevitably to considerations of the Prophets, too, but neither the Law nor the Prophets occupied me or Steve Wizner in the early days when I went to his office to see what he had to say about this case. The *very* early days, when the project of getting Bandit back home to Henry Street was still alive.

I showed him the statute under which the dogcatcher had ordered the fence built and the disposal order written, Connecticut 22-358, which reads in part: ". . . the commissioner, the chief canine control officer, any canine control officer, any warden or regional canine control officer may make any order concerning the restraint or disposal of any biting dog as he deems necessary."

Steve Wizner bent over this object studiously, peering through his glasses, then reading it without his glasses, and said, "That's just *got* to be unconstitutional!"

At this point I cheered up, which shows you how wet I was then. What I thought was that if the Yale Law School said that something was unconstitutional, then you could just get a lawyer to explain it to a judge, and then any action taken under the statute wouldn't be legal anymore, and then they wouldn't get to kill Bandit, who could go back home to Henry Street and protect the public there, which as I have indicated wanted to be protected, not *from* Bandit, but *by* him. When Steve said "unconstitutional," I was filled with a vision of Bandit back on his porch, next to Mr. Redd, and of Mr. Redd no longer waking up in the night, or half waking up, walking around and talking about Bandit and worrying whether there was enough of that expensive dog feed for him, the kind in cans that he likes, for when Bandit came home.

Realizing that all of this was wrong, I began also to suspect that the Yale Law School does not exist, but more of that later.

According to *A Recent Study,* losing a dog is hardest on the old and the young. According to *A Recent Study,* it is especially productive of what used to be called delinquency, a failure of respect for societal values, you see, to lose a pet to the deliberate actions of parents or authorities.

I would say this sort of thing to Steve Wizner, because the man persisted in using the phrase "animal rights" and I persisted in saying, "This isn't an animal rights case, Professor Wizner."

"Call me Steve," he would say. "Everybody calls me Steve."

Then he would say, "You keep saying that, but I don't get it."

I responded somewhat shrilly by saying that the only person in this case in relationship to whom Bandit could be said to have rights was Mr. Redd, that Mr. Redd's rights were being trampled on by careless, inauthentic, violent, ignorant bureaucrats, that it was redundant anyhow to put those adjectives in front of the word "bureaucrat," that everyone was entranced, out of their minds, because they could not see that Mr. Redd's rights were the point. Steve countered by urging on me a charitable view of Frank Intino, chief Canine Control officer of Connecticut, the fellow who kept wanting to uphold the disposal order on Bandit. I won't say that Intino actually wanted to kill Bandit, because he never said so directly; he talked mostly about protecting the public and the integrity of the disposal order. That looked like killing Bandit to me, but Frank Cochran said at one point that I must be more literal, i.e., careful, i.e., perhaps it wouldn't be all that good an idea to say in this book that Intino wanted to kill Bandit, only that he wanted to protect the public, which is no doubt true and would comfort me more if there were any indication that the state thought of me as part of this mysterious public that needs protecting.

Now, Intino did want to engage in action that would result in Bandit's transformation into a corpse, but how much does any of us know of what our fellows have in mind? I don't, for example, know whether any images of the corpse of Bandit actually inhabited Intino's consciousness as they did mine, so I wouldn't be speaking from real knowledge if I said that he wanted to kill Bandit. Maybe he didn't realize that if he upheld the disposal order Bandit would never again look at me or anyone with that uncanny expression of "At your service, ma'am." Maybe he doesn't know what it is to cause death—not everyone does. So all I will report is that in my naïve way I kept thinking that "protecting the public" by means of a disposal order meant Bandit as a corpse, and that that meant killing Bandit.

Hence Steve Wizner was not the only person to urge upon me a charitable view of, or at least a charitable account of, mine enemy and attorneys of mine enemy—even my lawyer was preaching charitable caution. Steve's motives were more—dare I say it?—Christian than Frank Cochran's were. Frank wanted me to stay out of trouble, Steve wanted me to practice the virtue of understanding.

"Think of it!" says Steve. "Think of how much this man wanted to do his job. All he wants to do is protect the public, and now he doesn't get to. Think of how it must feel to be defied and defeated in your professional activities."

I said I knew a fair amount about that already, thanks to the blasted Department of Agriculture, and didn't need additional meditations on the topic, and Steve harassed me with the idea that I should think of what it is like to be, not me, Vicki Hearne, triumphantly in possession of the vicious monster dog Bandit, but him, Frank Intino, wanting to protect the public and defeated in this project.

When Steve needles me, it always works, every damned time he does it, so I said, "Hah! Protect the public, indeed! Kill Bandit, that's all he wants to do, he just wants to kill Bandit!"

Steve greeted this outburst serenely by repeating some bits about how Intino is human and he has his woes too, and it isn't good for dogs to chew up little children, and I asked if he had ever had to confront the primal anger of a mother taking a broom to the guy who did wrong by her daughter. Effie Powell was by her own account in a dangerous mood, I said, since she was too angry to speak, so had to grab up that broom and commence beating Mr. Johnson with it, and Bandit was just doing his job, keeping the peace, when he bit Effie Powell, *and:*

"Bandit has never bitten any innocent little children!" I screeched, and added sternly to the law professor that Frank Intino's woes were none of my business anyhow, any more than mine seemed to be any of his, except insofar as he increased them despite or because of his fancying himself to be a modern St. Francis. I added, in case Steve hadn't read all my books, that the dog trainer's gods are Apollo and Diana, which means that Christianity and charity aren't in it. Truth is.

I didn't tell Professor Wizner the two stories that drove me to his office and the offices of other lawyers. In the fall of 1987 there was a week-long ABC special on pit bulls. I watched one of the episodes with my friend Sara, who has a television. You had your intrepid reporter going into one of Those Neighborhoods, dedicated to truth but all a-tremble because: "There might be pit bulls anywhere!" The intrepid reporter is eventually seen interviewing a nine-year-old boy, along these lines:

Q: Is that your dog?
A: (Proudly, fondling the ear of a more or less bull-type dog who looks about as ferocious as Bill Cosby, though not nearly so energetic.) Yes! His name is Spike, and he's my dog. He's a good dog! [We hear a fair amount about how Spike is always there, and never deserts his friends, and doesn't wet in the house, and never refuses to play.]
Q: Do you fight your dog?
A: Yes. I fight with my friend. We fight every day after school. Sometimes my friend wins and I pay him money, and sometimes I win and he pays me money.
Q: Do you like your dog?
A: I *love* him! He does everything with me. Other people—my mom gets mad with me, but he don't.

At this stage, an ASPCA or generically Kind truck appears, and gentlemen with snare poles leap out and "capture" Spike, who responds with good humor and is dragged off to the paddy wagon by men who are having a hard time making the capture look dangerous enough to justify rolling the minicams.

The child—of course the child runs after the men, crying, crying, crying. Crying out: "Please! Help! Stop! They're going to kill my dog!"

The description of the "dogfighting" activities, by the way, together with the obviously unscarred hide of Spike, makes it clear that this has about as much to do with organized dog-fighting as Tom Sawyer's piracy club had to do with the Co-lombian dope trade.

The child cries, "Stop! Stop!" The voice-over asks the audi-ence, "What are we going to do about this horror?" The horror I saw was a child terrified and brutalized because the state—in the form, as I recall, of the ASPCA, which has a contract to handle animal control in New York—was impounding his best friend, but the horror the newscaster had in mind was the child himself, not the child's terror and grief. The child was the em-blem and instance of the overwhelming specter of dogfighting and the dope trade.

I did not tell Professor Wizner about Mr. Redd's defense of Bandit either: "The white ladies like him, too." I have men-tioned living in Lake Charles, Louisiana, in the 1950s. It is as true of Louisiana as it is of the Northeast that, in Cover's words, "Between the idea and the reality of common meaning falls the shadow of the violence of law, itself." It is as true in Louisiana as it is at the Harvard philosophy department that black and white are among the divisions diction has trouble crossing suc-cessfully. But there is also something to the stories you may have heard, stories, for example, about naval vessels during World War II on which it was discovered—by whites at any rate—that Southern blacks and whites had more in common with each other than Northern and Southern whites did. And in my childhood, "Yankee" was not a polite word, because Yan-kees themselves were everywhere understood to be unmannered, boorish, scarcely able to speak. (This sort of thing led my mother, herself a Yankee of sorts, to produce more than one assault on the supposed godliness of our neighbors on Lake Street and certain of our relatives on my father's side, also to insist rather heavily on her relationship to the Episcopal Church, which in Southern Baptist territory is assumed to be a den of iniquity.) I did not tell Wizner that there was something of my feelings as a Southerner in the forces that led me to tend for several days after Mr. Redd's testimony to weep in a long, quiet way—I wept for lonesomeness perhaps, a kind of political lonesomeness or nostalgia for the time that may never have existed, and I visited the houses of Harriet Beecher Stowe and Mark Twain.

Lawyers don't have time for these stories, not if they're any good, and this is as it should be—I have learned from the impatience of lawyers. So I didn't tell Steve Wizner about any of this, not up here in Yankee territory, no sir. Besides, he was already listening to me, and was fond of *Bleak House*. I didn't want to queer this wonderful situation in which a law professor was paying attention to me. So, by way of providing support for my claim that this was not an animal rights case, I asked him if he had a television. He said he did, but he denied that he ever watched it. I said did it ever happen that he walked through a room while it was on? He allowed as how this occasionally happened, through no fault of his.

"Aha!" says I. "What do you know about pit bull owners? What do you *know* about them?"

"Well," he says, "I know that they are vicious, violent, scuzzy people, and that they are, uh, black and Hispanic."

"Yeah. So like I said, this isn't an animal rights case, Professor Wizner."

I no longer cheer up when a lawyer looks at a statute and says, "That's unconstitutional!" Because all it means is that someone is going to be done in, most of the time. I do not give up in the face of an unconstitutional statute, however, because these pit bull wars have drawn me into a circle of people and dogs who know what dead game really means. I was talking a few years ago to a man who had a dog who is a piece of history, word has it. There was a difficulty about her that was a function of her dedication to blood sports. That is, she liked to fight other dogs. I suggested a maneuver that would enable him to take her for walks without worrying about her going for other dogs, but he was dubious. Like many people who own dogs from game breeds, he was as exactly ambivalent about her prowess as nations often are about the prowess of their poets. He said, "Look. It isn't when they're winning that you find out what a dog is made of. It's what they do when they're *losing* that tells you."

The maneuver I suggested was simply longeing, the about-turn I have described using with Bandit. The owner, not yet realizing that just because a dog takes her sporting activities seriously, that doesn't mean she will regard a training situation as an adversarial one, doubted that the maneuver would work, because this was not a dog to "give in." Because training is not, by and large, adversarial it actually works better on dogs who have the kind of gumption he was at once admiring and asking my advice about. If the only idea you have of dog training is the idea that it is wholly a matter of "dominating" the dog, then you would be quite right to doubt that training would work on a game pit bull, because anything presented to such dogs as a contest only spurs them on. Not to bite you, rarely to bite you. But to refuse to submit. That is why I do not rely on submission in training. It doesn't work on wolves because they are too submissive. It doesn't work on the stalwart terriers and bulldogs because if they are any good submission isn't in their makeup.

I should here say a bit more about dogfights. There are dog-fights that are organized by the dogs themselves, called "fence fights" or "street fights" or "kennel fights." There is also what is called "rolling" a dog, which is matching one dog against another to teach them that there is such a thing as fighting and to find out if they want to do that. (Some dogs do not; they "test out cold," as people say.) And there is game-testing. Dogs who have been game-tested and proven sound are those who keep fighting even when they are losing. Game-testing and rolling are of course considered brutal and deplorable, largely because they are done by people rather than Nature. When Nature game-tests animals, as she does on a global scale, then it is magnificent or something, and the loser and the winners are said to live "in harmony with Nature."

Bandit, by the way, has not to my knowledge been game-tested—unless you count his incarceration in the Stamford pound as game-testing. In which case an evaluation might say that while he did show some loss of nerve (with his frantic circling), no fighting dog is ever tested the way he was, for months on end. Also, the fact that he came out of the pound ready and willing to work with me despite the fact that his heart had been battered by evidence that people are not worth working with, that he was bound to lose a fight for friendship with people, tells me that he tested out sound. He is bullheaded, annoyingly so, but he is a dog who, once he gives friendship, does not lightly give up on it. He is game.

We say of a game dog or person that they will "fight to the death," as in the stories about Patrick Henry crying, "Give me liberty or give me death!" This is that dreaded quality "dead game," which might just as well be called a willingness to fight to the life. Helen Keller, for example (she owned a pit bull), was a person who was game-tested and proved sound.

One of the most important figures in the dog wars was Ralph Greenwood, who in the early seventies, realizing long before anyone else did that pit bulls were in serious trouble, bought the registry I mentioned earlier, the American Dog Breeders Association, headquartered in Salt Lake City. Greenwood instituted ADBA conformation shows, weight pulls, and other activities for pit bulls and their owners because, as he said, "We had to give these dogs something legal to do."

Greenwood would sometimes protest that he was not prejudiced about breeds of dog, but he revealed his true colors one day when he said to me, "Of course, we have some dogs come into the kennel that are a little rough, and I handle them myself, don't let the inexperienced kennel hands deal with them. But those aren't the pit bulldogs. Those are the streetdogs." Here, "streetdog" means any dog not a pit bull, and "pit bulldog" is synonymous with "gentleman," just as in certain areas of this country "cur" means any dog that is not a well-bred foxhound, the only animal worthy of the name "dog."

Ralph Greenwood died last year. I got the call at around midnight, from a friend in Virginia, who announced the news thus: "We're in trouble. No more one-way tickets to Salt Lake City." This was a reference to a story that may have some truth in it, or may be a jive story, that when idiots called Greenwood and started giving him a hard time, he would offer to buy them a one-way ticket to Salt Lake, on the grounds that they would not be needing the return fare, for a while at least. An outrageous way to conduct political and business affairs, perhaps—to invite your opponent to come slug it out—but the interesting thing is not that he did this, or how often, but that the story is told, together with addenda such as that no one ever took him up on it or threatened to sue him. These stories about Greenwood, then, are stories about a man who was gentle but not to be bullied, who could with a word call bullies on their posturing.

So it is perhaps a good thing Greenwood cleared out when he did, because this man had the imagination of mountains and taught other men to be dog men.

Greenwood said to me one time—he was an old-style union organizer and knew when he was talking to the press—he said, "Here's what a dog man is. You don't find him in bars, because he's got to get home from work and take care of his beauties. And you don't find a real dog man lying or cheating, either, because he has to live up to his dogs."

He credited me once with being a dog man, so we are not contemplating the powerful impact of the women's movement just at the moment, though Kate Greenwood, his daughter, has recently been game-tested and proven sound in battle royal, in court. And I must add, in the interests of full disclosure, that even though Greenwood was a disgrace to the Mormon church

I do not know exactly how much can be inferred about his ideological soundness from my generation's point of view. Even a person who was both a "disgrace to the Mormon church" and an "old-style union organizer" might not have been politically correct.

He knew at least four months ahead of time that he was dying, and he told no one, not even his best friend, who was both a physician and a dog man. The result was that his enemies were still putting out literature trying to Do Something About Greenwood when he was a month or two in his grave, so he had learned something from his dogs about what "dead game" is all about.

Am I saying that this man admired *fighting dogs?* And that I admired him? Oh, yes, yes, I am saying that. And that America has no virtue but *virtù,* just at the moment at least, and one time, one time in Stanford, California, I was engaged in decent battle with the British poet Donald Davie, who is the author of the poem in which the line about desiring one's own and not another's kindness occurs. He said to me, "*Why* must you American poets always dive straight for the metaphysical? *Why* don't you write about the actual details of the American experience?" I said, or I hope I said, "But Donald. The American experience *is* metaphysical. Have you ever been to a dogfight in Lafayette, Louisiana?"

Actually, I have never been to an organized dogfight, not even in Lafayette, Louisiana, where the great fight of 1954 took place, a fight legendary in dog circles. I rather strongly suspect that I would not like a dogfight. But I like fighting dogs, their spirit, their élan vital, their refusal to respond to any but honest, straightforward training methods, their courage. Their hearts, above all their deep hearts. Hence I stand as most contemporary pit bull fanciers do in an exactly ambivalent relationship to the dogs. This is a microscopic version of the way we stand in relationship to Nature itself. On the one hand, out of Nature come so many magnificences: lions and tigers and elephants. And so many beauties: the exact angle of a grasshopper's leap, the grace of the house cat, the mysterious and complex relations of the branches of trees, which can be seen best in the winter, in the cold, when the branches are shagged with ice.

To call the courage and heart of a dog viciousness, and to oppose it with images of sweet, fluffy innocent animals—to do this is not only to trample on language, but to attempt to deny the world.

Mr. Redd not only said, "The white ladies like him, too," he also said, of the time Bandit bit him, "He notified me, g-r-r-r, g-r-r-r-r!," thus articulating a capacity for respect largely unknown to the animal rights and animal welfare movements. The HSUS, in urging that any dog used primarily to guard public or private property be seized and destroyed without a hearing, has demonstrated that it is, as an official body, incapable of seeing beauty, incapable of seeing animals for what they are, incapable of being commanded by the realization that beauty is the beginning of power, a marker for the possibility of loss, and thus the beginning of terror.

But beauty is all that we have, and the idea of universal human rights, like the mathematics that made the atom bomb possible, is beautiful.

While the Bandit case was appearing in local papers and on TV stations, I got a lot of calls at the kennel from people who were eager to help. Eager in particular to help rescue Bandit from Mr. Redd, and quite sure that the important thing was to prevent the state from returning the dog to "that environment"—i.e., the porch on Henry Street. The callers standardly opened by talking about various people their animal rights group had indicted, driven out of town, driven out of the state, put down. I would say, "That is fascinating to me. Do you have documentation for that?" The callers would get a little blurry at this point about the details—so terrorists lie, so what else is new? said my poet friend John Hollander when I wept on his shoulder about that one.

The callers would praise me for my good work in the field of animal rights. And then would offer to find Bandit a good home, together with outraged remarks about the abuse that had

made him mean. That is to say, they figured Bandit wasn't
rescued enough, and needed more rescuing, even though he had
already been ~~stolen~~ taken from his owner, which is how animal
rescue generally goes.

Bandit—I should repeat myself here—Bandit himself has an
elaborate sense of *neighborhood*. Most dogs do not, most dogs
share their owner's sense of neighborhood, which is to say, no
sense at all. But Bandit's sense of the territory in which dwell his
fellows, his neighbors, includes most of the block on which 189
Henry Street is situated. The same neighborhood where, as I
was telling you, people say "Mr. Redd" and "Mrs. McClean,"
instead of Sally and Bob and Tom. This is very Southern, of
course. As is Bandit's addressing me as "ma'am," and his care
to ask for help with his bladder in a respectful manner.

A facet of the question about nature and nurture is here revealed for those who seek it in the facts of Bandit's good manners and the formal modes of address that prevail at 189 Henry
Street, or "that environment."

So this lady was threatening to find a good home for Bandit.
I found my voice growing hard and angry and crude and cynical
and coplike. "No ma'am!" says I. "This dog is not going to a
good home!"

"And will you tell me why not?"

"Because I do not believe in good homes."

Then there would be some more from my caller, who was on
to me now and would demand to know how I envisioned Bandit's future. I said, "He will be a Companion Dog." One caller
asked suspiciously what that was, so I asked if she had ever
heard of AKC obedience competition (in which dogs who have
mastered manners so deeply that in some cases they become
graces, even dances, are awarded titles for their work, including
the titles Companion Dog and Companion Dog Excellent), and
of course she had not, because people in animal rights have
rarely heard of any discipline in which understanding in detail
the happiness of animals is central, and know little of the com-
panionable excellences dogs are capable of, in and out of the
show ring.

She said darkly, "Well, a dog that belonged to a hunter—that could be a Companion Dog!"

"I do believe you're right about that," says I, and this really sets her off.

She says, "Our group operates throughout the state of Connecticut, and you will be hearing from us soon!" She would not give me her name.

It is not news that trainers and the humane movement are rarely on the same side in any case. I trained Bandit in order to save his life, to try to get him back home, to give him some coherence, friendship, peace. Bandit is not the only such dog in my life—with Mark Vandenberg I make rather a habit of taking in dogs, boarding them at Silver Trails, and training them so that they can, I hope, find homes. (Good homes! I lied to the lady on the phone. I believe in good homes.) I am not the only trainer to do this sort of thing, so you would think that humane societies and shelters would be eager to help, at least by working to find homes for the dogs I train, since such dogs are the ones least likely to be returned to the pound or shelter in a few weeks or a few months to be killed because the new owners can't figure out how to work with them. But this is not so—trainers are usually the enemy. There was at one point a proposal that Benjy be rescued from his trainer, Frank Inn. Benjy rescued! PETA tried in 1989–90 to rescue eight orangutans from their trainer. In that case, the trainer sued. A witness to the trial, which lasted for six weeks, said to me, "Taking those orangs away from the trainer—that would be abuse of animals." I am reminded, too, of the argument I heard on a talk show while driving in the Los Angeles area. The argument, from the representative of a local animal rights movement, was that veterinarians are basically sadistic people who hate animals and that is why they go into veterinary work.

How it comes about that proponents of the humane movement often oppose people whose knowledge saves animal lives and hearts is a complex topic; and I am not even sure why it is so. Perhaps Hannah Arendt is on to something in *The Human Condition,* where she argues that goodness that goes public inevitably becomes the worst sort of wickedness. This is possible—that there is some logic outside of the individuals involved that makes the whole animal welfare enterprise, or any human rights or human welfare enterprise, tend to go bad at crucial moments, and even that this is the something that makes cops so cynical. This does seem possible. I am aware that to most people the idea that pit bulls and other animals are vilified by humane organizations is startling. What startles me, what at once cheers me up and worries me, is that there are so many people in the animal welfare movement who are sincerely and genuinely devoted to animals. There are even some who understand something about animals.

If Hannah Arendt is right, then to the extent that this book has as a goal increasing tolerance in the world, it is to that extent a wicked book. To the extent that I imagine myself to be publicly attempting to help pit bulls, I am to that extent a participant in the worst sort of wickedness, in the worst intolerances of human history.

It is possible.

Sometimes I would cut a caller off before the part about my good work in animal rights segued into the threat part; other times I would listen through, to check to be sure that things hadn't changed. They hadn't and haven't. Now, as in the beginning of the humane movement, animal rescue is effected with threats, prosecutions, and shotguns, mostly. Or at least—I hasten to say this—so it sometimes looks to me. The first thing the great Henry Bergh, founder of the ASPCA, did in his rescuer capacity was to assault some poor cab driver on the street and haul him into court. Humane society literature doesn't say what happened to the cab driver's horse, the first American horse to experience animal rescue, but mercy killing is often the only thing you can do to rescue an animal.

There's that word "kill" again. Time to run some more manuscript over to Frank Cochran.

I talked to a young lawyer in California the other day. He had sent me the ordinance under which his clients' dogs were being disposed of. It said that the officials could declare vicious, and dispose of, any dog that showed a disposition or tendency to menace persons or animals. I pointed out to him that this was about as vague as laws get, that it gave officers too much discretion, that a dog who looked at someone cross-eyed from behind a fence could be held to have shown a tendency to menace. "Menace" is vague enough—what is a "tendency to menace"? That ordinance, I said, is plainly unconstitutional as all get out.

"You're right!" he said. "That's great!" I was startled by his naïve response, then recalled that I too had once cheered up when Steve Wizner said, "That's *got* to be unconstitutional!"

Why do people get themselves into these things? Why do perfectly cynical people, who know enough to know how it comes about that the word "cynical" comes from the Greek for "dog," and that Diogenes in his barrel, reading a book to an assembly of dogs, is learning, shall we say, that the realm of the sacred is expressed in a language that has a grammar for Thou Shalt, which is felt as a singing, and no grammar for Thou Shalt Not—why do they go to bat for this, that, or the other dog or person, knowing everything, knowing that there is no just city?

George Bernard, ex-cop and kennel proprietor, kept calling Bandit "Bullet." So have a couple of other people, possibly because there is a racial memory somewhere of Roy Rogers's dog, whose name was Bullet. George would say, "Bullet's doing well," as he watched the dog work.

I would say, "Bandit. His name is Bandit."

"That's right," George would say agreeably, "his name is Bandit."

Then in an hour or two would be back to calling him "Bullet," watching him do Up and Off on the truck bed or the grooming tub and saying, "I *still* say that Bullet is a good dog."

"Bandit," I would say. "You mean that *Bandit* is a good dog."

"Yes," he would say, "Bandit is a good dog." At such moments I worried a little about George, because mild vagueness is unlike him.

One evening, after a particularly tricky passage in the case had been successfully negotiated, the Scotch flowed. Lillian got out the scrapbooks and showed me pictures of the kennel in various stages of construction. "This is how it was when we started, this is the first stages of D Building, this is the drainage ditch for the grooming room."

Flipping through the albums, I came upon news clippings and pictures of a young, skinny cop, one George Bernard, and his police dog, a German Shepherd named Bullet. I heard a great deal about Bullet that evening, and on other occasions. A good dog, Bullet, if you believe George, and there isn't anyone else to believe about him.

Who one day bit a man who was in the habit of throwing rocks at him. Frank Cochran once asked me why it is illegal for dogs to bite juvenile delinquents, and of course I told him that it was his job to *answer* that sort of question, not ask it, but I was wrong about that. Frank has many splendid variations of himself, and some of his best moments come when he demands to know why it is illegal to take corkscrews into a courtroom, or for dogs to bite juvenile delinquents.

Anyhow, the town ordered Bullet put down—we won't say "killed"—because the dog, who had served the town even though of course he was just a dumb dog, had turned out to be vicious. The thing was that the man was not hurt, the skin was not broken. Bullet had just grabbed his throwing arm for a moment and said, "Stop that!" But it *scared* the man! Scared him! And he had an uncle or a cousin or something who was a lawyer, and the cousin or something said the town would probably pay him a bit of money to shut him up if he created a stink, and that is what happened. The town paid the man one thousand dollars and got on George's case, saying that Bullet had to be ~~killed~~ euthanized unless George could build a kennel for him, cement floor, chain link, covered top.

George was a patrolman with three kids in those days and he couldn't do it, no way could he do it, because cement and chain link and such are expensive, so Bullet was put down because George had no place to keep him, no proper kennel to satisfy officialdom. It would be as much as my hide is worth to psychoanalyze George here, but it did turn out some years down the pike that George had himself a nice, legal, licensed kennel, and there was room for Bullet, no, for Bandit, at Silver Trails, The Animal Inn.

Bullet was a police dog. In the *Republic,* Socrates gives over to dogs the problem of knowing where the just city is located, and of guarding it by that knowledge. I think of Henry Street, now unguarded, because Bandit is no longer there to sit on the porch and conduct his proper business of knowing the justice of Henry Street.

I keep thinking, too, about that nine-year-old boy whose "pit bull" was rescued from his clutches on television. We have his testimony that his dog went everywhere with him, which means that his dog knew him, so he is now stripped of the protection he had from the continual presence of his dog's knowledge. I wonder how he will fare in the world, unfortified by Spike's adroit recognitions of him, how he will manage now to sort out real language from the pseudolinguistic behaviors that are the form in which justice and truth will be presented to him, most of the time. That is, how smart will he be without his dog and therefore unable to locate the just city?

Tests of intelligence and achievement typically present the subject with a few paragraphs of prose and a limited time in which to read them. Then there are questions about the passage of prose. The passage might be from a textbook on pit bull aggression, and it might go like this:

Over a three-year period, 20 out of 28 people killed by dogs in the United States were victims of pit bull attacks.

Pit bulls are especially dangerous because of their double jaws, which are developed by inbreeding so that they can hold on with the front jaw while they chew away behind. These dogs are genetically vicious and their training is part of their genetics.

Also, families may honestly believe that their dog is a gentle pet, never realizing that they might be harboring a dog who suffers from the Jekyll–Hyde syndrome and might turn on the children at any moment. Funding for expert evaluation and investigation of this crisis is required immediately.

The threat represented by these dogs, one of the many tragic results of the increasing drug trade in America, is insidious and urgent.

Then you have your test questions. For example:

1. How many persons died of dog attacks in the study period?
2. How many of these deaths were caused by pit bulls?
3. Why is the apparent docility of a family pet misleading?
4. What causes the Jekyll–Hyde syndrome?
5. What is unusual about a pit bull's jaws?

The students have no time to question this material, only to believe it quickly so that it will stick in their heads.

This is why Charlie, who takes care of the cows, and George, the ex-cop, are not as interested in learning Dan Rather's abstractions as the high school student who is taking the test with an eye on a career in communications. This may also be why it is harder for blacks and Hispanics to believe what they read on comprehension tests, at least to believe it in time to answer the questions. Cultural competence so often becomes a matter of managing to believe things quickly enough, and cynicism entails slow belief, at least of certain things. Specifically, cynicism means being slow to believe anything a dog can't believe, and one of the things dogs have trouble understanding, and thus believing in, is the righteousness of the ASPCA uniform.

Which is not, by the way, to say that dogs don't believe in cops. Bullet, for instance, seems to have believed in George—at least, I have heard nothing to indicate that he was a mutant, and police dogs believe in cops. But not in their uniforms.

The child—of course, long before my fantasy IQ test, there is the episode in which the child runs after the men, crying. Crying out to ABC: "Please! Help! They're going to kill my dog!"

And how foolishly, too, for it is to representatives of the media, in this and other episodes, that people who are afraid of losing their dogs have cried out, "Help! Help!" The media, by and large, have not answered this cry, and poetry cannot answer the cry, being promised to a different territory of the Ideal—to truth, rather than justice. The poet's response might be, if the muse approved the project, to sing a song of Spike, celebrating perhaps even the small boy's pride in Spike's vaunted fighting prowess, and that would not help at all, not even if you explained to the AAG that the dog wasn't really a fighter and it was the boy's yearning for a dream of prowess that was being celebrated, which is to say the song's yearning for prowess and nothing to do with small boys anyhow, and justice would not be served thereby.

I have sung of Bandit's prowess, of what a good dog he is, and it has not helped me to understand the State Office Building, which is one of the projects of this book. Further, I have been trying to tell myself and others that Mr. Redd had a right to have Bandit, that Bandit had a right to have Mr. Redd and Henry Street, and while I still believe that, I believe it in somewhat the way I believe that our heart joy in beauty is wisdom. My heart feels joy in the face of the beauty of dogs, and of certain extraordinary ideas, such as the idea of universal rights. I do not understand these beauties, but continue to believe, unwisely, that my heart joy in them is wisdom, or all the wisdom I am born to.

I am driven beyond rights, or rather behind them, to something prior to such a codification, prior, that is, to the Law, to justice itself, to an attempt to recover Plato and the original chat about the just city. I am carried to my topic kicking and screaming, eyes darting about for a way of escape, for I am a poet and therefore expelled from philosophy's Republic, an undesirable alien there, liable to unseemly outbursts that might lead to a second and more final expulsion, to a complete exile, and no chance of return even through the understanding gained from peering over the walls of the city whose home is the Ideal.

But I must go there in order to discover if dog bites are allowed, and thus if Bandit is allowed, if life is allowed.

My hope is this: Socrates admired well-bred dogs, and Bandit is a well-bred dog, so perhaps there is a clue here as to how the poet might return, warily, her prodigality chastened by the court.

···

SIX

Some Notes
On Dog Bites
(Just Before the Just City)

The work of humanization is still to be done. While men
believe in the infinite some ponds will be thought to be
bottomless. So long as we will not take our beliefs all the way
to genuine knowledge, to conviction, but keep letting ourselves
be driven to more or less hasty conclusions, we will keep
misplacing the infinite and so grasp neither heaven nor earth.
—STANLEY CAVELL, *The Senses of Walden*

THERE WERE urgent memoranda about dog bites
for a while there, but there was no dog-bite epidemic, and there
was no pit-bull-bite epidemic. Among the places supposed to
have a serious enough pit-bull-bite epidemic to justify special
laws was New York City, where Mayor Koch, in what some
read as part of his bid for reelection in 1989, asked the City
Council to ban pit bulls. Councilwoman Maloney, on her account, was happy to comply, but then pit bull owners brought
their dogs to her office, and she said, "I couldn't ban them—
they are too sweet." She began writing a generic vicious dog
law instead, and Mayor Koch, disappointed with the City
Council, attempted to do an end run around Maloney and went
to the Department of Health. Since Department of Health regulations and enforcement activities are administrative, like those
of the Department of Agriculture in Connecticut, they are difficult to appeal.

The Department of Health offered the report that over an
eleven-month period ending in the fall of 1988 there was a total
of 3,057 dog bites, or 278 a month. (If that is right and there are
eight million stories in the city, one person in approximately

135

29,000 was bitten in the eleven months.) According to the report, "pit bulls" were responsible for a disproportionate number of these bites, but the figures were so wacky to begin with that it was hard to work up any faith in the means of breed identification and counting that had been used. In a 1974 article in the *Bulletin of the New York Academy of Medicine,* Dr. David Harris of Mount Sinai Hospital and his coauthors cited ASPCA figures of 37,896 bites in 1972, or 3,158 a month—that is, more bites per month than were being cited by supporters of the breed ban for a period of nearly a year. The numbers in the Harris study seem more reasonable, given the usual numbers reported in other bite counts—but bite counts are in general unwieldy things to interpret, since it is not clear what counts as a bite even when the authors of the study are doing their best to be thorough. A study done in De Kalb County, Georgia, reported 40,000 bites there in 1980.

There had plainly been a miracle of social reform in New York City, or else the Department of Health was using very dubious information.

However you read the figures, they add up to a lot of dog bites in the nation, but again, it is virtually impossible to interpret them. At Silver Trails, there is barely a bite a year. Given staff fluctuations, that means one bite per four to eight persons, a high incidence, but there are over a hundred runs at Silver Trails, and everybody is handling dogs that are strange to them and in a strange environment all day long. Sometimes the momentary brushing of a dog's teeth against someone's skin is recorded as a "bite" because of fear of rabies and tetanus. I have been bitten by dogs, once seriously, but I am clumsy and injure myself far more frequently by smashing my hand against some bit of the car or absentmindedly crashing into a bookcase. My subjective impression is that cars, kitchens, and bookcases are far more dangerous than dogs are, because dogs look out for me, get out of my way, and inanimate objects just sit there stupidly. I recently spoke with Judy McBau, professor of the history and sociology of science at the University of Pennsylvania, who noted that with the industrial revolution and the

introduction of machines into everyday life, horses suddenly
became much more dangerous, possibly because people lost
their sense of how to move around horses when they started
riding railways, possibly because the typical object of fear
changed. For me, the responses of animals are comforting, reassuring, because animals are an intelligence outside of mine, so
I don't have to worry so much about them. For others, the same
fact, that animals are another intelligence, outside of the movement of our wills, is terrifying.

Be that as it may, there are other reasons to doubt the facts
and figures offered in support of pit bull breed bans. At a hearing in March 1989, before the New York City Department of
Health, an elderly gentleman rose to testify. He identified himself as Dr. Levine, a veterinarian, a retired gentleman who had
a story to tell. He was retired from the Department of Health,
had been retired for all of eleven days. And he had done the
autopsy on the dog involved in what was said to be New York
City's only "pit bull" killing, in which a monster pit bull from
hell was said not only to have killed the victim but then to have
consumed him. Levine also worked with the coroner who did
the autopsy on the victim. The occasion for the consultation was
apparently this: There were no dog-bite wounds on the victim's
body. There were a lot of razor wounds, but no dog-bite
wounds. The autopsy, said Dr. Levine, suggested that possibly
the murderer had cut up the victim and fed him to the dog.

Statistically, it would not matter if this had been a death from
a dog mauling, of course, since 1 is not a statistically significant
sample. But: There was no pit bull killing. At that hearing I
testified about the statistics and also gave testimony about boxers, bulldogs, hounds, and other dogs that were mistakenly or
falsely called pit bulls. Dr. Levine gave his rather dramatic testimony about the phantom pit bull killing. This did not slow the
Department of Health from approving a breed ban in New
York City (though it does not seem to have survived legal
scrutiny).

New York was not the only place where a pit bull was blamed
for a death caused by people. There was the case in Rochester,

New York, where the victim died of an embolism and there was evidence that the hospital had not properly monitored the anti-coagulant medication.

I became more than just casually suspicious of the statistics that showed that all of a sudden pit bulls were doing so much killing when I noticed two things. One was that the total number of dog-attack-related fatalities had not risen according to the HSUS statistics that were everywhere offered as evidence of the ferocity of pit bulls. That meant that all of a sudden all those other breeds had stopped biting people seriously enough to kill them, which meant that for all breeds except pit bulls a sudden increase in sensible breeding and handling had taken place, and there would have been other evidence if that were so. If pit bulls had been killing a lot more people, there would have been a rise in the total number of deaths, and there wasn't. If anything, there was a slight drop, according to the HSUS, depending on which of their figures you choose: either 15 to 17 deaths a year nationwide, or 12 to 13, in the period from 1975 to 1986.

Their figures were not to be trusted, even the total numbers. Dr. Randy Lockwood, the compiler of these stats, told me he based them on data from a "clipping service." Data from the Centers for Disease Control show a steady number of dog-attack-related fatalities throughout the period of hysteria in question, the late 1980s. The CDC stats do not give breeds. The only way to find out for sure what breeds were involved would be to look at each dog, since breed ID is made by victims, excited witnesses, cops, and reporters, and breed ID is a tricky business.

Mysteriously, in the piles of articles and studies I have read about both bites and attack-related fatalities, the breed of dog is never listed as "unknown." Since the dog in question is often either dead and buried or has been transported elsewhere, there can be no certainty about breeds.

So the statistics are useless, by and large, but those that look even remotely reliable suggest that there was no dog-bite epidemic in the 1980s, whether nationally or in any particular municipality, although it appears that there *was* an increase in dog bites in the late sixties and early seventies, in New York City at least. The paper by Harris *et alia* is not nearly so sleazily done as the "studies" of the mid- and late 1980s, though that may be because you had to be somewhat more literate to graduate from college twenty years ago. In any case, according to Harris *et alia,* the number of dog bites rose from an average of a little over 25,000 a year to nearly 38,000 in New York City from 1965 to 1972. This study does not say whether the total number of dogs increased in this period, so it may be that there was no increase in bites per capita.

The authors suggest that rising fear of crime in that period caused an increase in the popularity of "larger, more aggressive" dogs. Size does not make dogs more aggressive. If anything, larger breeds tend to be less meaninglessly aggressive, since it is easier to tolerate a Miniature Poodle with a screw loose than a German Shepherd. My memory is that larger dogs did become more popular in the late sixties and early seventies, though "larger" is a relative term; my old German Shepherd cross Stevie was a humongous dog by comparison with the other dogs in his obedience class in 1966. A few years later sixty to eighty pounds was pretty much an average size for dogs in obedience classes in the Southern California area.

So as I have said, this thought occurred to me: It was not only *fear* of crime but crime itself that increased in that period. People were not behaving as well from, say, a German Shepherd's point of view. I do not know if this was noticeably true in New York City, but I do know that in 1965 a woman took walks alone at night in Riverside, California, and by 1975 she didn't so much. I also know from my experience of walking at night, not alone but with dogs, that in 1965 nothing happened on the streets to tell you whether or not your dog had the natural drive needed to protect you if you were attacked, but that by 1975 you found out what your dog would do in an emergency.

It may be that I did the Department of Health a disservice when I suggested that their figures, showing only 3,057 bites in eleven months in 1988, were careless or tainted. Perhaps there really was an enormous decrease in dog bites in New York City from 1972 to 1988, perhaps as a function of the decrease in evening strolls taken by dog owners and everyone else. Presumably a lot of people learned some version of what I learned: It is not such a bad thing to find out that your dog will be there for you if needed, but it isn't a *good* thing to take a walk expecting your dog to have to come to the defense. Also, you worry about people with guns.

Once or twice I have gone to New York by way of Stamford, leaving my car at the train station there. Coming back, I drove by Henry Street. Sarah Arnold, an anchorwoman who covered the Bandit story, asked me one time whether or not Mr. Redd had another dog. I said I didn't know, that I had been by a couple of times and had not seen a dog in the yard, but that it had been fairly late at night, and in the wintertime.

"You don't drive through there at *night,* do you?"

She went on to tell me that a particularly grisly murder had occurred on Henry Street since Bandit left. A decapitated body was found across the way in an artist's loft. The murderer was not found, but more terrifying still was that there was no known reason for the murder. Some people thought that because of the location of the crime, it wouldn't have happened if Bandit had been there, or if it had happened Bandit would have stopped the murderer, whose flight would have taken him past Bandit's porch. It was after she told me this that she said, "When Bandit was there, Henry Street was such a lighthearted, innocent place."

Burglary, assault, break-ins—these cause dog bites. Not *fear* of crime, but crime.

There was no dog-bite epidemic in the eighties. There *were* appeals for funds—"Help us to fund this crisis," wrote John Hoyt, president of the HSUS, unconsciously telling the truth about his intentions, perhaps, or at least about what seemed to be happening—but there was no dog-bite epidemic, only specters and apparitions constructed out of words. In a 1986 "fact sheet" the HSUS linked the miraculous ability of pit bulls to hold on in front while they chew away behind with dope dealing and illegal firearms. *People* magazine, using Pat Owens of the Women's SPCA as a source, as near as I can tell, reported that "typically the creatures are starved or fed irritant substances like hot sauce and gunpowder to make them mean." *Playboy* published a novel in which a dogfighter prepares his dog for combat by feeding him rattlesnake serum. The words "urban," "poor," "black," and "Hispanic" appear everywhere in media treatments of pit bulls.

In seizing an occasion to stir up public fear of dogs and to mix it with class hostilities for the sake of a hearty financial and legislative stew, the HSUS and others were here following in the traditional paths of humane societies. Harriet Ritvo's *The Animal Estate: The English and Other Creatures in the Victorian Age* contains a meticulous and enlightening account of the rise of the first humane society, the RSPCA, in a section called "Dangerous Classes," consisting of two chapters dryly titled "A Measure of Compassion" and "Cave Canem." The former describes a familiar feature of social hygiene movements, the tendency to set penalties, fines, and requirements in such a fashion that it is the poor and working classes that feel their bite. Ritvo presents a great deal of evidence that the class-oriented nature of RSPCA rhetoric and legislation was not accidental or unconscious, but quite deliberate. For instance, one "legal member" of the RSPCA, in the course of an argument for punitive legislation, wrote, "Now the liberty of the lower orders had arrived at such a pitch that if a gentleman . . . witnessed any act of cruelty, he dared not inflict any punishment on the perpetrator."

I have already mentioned Professor Ritvo's account of the rabies "crisis" of the 1880s. The RSPCA used its resources to exploit the fear of rabies, and there was as much nonsense published in the British press then about dogs as there was in the 1980s in the American press. Then as now dogs were shot and clubbed on the streets. Nowadays the tale goes around that it is raw meat and gunpowder and dope dens that make dogs vicious. In the Victorian era, the story was that the dogs of the lower classes were especially subject to rabies because they were oversexed. (In the seventeenth century, the theory that there was such a thing as being oversexed and that it led to viciousness buttressed the witch hunts.) In Nottingham, strict enforcement of laws and programs "meant killing all unmuzzled dogs, a duty that police carried out with energy and often in full view of the public." One legacy of the RSPCA's enthusiasm is still with us, in the form of Britain's inhumane and deranged law that requires animals entering Britain from other countries to be quarantined for six months, no matter how many rabies shots the animal has had. This restriction applies even to guide dogs. The incubation period for rabies is less than two weeks.

There does exist, of course, a real disease, rabies, just as there really do exist dog bites. There are also people—very, very few people indeed—who die from dog-bite wounds. And this is plainly a compelling fact, a cynosure. But it does not account for the startlingly superstitious idea that tattoos and unusual hairdos on the owners cause strange mutations in the genes of the dog. I recall a cover story in *Sports Illustrated* that featured photographs of Hispanic men playing tug-of-war with pit bulls. There was also a white man with a shaved and tattooed head, smiling at his dog. Captions and text invited the reader to make the leap from socially unacceptable inner city males to pit bulls to the concept "Rambo of the dog world," as *People* magazine put it in a similar article. The use of pictures was more powerful than statistics could have been in creating the impression that the dogs were linked to crime and hence evil, though the word "evil" was not used, but rather "irresponsible," as in "irresponsible dog owner." Everywhere there was assurance that the pit bull problem was not the fault of decent citizens; in *People*'s words, "Pit bulls are, in fact, less popular among ordinary dog lovers than among back-alley types. . . . In Philadelphia, where poorer neighborhoods are overrun with youths who train their dogs to fight one another, the number of pit bulls has grown."

If popular media are any guide, biting dog = pit bull = child abuse = hit men = sex = cigarette smoking = crack = rape and pillage = voodoo rites = the fire next time. I am not knowledgeable enough about child abuse or hit men or voodoo or sex gone wrong to comment on this vision, but there remains a real question here, one that may not lead to any illumination of the winter of our discontent or the corruption of our times. The question is:

What *is* a dog bite, anyway? This is not the same thing as the question about a "vicious" dog. There is no such thing as viciousness in a dog, though some dogs are real problems to deal with. Some dogs, but not many. If many dogs were serious problems, there could be no such thing as a boarding kennel. At Silver Trails, there are over a hundred runs, some of them double runs. During holidays and school vacations, the runs are full. There is also at Silver Trails a snare pole, for use in emergency handling of a nasty dog. Sometimes nasty dogs come in for boarding—dogs that Lillian calls "snotty"—but even they can usually be handled without the snare pole. In fact, in the three and more years since I brought Bandit there, I have not seen anyone use the snare pole, and am uncertain where it is stored. Silver Trails is, as it happens, one of the best kennels I have ever seen anywhere, bar none. The Bernards take care, not only of their own dogs, but of everyone's dogs, in somewhat the way Jack London describes Thornton taking care of Buck—not out of a sense of duty, but because they cannot help it, it is just in them to take care of the dogs. I can more easily imagine the sun failing to rise than I can imagine a personal crisis or any sort of crisis causing the Bernards to neglect the dogs. Nonetheless, being left in a kennel is stressful for dogs, especially before they learn how reliable the people there are, and the problems that crop up in handling are as tough as any that crop up in animal shelters and pounds.

In a kennel one encounters a cross section of dogs, including dogs that, let us say, I would not be delighted to have to train. "Snotty" dogs or dogs with "a screw loose." Biting dogs. No vicious dogs—that is a human category. The difference between difficult dogs and vicious human beings is that difficult dogs do not rise to positions of prominence in the community. A fear-biting dog says as plainly as possible when you open his run, "I am afraid and angry—don't get too close to me!" A vicious human being makes speeches about public health and safety or the American way or human rights. Or, sometimes, animal rights. Vicious human beings can learn quite a repertoire of tricks—shaking hands, laughing at jokes, putting on a show of respectful good manners. Dogs can put on shows, but not of good citizenship, and not in anything like the extended, detailed way people can.

Let me sneak up on the dog-bite question, thus: Is a biting dog a happy dog? If happy, then what kind of happiness is a dog bite? Is it wholesome?

Bandit is not biting anyone at the moment, hasn't for years in fact, but I guess you could say that he is a "biting dog." And in the period when the state allowed me to train him, this dog would do *anything* for me, anything. I do not mean that he is eager to please.

Is that wholesome, if I am right—I have no way of proving it—that he would do anything for me? What do I mean—"He would do anything for me"? I mean: He has a working heart. A great big loyal working heart, which everyone involved has betrayed, including me, since I am not willing to risk having the state seize and kill him should someone discover me violating the terms of the agreement reached in Hartford on July 29, 1988, terms that include the requirement that he wear a muzzle in public. This means that I cannot finish training him to retrieve; all he needs is a little more experience retrieving in different situations—i.e., in public, even if "public" only means the local game preserve. So his retrieving work sits there, halfway done, like a heart having completed half a beat. And he knows this, and wonders why I have not kept my promise to him.

I can't continue Bandit's work, so will look elsewhere for an example of "willing to do anything," an exemplary reality. There exists a dog, a pit bull—a real pit bull, that is, an American Pit Bull Terrier—named Puller, who belongs to a trainer named B. W. Lightsay. Puller is a Search and Rescue dog, which means that Puller and B. W. are among the search teams likely to be called out in the event of an earthquake, a lost child, someone with Alzheimer's who has wandered away.

A search will often entail twelve-hour days and more, sometimes three or four or more days in a row. It might come about that it is eight hours into the third day, that Puller is down in weight, has a fever, won't or can't eat, has raw pads and also raw, torn front legs from the brush he has been negotiating. If and when he finds someone, he returns to B.W. and jumps and barks, to signal the find, and B.W. then follows him for what is called the "refind."

Usually, except in training exercises, there is no find. The dog's evidence is valuable but generally negative, telling you that there are no live victims in this pile of rubble, or that the lost child is not in this particular quadrant. A dog is small and the search areas are large. The dogs know this, and keep searching.

Late into the third day of the search, running a fever, unable to eat, with raw pads, Puller is still working, like other Search and Rescue dogs.

Search dogs work off lead. They run across loose dogs, upset people, do not attack the loose dogs or upset people.

B.W. and Laura Lightsay say that they attack-train their dogs because that makes them better search dogs. That is to say, they claim that Puller, and also Laura's little pit bull bitch, Jo, are good search dogs *because of* rather than in spite of their bite work.

How do they come to talk this way? I do not ask whether or not they are mistaken, because you cannot do this sort of work with a dog without knowing what is going on. Laura and B.W. are not dreaming, are not faking it, are not deluding themselves.

When Laura and B.W. Lightsay say that Schutzhund, or protection dog work, or bite work, builds the dogs' confidence, they have in mind, not exactly that bite work teaches the dogs courage or a sense that they can triumph or conquer, but rather that it teaches them confidence in their own judgment. The important point is not the bite itself, but the fact that the dog makes the decisions about it. Dogs are not, according to certain philosophers, capable of judgment, decision making, and so on, but Puller and Jo are.

Now look: Aggression isn't in this. Schutzhund is a sport,

and the principal complaint about Schutzhund is that the dogs become "sleeve happy" and are therefore no good for a situation where you need a man-stopper; in Schutzhund the dogs, if you like, "fight" a human being, but they are fighting to win, not to kill. You are safe with a properly trained Schutzhund dog, just as Marianne Moore was safe the day she had lunch with Muhammad Ali.

If you have a pit bull or one of the other "game" breeds—a good Airedale, say—you can bring the dog to a Schutzhund III title *without ever inspiring any aggression toward human beings in the dog*. For Schutzhund III the dog must not only bite hard on the sleeve, but must hold on and not give up while taking "hits" from a flexible stick or crop called a "schlagstock." Not everyone can do this with every dog, but good trainers can do it with dogs from the game breeds, train them for the sport of Schutzhund without developing aggression toward human beings.

The AKC, which claims to make it its business to understand sports involving purebred dogs, recently outlawed Schutzhund demonstrations on AKC showgrounds, and says it will deny membership to clubs that sponsor Schutzhund and related events, that is, any events involving "aggression" toward human beings. The justification for this ruling was not that these sports are in and of themselves bad, but rather that it was bad PR for the AKC to be associated with them. Shortly before this policy was instituted, the AKC had elected a new president, a former breeder of Bouviers. Bouviers were originally a stock breed, but from World War I on fanciers discovered and developed their abilities to do ambulance and other war work, as well as police work. *Dog World* quoted the new president as having said that he didn't believe that, but that if it was true, he was going to put a stop to it. I do not know whether he knew that in their native Belgium, Bouviers cannot win breed championships without first showing that they have working ability, and that working ability means the ability to do police work.

Shortly before the new policy was made public, I chanced to be in conversation with Allan Stern, the AKC's vice-president of communications. I had some questions about Poodles in field trials, but Mr. Stern, out of nowhere and for no reason that I could discern except that he assumed I was from the media, informed me that there had been a "study" of "police dogs." "What breeds?" I asked. "Just police dogs," said the spokesman for the AKC. Anyway, it was a three-year study. And in three years "they" had been "unable to breed the aggression out of the dogs!"

I expostulated that for one thing, it is about three years from whelping to full-fledged working in a police dog tracker, especially in the slower-maturing breeds. And for another, as I had already said to a number of AAGs and DAs, thirty to a hundred years is the average time it takes to develop a trait in a line of dogs, in part because you do not know for two or three years whether a given pup really "has it," and because it takes two to eight years of dedicated work to find out what a dog's capabilities really are, much less to breed for them. How, I demanded, could there possibly have been a study of inherited behavior of this sort that lasted only three years. Could he give me the citation on the article?

He could not at that moment lay his hands on it.

Aggression is a pretty fuzzy term; bite work is not, let us say, assertiveness training, such as marines are shown receiving in Hollywood versions of war, or not necessarily. You can, of course, agitate a dog with no other goal than making the dog into a frantic aggressor, but that isn't training. As I said, an important detail about Schutzhund training is that the dog makes his own decision about when to bite, when to wait. What the trainer does is to set things up so that when the dog makes the right decision, the dog knows it. The "decoy," as the person wearing the bite sleeve or padded suit is called, behaves sometimes reasonably, sometimes unreasonably, and the dog learns that if he goes in and bites when the decoy is behaving unreasonably he can keep the decoy under control.

Or, if the dog is a good pit bull or Airedale and the trainer understands the breed, the dog learns that there is a good game to be had if he judges the decoy's behavior correctly. A properly bred and trained pit bull in a Schutzhund III contest just cheers up when the decoy hits him. And holds on harder, shakes harder, flying through the air. The decoys learn, with these dogs, to spin as the dog hits, otherwise they go ass over teakettle, in the words of trainer Diane Jessup, because they underestimate the dogs. Having gone ass over teakettle, the decoy is then on the ground, with an attack-trained dog on top of him and—nothing happens. The dogs, understanding perfectly well that this is a sport and that the rules include the one that says they must bite the protection sleeve and not the decoy, do not go for faces or throats. Not all dogs are this bravely reliable, but many pit bulls are.

The dog who can take the hits and keep coming at the decoy—we say that this dog is confident. Such a dog is also under control. The handler is required to be able to drop the dog with a quiet *"Aus,"* or, more harshly in English, "Out." When the handler is Diane Jessup working her pit bulls, this is all a joy to behold—the game little dog leaping onto the sleeve worn by a decoy perhaps five or more times her size, tearing away at the sleeve fiercely, then plopping instantly and cheerfully to the ground at the word *"Aus!"*

Cheerfully. Responding to the call to come off the decoy is, for her dogs, as much of an accomplishment as latching onto the sleeve in the first place. Virginia Isaac, another trainer who was at the seminar where I saw Diane Jessup work, said, "At home she works the dogs on a spring pole. She sends the little bitch, who leaps up—eight feet, ten feet, more—and grabs the hang. Then she sends the male. He leaps, too, and if he can't find a hold without hurting the bitch, he drops down and jumps again. And they hang there, working the spring pole together. Then both dogs drop, wagging their tails, when she says, *'Aus.'* I never saw anything like it."

Virginia Isaac added, "I'd love to do that with my little bulldogs, but I can't because we have a paraphernalia law in California."

Understand, please, that the work on the spring pole is no different from Scoop Ball or Frisbee for a dog who likes to do it. A dog running to jump and grab the spring pole, or to grab the burlap sleeve worn by the decoy, is no more likely to change her mind and bite a spectator than your Golden Retriever is to go for your child rather than the tennis ball. In fact, if Diane Jessup is the trainer and the dogs are pit bulls, they are *less* likely to menace a human being than an untrained dog, because they understand that it is a sport.

However, this form of working with dogs, which is really a developed game of tug-of-war, is more than just socially unacceptable. In California, as Virginia Isaac indicated, it is a *felony* to own a spring pole or a treadmill—which is used for dogs as it is for people, as a means of exercise when other possibilities are limited—largely because the only use a bureaucrat or politician can imagine for either the equipment or the dogs is violence, killing children, aiding and abetting the Colombian dope trade. If anyone can use a treadmill to train dogs to eat children, he is a cannier trainer than I am. You can buy a pair of Nikes and jog and jog until you are fast and strong enough to pull off a mugging. You can study self-defense techniques and use them for offensive purposes. That is not a reason to outlaw martial arts or Nikes.

So our bureaucrats and politicians have violent imaginations, but our dogs do not. We live in an extreme poverty of heart, and have taken despair at the possibility of a dog's having a heart at all to be good citizenship and rectitude. To paraphrase Stanley Cavell, we have not mastered, or we have forgotten, or we have distorted or learned through fragmented models, the forms of life that could make the ordinary utterances of real dog training carry us through to knowledge.

Also at the seminar was a woman named L. Maugh Bail, who had with her two Airedales. She took her dogs, as I took mine, through the Challenge Agility course, under the instruction of Virginia Isaac. Her male came through for her especially well, climbing, balancing, crawling, leaping over and through the various obstacles without hesitation. She said, looking at him, "He has so much heart!"

"Yes," said I, "yes, he certainly does."

Later, during a break, her male was scampering about, romping on a twenty-foot line. There were perhaps thirty people there with as many dogs, all of them moving about, some resting or playing, some concentrating on the obstacles. Maugh Bail's dog has a Schutzhund III title, which means that he will attack a person as he attacked the obstacles—without hesitation, and without the fearful defensiveness of the unreliable, tricky, or as Lillian would have it, "snotty" dogs that one does in fact worry about.

No one worried about getting bitten, because there was no reason to worry, because a Schutzhund III dog has so much heart.

It is as though the legislature were to begin to worry that poets and artists, because they have so much expressive power, might hurt someone's feelings, so that there ought to be a law against it. It is as though *Tom Sawyer* had been banned in Brooklyn (which it was), or as though *The Koehler Method of Dog Training* had been banned in Arizona (which it was), or as though in Prague it had been as much as your life was worth to own a volume of English poetry or philosophy, or as though there had been a time in America when women were burned at the stake for witchcraft, or as though it were illegal for a black to ride in the front seat of a car with a white, or as though rape victims were sometimes stoned.

But to return, what if someone had had occasion to worry about being bitten? What would that have meant?

Most likely that they didn't know much about dogs, but possibly that they were behaving badly or planning to; people tend to mind their manners when a dog that is at all formidable—which means, generally, a dog that weighs more than ten pounds—expresses a negative opinion. (Though I once got a call from a family whose six-pound Yorkshire Terrier had barricaded himself in the downstairs bathroom and kept them out of it for three days, just by baring his teeth and snarling emphatically.) A snarl or a hard stare or raised hackles or a lowered head can mean, "Mind your manners, I don't like the cut of your jib or the way you are behaving," or "Let's just

straighten up and fly right, here," as when my dog has effected
a reversal in the way a would-be mugger perceives the power
structure. The mugger pulls a knife or feels about meaningfully
in his pocket or touches my clothing. He acts "confident," that
is, until my dog says, "Cut that out!" Then he backs down. (In
my experience it has always been a "he.")

A dog can be inspired to menace or attack a human being in
three ways, or in a variety of ways that can for convenience'
sake be classified under three headings: defense drive, prey drive,
and protection drive. These are the terms used in bite work, or
protection work, or attack training, much of which involves a
combination of the three drives, or at least of the first two.

We say a dog is motivated defensively when a real or perceived threat to the dog himself or his territory is the prelude to
the bite. In ordinary life, an excessively defensive dog is the
most worrisome, because he is liable to perceive ordinary behavior as threatening. When defense drive is too pronounced, it
is diagnosed as "fear biting."

In attack work as I have seen it, the defense drive is not
enough. The dog motivated by defense might bite, all right—
with or without attack training, fear biters can be a problem—
but that dog is looking for relief from the threat, and so is likely
to run away or stop biting too soon. And in my experience, a
dog driven only by defense is not likely to be effective off his
own property.

Relying on a dog who is biting out of defensiveness is risky.
A defensive dog is not thinking properly, is liable to bite anyone
in sight, is certainly not attacking either out of courage or out of
the sense of sport that motivates a hunting dog, whether the dog
in question is a pointing, setting, or retrieving breed that doesn't
kill or sometimes even touch the prey, or one of the breeds that
must actually go in and fight dangerous game.

A dog driven by the prey drive alone is something else again,
though the term "prey drive" is misleading—I prefer to call it
"varmintiness," since you can have a hound who will track a
bear indefatigably but not go in after the bear. ("You want,"
said an old dog trainer to me thoughtfully, "a certain amount of

caution in a bear dog.") The "varminty" puppy is the one who will pounce on that tennis ball or sock, worrying it, throwing it, and leaping after it, and preferably bringing it back to you if you are checking the puppy out for certain kinds of work.

Guide dog work, for instance. Clarence Pfaffenberger, in a useful book called *The New Knowledge of Dog Behavior*, reports that the "fetch test" is a better indicator of which of a litter of eight-week-old puppies will work out as guide dogs than anything else. Of course, he is talking about puppies from lines already bred for guide work, but varmintiness is an indicator also of responsiveness to people, it is sort of like a language skill.

Varmintiness, or prey drive, is not the same thing as what some police dog trainers call "play drive," though often you will have both in the same dog in a terrier breed. Play drive is what makes the dog willingly and happily learn to negotiate a police dog obstacle course—climbing chain link, jumping in and out of a cruiser, etc. Prey drive is what makes the dog courageous enough to chase down an armed suspect, off his own territory and at some distance from his handler.

There are aspects to "varmintiness." There is . . .

But if I am not careful, this will turn into an essay on the happiness of the police dog, and that is another topic altogether; this book is about the diminishment of truth and happiness, and this chapter is only about dog bites in the sense of things that We Do Not Want in Society.

When Bandit bit Effie Powell, the motivation was very likely protection, I would guess, going not only on witness testimony, but also on his behavior—he is fairly cold. That is to say, he is low on aggression but high on drive, and is in fact one of the rare dogs whose protection drive—the impulse to defend, not just himself or his property, but his friends and family—would be strong enough by itself to motivate the bite. Normally, protection drive is too weak to motivate a dog by itself, without prey drive, but Bandit has virtually no prey drive in relationship to people, and though annoyingly bullheaded, he is also bullheadedly loyal. In the period before the hearing of July 29, 1988, when Bandit and I could take walks, if I released him on an Okay, his position of preference when the territory was strange to him, or when there was some unexplained noise or bother, was slightly in front of me, between me and the noise, interposing himself protectively and with pronounced determination. He is not as sporting a dog as many of the bull and terrier breeds, including pit bulls, or the Airedales. Loyalty comes first, then sport.

It was not until Bandit had been in the Stamford pound for six weeks, and became unclean on the porch, and was switched for it, that he bit defensively—bit his own master.

There is no end to the topic of dog bites in the sense of an "epidemic" or other Things We Do Not Want in Society, largely because there is no dog-bite problem to speak of in this country. It is a nontopic and therefore endless.

There are real topics that entail an understanding of what happens when a dog's mouth opens and then closes with something human between the teeth, but they are not topics that can be introduced here. Dog bites are real—I am not saying they are not—and it really is important to diminish the chances of dog bites, but the sort of thing that would genuinely help is not the sort of thing that occurs to bureaucrats or humane societies. This is partly because the language in question is confusing. The term "epidemic," for example, suggests a causal model. AIDS is caused by a virus that can enter the body in certain ways. Flus and colds are caused by airborne viruses. Rabies can be prevented by a vaccine. Dog bites are caused by—

This is where the medical analogy leads us astray, because we expect a noun or noun phrase to appear after the preposition "by." But dog bites are a social phenomenon, a function of complex interactions, agreements and disagreements between people and dogs. A dog bite may be a form of communication. It may also be a breakdown in communication. It is, in part, a grammatical problem, like divorce.

I could say that the cure for dog bites is community, social enrichment, flexibility, public trust, and I could mean something by it, but it would take a book or two to talk about what I mean by it, since the cure for dog bites is: happiness.

The topic of dog bites includes the topic of the happiness of police dogs, and this topic is related to the topic of guide dogs. Most of the German Shepherds on the state police in Connecticut are donated by Fidelco, a company that breeds and trains guide dogs. The same qualities that make a good guide dog make a good police dog. That is to say, judgment, and the kind of work in which judgment is expressed as the happiness of competence.

As for Puller, other search dogs, dogs of happiness and in fact devotion and in fact courage—all of that Lassie and Rin Tin Tin stuff—that is real, that is true, that actually exists. It is not in the ken of the state, at least not the state in the persons of anyone I have met at the State Office Building. Some of them know this.

There are people who are experts in the exact details of many rich landscapes of animal happiness. Dick Koehler, for instance, who flew from California to testify in late July 1988. Left his business and flew out here, and at one point had a small conversation with one of the state's "experts." Who said, after the conversation, "I'm sorry, I can't help with this case. Koehler knows too much about dogs."

This is not the book in which I can tell you much about Puller or Dick Koehler, because this is not, as I have said, a book about animal happiness. It is, rather, a book occasioned by state activities that precluded things making enough sense for happiness to get into the discussion.

Happiness comes in with knowledge, for grown-ups at least. In the case of the wonderful variety of activities in which people use their hands, and dogs their mouths, knowledge and happiness become one. Sometimes a little of the true knowledge of dogs makes it into the general culture, usually in the form of movies and children's stories—Toto in *The Wizard of Oz,* or Rin Tin Tin. And sometimes knowledge is driven back by the state, replaced by false ideas of infinite viciousness and infinite pity and compassion. (These two heady ideas tend to go together.) It is possible that the belief in infinite viciousness is like the belief in a bottomless pond, and it is even possible that those beliefs are like the infinity sign or the zero sign in an equation; they are handy for marking time when reality is too complicated, restless, and wooly for our understanding to settle into. They make some equations come out right, but they are fictions.

What is it about a fiction that tells you when the fiction is going wrong? (The fiction of infinity, for instance, or the fiction of the infinitely vicious dog? The fiction of democracy?) How can we know when our happiness is false or true; how can we know when the infinity sign in the equation is carrying us and our neighbors, all unwitting, into misery? There are clues. One clue is when it begins to seem reasonable that someone else stop living for the sake of our favorite fictions and infinities. But I do not know much about how to be alert to these clues now with Bandit; my dissatisfactions with the life Bandit must lead, with his displacement from the porch on Henry Street, tempt me to a belief in the infinite deficiencies of the state—any state. I do not know whether that is one of the infinities that prompted Cavell to write, "The work of humanization is still to be done. While men believe in the infinite some ponds will be thought to be bottomless. So long as we will not take our beliefs all the way to genuine knowledge, to conviction . . . we will keep misplacing the infinite and so grasp neither heaven nor earth."

The project of grasping heaven, or at least earth, belongs to some other story, not the story of my good Bandit. Even Bandit's happiness, the happiness of *der Hund am sich,* or even *der Hund* as I know him, belongs to some other story; this is the story in which all of my knowledge, and all of your knowledge, and all of Bandit's knowledge, was for varying periods of time lost.

In this case: to imagine that there is such a topic as dog bites is to lose the knowledge of dogs. Puller and Jo, for example, searching through fatigue and brush and weather and illness, are not the same thing as the Lhasa Apso who snaps at you when you go to change his water dish. We are misled here by our mind's stately prowess at creating the literal, the hubris that fails to foresee that the literal fact of teeth, discovered in the newspaper or on television or in a courtroom, is bound to be followed not only by the literal fact of the snapping Lhasa Apso, or by the literal loss of the work that is a Lhasa Apso's true heritage (guarding the meditations of monks), but also by the literal fact of Puller out on a search. That hubris is not unlike the pride in moral knowledge that fails to foresee that the literal fact of a book or a pamphlet, penned by a human hand, urging one man to kill another, is bound to be followed by, or at least presages, not only the literal fact of murder but also the literal fact of Shakespeare's hand, creating a new world in which we can walk away from murder.

The project of grasping heaven, or at least earth, belongs to intellectual courage. Early in this book I quote Russell, who distinguished between the intellect and intuition, and gave higher honors to intellect. It was human intellect that created the literal fact of Bandit the "aggressive" dog, Bandit the "vicious" dog, but it was also human instincts that did so. There is greed—the pit bull publicity inspired many appeals for funds. And there is the protective instinct, or drive, that in improperly trained human beings no less than in improperly trained dogs can become uncontrolled aggression for the sake of the pleasures of the sport of hunting down "vicious" dogs. Then there is the defense drive, which in humane societies and government officials no less than in individuals is dangerous because a defensive animal makes mistakes, sees threat everywhere. When defense drive is accompanied by the appearance of reason—when it becomes part of the intellect—that is when intellectual courage is most needed.

And hardest to come by, in dogs or people.

SEVEN

Guarding the Just City:
A Pastoral

> . . . *but that was the pastoral era*
> —CHARLES TOMLINSON, *"Elegy for Henry Street"*

IN 1987, Bandit either defended himself, his master, and his friend, or else he perpetrated frenzied attacks. I said he was doing a job, Lily Mae said so too, said he didn't bother anybody unless they were disturbing the peace, but Frank Intino said he wasn't doing a job, said that Bandit is a naturally aggressive dog who was looking for a fight.

At a party once, I heard a shrink discourse on animals, which in dreams, he said, always represent something about ourselves that we can't say directly. Not necessarily something bad, but something unacceptable.

And we are *always* dreaming when we think of animals, he said. If that is right, then the problem of figuring out anything about Bandit is hopeless, since we are always dreaming. Not just me and Lily Mae and Mr. Redd and Frank Intino, but also the psychiatrist, dreaming that animals are nothing but dreams and never themselves; if you believe the psychiatrist then *das Tier am sich,* the animal himself, is beyond us, beyond our powers to know the animal, further beyond us than *das Ding am sich.* Certainly animals will continue to be more mysterious to us than things—stones, for example, which are, as Stanley Cavell noted, open to ocular proof. You look at a stone and know by looking that it is there, and in what form it is there. You may have to touch it to know if it is cold or hot, but by and large looking is enough. You can look at Bandit, too, or your friend, but you may or may not know by looking that the person is there, or in what form. Because people speak and respond sometimes—quite often indeed—in ways opposed to our views

of them, and because Bandit, too, may respond in ways opposed to the images of him the eye presents, persons, whether
human or canine, are not open to the eyes in the same sense.

Does Bandit exist or not? Will he bite me or won't he?

There is something wrong with this question. Why has there
been, for three years now, all this focus on *Bandit's* aggression
when the entity that continually announces hostile plans is the
state? Is it possible that when a state starts telling horror stories
about animals or women or Jews or blacks or dope dealers or
children, it is projecting, as the shrinks say? Revealing itself? Or
dreaming, anyhow, dreaming something up, something our
dogs cannot comment on.

In some video footage of an arrest of Bandit, you see cops and
snare poles and a lot of shouting, enough paraphernalia to make
a TV series about hostage situations. Good enough for "The
A-Team." In the middle of all of this you see Bandit, walking
along lugubriously with his captors, looking puzzled.

In 1987, the Humane Society of the United States produced a
publication called *Guidelines for Regulating Dangerous or Vicious
Dogs,* and there proposed various sorts of laws. Of course, laws
don't control dogs, because dogs cannot read, but they proposed laws anyway, instead of training. In Plato's *Republic,* our
first book of justice, our first book of philosophy, it turns out
that the philosophy of justice is virtually synonymous with the
philosophy of education, but the "education" touted by humane
societies consists entirely of words and pictures—that is to say,
it is no sort of education at all for Bandit.

Justice entails education in Plato, and education is as distinct
from punishment as it is, or ought to be, from rescue.

Education is for the *citizens,* including the guardians, of the
just city. But education is not among the ideas proposed by the
HSUS as a response to unruliness among dogs; the idea that the
dog is a citizen is not yet available to official kindliness, because
when kindliness in its most energetic modes is not announcing
that your animal is vicious and needs to be destroyed, it is
announcing that training is sadistic and brutal and needs to be
destroyed. The two images that are the cornerstones of humane

PR about domestic animals are these: Vicious Animal, Sadistic Trainer.

So, instead of trying to learn something of what trainers know about teaching dogs the manners that enable them to have a place as citizens of their households and neighborhoods, the HSUS proposed in part:

> The following characteristics should *automatically* [their emphasis] characterize an animal as dangerous. That is, no hearing should be required. . . . "Dangerous Dog" means . . .
>
> (3.) Any dog owned or harbored primarily or in part for the purpose of dog fighting or any dog trained for dog fighting.
>
> (4.) Any dog not owned by a governmental or law enforcement unit used primarily to guard public or private property.

Additionally, there are "potentially dangerous" dogs, to wit:

> (1.) Any dog which, when unprovoked, chases or approaches a person [on] any public or private property in a menacing fashion or apparent attitude of attack. . . .
>
> (2.) Any dog with a known propensity, tendency or disposition to attack unprovoked, to cause injury, or to otherwise threaten the safety of human beings or domestic animals.
>
> (3.) Any dog which, on three separate occasions, has been observed being unrestrained or uncontrolled off its owner's premises. . . .

Guidelines notes that these are "catchall" categories, though not that the wording is vague and extremely broad, the sort of thing frowned on in the Constitution. *Guidelines* notes also that even well-behaved dogs can be a nuisance, and the word "nuisance" transmutes easily in the prose of the booklet to "dangerous." The phrase "otherwise threaten the safety of human beings or domestic animals" does a magnificent job of including any dog alive in the category "dangerous," since existence itself is bound to be a nuisance to someone.

One section of *Guidelines* is headed "Indications of a Dangerous Animal Following a Hearing," which could, I suppose, be construed to refer to the presence of a reporter taking critical notes instead of listening with glazed approval. (One of the difficulties I have with this literature is that, like the literature handed to one on the street about the Second Coming, it provokes the English teacher in me.) *Guidelines* was primarily addressed to dog wardens, animal control officers, and other bureaucrats, which may be why it has the odious and clumsily authoritative sound of government itself. Theoretically, the HSUS is a private charity and not government; the trust they were willing to put in the government was touching, equaled only by the faith the English must have had in their rulers in the period when it was a capital offense for a commoner to own a staghound.

The footage of Bandit being arrested is smoky, like an interior urban scene in a film of a story by Charles Dickens, or any film of major political catastrophe. Smoke and confusion. In the middle of it, Bandit goes along looking puzzled.

Mr. Redd said he wanted a dog for protection. He went further and said that when he was a young man he didn't love dogs, didn't see the point of them, but changed his mind when he got older, and really changed his mind when he got Bandit.

Most people who consult with me about buying a puppy these days want a dog who can protect them; quite often they have their children in mind, or else, as Lily Mae did, an aging parent. "When that dog was here," she said, "I could work in peace, go anywhere I wanted to in peace, and not worry about someone doing something to my daddy."

Many women become aware that a dog, attack-trained or not, is the best deterrent against rape; even a small terrier in a cross mood tends to ruin the romance. In the spring of 1989, an assault on a woman jogger in Central Park was followed by TV programs in which some people proposed laws that would require that rapists be castrated; discussion of this project coincided with the attempt to have pit bulls banned in New York City.

I do not know how the HSUS proposed to decide that a given dog was "used primarily to guard public or private property." What if, as happens, someone adopts a dog, rescuing her from the streets or the pound, and then makes the discovery, if they live in a city, that it is after all safe to go jogging if they take Heidi along with them? What if a decision about keeping Heidi rather than sending her to live with relatives in Connecticut— say the owners have to move because of a No Dogs rule in their apartment, and it is expensive to move—is based in large part on the discovery that no one breaks into their apartment with Heidi there and that the streets are much safer with Heidi? Does Heidi thereby become "dangerous," or is she only dangerous if her owners knew before they got her that they would be safer if they had her? One of my clients is a woman of about sixty-five who brought her West Highland White Terrier, about fifteen pounds, for training. While the dog was with me, the owner was nervous, because she lives alone and the dog is a good watchdog. I suppose that if HSUS investigators knew the content of my consultations with most people who want a dog, they would decide that *any* dog my clients purchased fit the definition, including a small dog selected for value in giving the alarm, and would seize the dog forthwith, since protective abilities are almost invariably mentioned as a reason for getting a dog.

Another legal question: At what age would a puppy become dangerous? Or is it poundage rather than age that determines how dangerous a dog is? Would the puppy's potential for viciousness or danger be reason enough to destroy her right away, as a child's potential for understanding the Constitution is said to be reason to treat her as a citizen? If a two–year–old child's potential for studying law is reason to give her the right to counsel, is it also reason to prosecute her for assault if she bops her playmate on the head? In Colorado a couple of years ago a litter of *three-month-old* pit bull puppies was seized, declared vicious, and destroyed after another dog in the house bit someone. When certain kinds of animal rights supporters are testifying, the fact that one is a competent trainer is irrelevant to the puppies' survival, since the argument is that some animals are too dangerous to be trained humanely. Bandit was at one point said to be too dangerous to be trained humanely. In California, the same argument was made about elephants.

Before the state comes to the kennel, there is always a time that makes more sense. It may not be a better time, but it invariably makes more sense, the time when Bandit does the guarding instead of needing to be guarded. Once the dog becomes a hostage, things do not make sense, and in the idea of dogs as hostages of the state all of the bright valor of our knowledge of friendship with them is lost, to be recovered only in unreliable passages that lead through philosophy and oftentimes get stuck there. One name for a life in one such passage these days is academic psychology. Another is dog training as it is enacted in public discourse, and even in the discourse of trainers. The name of the darkest of these passages is: animal rights. None of these have the power to recover that time that made sense, when Bandit was sufficient, and not only because that time may never have existed.

Even if it existed, the time that made more sense must be the sort of thing frowned on by Marxists, by feminists of a certain sort, by child and animal rights societies, because property rights signify to Bandit, are part and parcel of his affections. Back when Bandit and I could take walks, he never, in the words of the HSUS, took an "apparent attitude of attack" toward anyone, but if there was a shout or running or any sort of excitement, he would move in front of me, as I said, positioning his body like a barrier between mine and what might be a danger. Taking care of his own.

The whole idea of people owning dogs and dogs owning people is coming into disrepute these days. When a dog protects master or property he or she is "vicious," and when a person protects a dog he or she is either insensitive to public welfare (if the dog is a pit bull) or an exploitative, "dominionistic" slave owner (if the dog is a hound or a bird dog).

Bandit's inability to tumble to Marxist insights about the unsoundness of his attitude toward property—he thinks there is such a thing and that it is Good—creates awkwardness for people who want to love dogs and get rid of property-based relations between people and dogs, which I guess is how it turns out that the best way to love dogs is to spay, neuter, and euthanize them.

Socrates, however, had praise for the unimproved nature of dogs. In Book II of the *Republic,* he and Glaucon have gotten so far in their fantasy of what the ideal city would be like as to propose some luxuries—not only bread but olives and cheese and spices—and so it seems that there will be a need for guardians. Socrates points out to Glaucon that such guardians will have to have contradictory traits, at once gentle and fierce, at once brave and docile, and Glaucon, ever the excellent straight man, agrees that the task is well-nigh hopeless in that case, because how can someone be at once gentle and fierce? The guardians of the just city are logical impossibilities because they must be at once ferocious to the enemy and gentle to the good folk. Since what we desire is that justice itself should be thus, this is one of the moments when the whole just city project seems to be bootless.

"By Zeus!" says Socrates in Allan Bloom's translation, "it's no mean thing we've taken upon ourselves. But nonetheless we mustn't be cowardly [he means philosophically cowardly] at least as far as it's in our power."

The guardians, like justice, must be high-spirited and must have "sharp senses, speed to catch what they perceive and finally strength if they have to fight it out with whatever they have caught." And Socrates troubles poor Glaucon, asking if the problem now won't be that if the guardians are like that, they will be "savage to one another and the rest of the citizens."

Glaucon's adrenaline is up, and he too says, "By Zeus, it won't be easy." He is on the point of giving up when Socrates pulls his rabbit out of the rhetorical hat—dogs. Dogs solve the problem, or rather, a true understanding of the nature of dogs does. In one of the most cunning pieces of anthropomorphism and its reverse known to Western thought, Socrates dismisses the problem of guardians by a trick that enables him to segue

directly into the banishment of the poets, which would not have
been possible had Glaucon only taken some psychology and so
learned to use the term "anthropomorphism" in its modern
sense. But Socrates does, in the course of banishing or at least
censoring poets, enjoin against an older sense of the term, attributing human traits to deities. In particular, he doesn't want
anyone suggesting that the gods acted out of revenge or petty
jealousy or weren't kindly to each other. Of course, as Nietzsche points out, it took some centuries of brutalizing the Jews
before a kindly deity would be produced; Socrates is too gay to
have pulled that one off, though he has a go.

The passage in Book II about dogs goes like this in Bloom's
translation:

> ". . . You know, of course, that by nature the disposition of
> noble dogs is to be as gentle as can be with their familiars and
> people they know and the opposite with those they don't
> know."
>
> "I do know that."
>
> "Then," I said, "it is possible, after all; and what we're
> seeking for in the guardian isn't against nature."
>
> "It doesn't seem so."
>
> "In your opinion, then, does the man who will be a fit
> guardian need, in addition to spiritedness, also to be a phi-
> losopher in his nature?"
>
> "How's that?" he said. "I don't understand."
>
> "This, too, you'll observe in dogs," I said, "and it's a thing
> in the beast worthy of our wonder."
>
> "What?"
>
> "When it sees someone it doesn't know, it's angry, al-
> though it never had any bad experience with him. And when
> it sees someone it knows, it greets him warmly, even if it
> never had a good experience with him. Didn't you ever won-
> der about this before?"
>
> "No, I haven't paid very much attention to it up to now.
> But it's plain that it really does this."
>
> "Well, this does look like an attractive affection of its na-
> ture and truly philosophic."

"In what way?"

"In that it distinguishes friendly from hostile looks by nothing other than by having learned the one and being ignorant of the other," I said. "And so, how can it be anything other than a lover of learning since it defines what's its own and what's alien by knowledge and ignorance?"

"It surely couldn't be anything but," he said.

"Well," I said, "but aren't love of learning and love of wisdom the same?"

"Yes, the same," he said.

"So shall we be bold and assert that a human being too, if he is going to be gentle to his own and those known to him, must by nature be a philosopher and a lover of learning?"

"Yes," he said, "let's assert it."

"Then the man who's going to be a fine and good guardian of the city for us will in his nature be philosophic, spirited, swift, and strong."

Allan Bloom has this to say about this passage:

> This identification of dog-like affection for acquaintances with philosophy is, of course, not serious. It only serves to prepare the way for the true emergence of philosophy in Book V and to heighten the difference between the philosopher and the warrior. The philosophers are gentle men because they pursue knowledge and not gain; their object does not entail exploitation of others. The love of knowledge is a motive necessary to the rulers of this city in order to temper their love of victory and wealth. But the philosophers are the opposites of the dogs inasmuch as they are always questing to know that of which they are ignorant, whereas the dogs must cut themselves off from the unknown and are hostile to foreign charms.

It is hard to know which of the mistakes here is the most exasperating, and whether the idea that philosophers are "gentle men" is more aggravating than the equally benighted idea that sheepdogs work for love of their handlers, as Bloom says in the next paragraph:

No mention is made of the fact that dogs do not character-
istically love the flocks but the masters to whom the flock
belongs and who teach them and command them to care for
the flock. . . . The dogs' nature opens them to the command
of philosophy but does not make them philosophers.

Socrates is not here discussing sheepdogs, of course, and even
if he were, a central question would be whether herding dogs or
flock-guarding dogs were under discussion. The chances are
that if Socrates had been mentioning sheepdogs, which he was
not, it would have been those of the flock-guarding breeds, such
as are mentioned in the Book of Job and in Psalms, because
herding breeds are latecomers. There are a number of major
differences between these two sorts of dog. The herding dog
lives with the shepherd, not with the flock, and is minutely
responsive to direction and command. The flock guard lives
with the flock and tends to be, in obedience work, more than
just a little knotheaded. The flock guard works for love of the
flock, not the master; the herding dog works for love of the
work, not the master. Many good Border Collies will work as
well for a stranger as for their master, if not better, so long as the
stranger knows how to work sheep; a Border Collie lives by the
work ethic. (As do many dogs, actually, if given half a chance.)
Socrates has it down a bit better. He does not tell us that
well-bred dogs guard things out of love for their masters, because it is not so. Like philosophers, they work out of their love
of knowledge, or learning, depending on the translator's pref-
erences, just as Socrates says they do—the joke is not an idle
one. And it is not, I think, lightly that he identifies the dog's
noble version of xenophobia with that which motivates the philosopher, though of course he does so humorously. Philosophy
is, or has become, above all the discipline of marking the limits
of knowledge. It took Wittgenstein to work out what that means
for philosophy, but it has been the case from the beginning that
however "problem" is defined, and however "knowledge" is
defined, philosophy arises when there is a problem of
knowledge—a problem about knowing where it is and safe-

guarding it by means of that knowledge, and being so fierce about knowing just where knowledge begins and leaves off that philosophy has become, not only in modern times, willing to repudiate the entire world if it cannot prove itself to philosophy. In the *Republic*, the problem is knowing, defining, the ideal or just city; dogs are the ones who know it by its familiarity to them. Socrates says in some translations that this means that a well-bred dog is a "true philosopher," loving (his own) wisdom so well that he acts always on disjunctions between what he knows and what lies outside his knowledge, *keeping the unknown out* so as to keep knowledge safe. This is philosophy's traditional chastity and discipline.

The breed that has been best at this, by and large, is the German Shepherd. By that I mean that Shepherds were great dogs in the days when there were cops on the beat, excellent at many forms of cooperation in the project of protecting the known and knowable by repudiating the unknown and un-knowable, as decisively as some philosophers will repudiate, say, astrology at a dinner party.

Like any good herding breed, Shepherds are maniacs for or-der, and often rather humorless about it, from some points of view. The fate of the just city can be seen, I think, in the fate of the German Shepherd, which, though still one of the finest working breeds, is falling somewhat out of favor with police departments here and there, a development that coincides with the disappearance of the cop on the beat.

When I first became old enough to be aware of police dogs, in the late fifties, Scotland Yard had approximately four hun-dred dogs and a program that was the talk and envy of the Western world. Most of these were German Shepherds, though eight were Labradors who patrolled Buckingham Palace, a sit-uation that required dogs who could deal comfortably with a change of handler. The German Shepherds, when possible, not only lived with their handlers, but lived *on the beat* with their handlers. This meant that the Shepherd's outstanding judgment could be used fully; Shepherds are masters of problems that take the form: What is wrong with this picture? They know what belongs, what is in its place and what isn't, and alert reliably on What Does Not Belong.

Of course, you have to have a scene in which you can tell what does and does not belong in order to use such a dog's abilities. In a neighborhood situation, a Shepherd will alert (without command) on, for example, an unfamiliar car, a piece of laundry blown off a line, a stranger in town, or a person behaving strangely. I modified the term "xenophobia" with the unlikely adjective "noble" earlier, because the Shepherd's alerts spring, not from "hostility to foreign charms," as Bloom has it—a Shepherd has as wide-ranging an affinity for the new and curious as any dog—but rather from love of what makes sense, what is in order, what is in that sense known and knowable, or "familiar."

In fact it is a great deal easier to teach a Shepherd to operate in a new neighborhood or with new concepts than it is to teach most philosophers, because Shepherds have a better grasp of the concept "neighborhood" itself than philosophers do. Hence it is possible to work the same dog sometimes in Brooklyn and sometimes in Grand Central Station; the dog in a few days says, "Oh, I see how this situation goes together."

So long as there is some sense in which the situation can be said to go together, that is. If there is no beat, no neighborhood, not enough of the known and coherent for there to be such a thing as an "unfamiliar" car or piece of behavior, then for the Shepherd the only neighborhood is the cop; the neighborhood is defined only as the territory around the handler's body, and in that case everyone is a suspect, an intruder. Justice becomes then so private as nearly to vanish, like a code language shared by only two people, too hermetic to be a social concept.

Here the pit bulls and some other terriers and other breeds become more useful. An Airedale has a more sporting relationship to the work. Suspects are game animals, say, rather than criminals, so if someone is behaving like a hooligan they are for the big game terrier an opportunity for something more like athletics, say, than justice. The Shepherd's universe is threatened if he is asked too many times to ignore obviously antisocial and criminal behavior, but the Airedale simply figures it is not his turn yet to show his prowess, as when he is told to leave that particular lion alone. Similarly with the bird dogs—a bird dog's heart is not demolished when it is not her turn to retrieve at a field trial, so long as you keep up her faith that there is always more sport to be had. But keeping things in order is not sport for the classic Shepherd, or at least not to the extent it is for some other breeds.

This does not mean that the terriers and sporting group dogs are less civilized than German Shepherds or Border Collies, but rather that the terriers are more likely to, say, take civilization for granted, or at least not to worry so much when the bottom drops out of the market—after all, it is a challenge, another opportunity to test yourself, show how quick on your feet you really are. Civilization is there, a backdrop, for the terriers; for the Shepherds it is the whole point of existence, and the meaning and foundation and center of existence is so incapable of getting along without me, Rin Tin Tin, that I might as well be said to be the foundation.

That is to say that a German Shepherd is quite often a walking social conscience. This can become a tad tiresome for the dog's intimates, and tiring, even quite nerve-racking, for the dog himself; there are many shy and spooky Shepherds who drive you nuts with their constant concern and vexation: Why Has That Tree Limb Moved? and When Is Something Going to Be Done? and even, There Ought to Be a Law.

Bandit is neither a herding dog nor a terrier, so neither of these types quite fits his case. He likes a challenge, of course— remember that retrieving bored him silly until he had to surmount a boulder or two in order to get to the dumbbell. Nonetheless, as a guard he is more like the Shepherd than the terrier. He is a bulldog, so does not quite have the abstract social conscience of the herding dogs, but has, say, a sense of being at work, on duty, and certainly a sense of neighborhood. Once I was being photographed for something or another, and an animal was needed, so I brought Bandit out because he can take a rather nice photograph. The photographer, Enrico Ferorelli, found him a cooperative enough subject, but not in the way dogs usually are—clicks and whistles and chortles and the rest all failed to cause him to cease his constant perimeter surveillance during an hour of work, and Enrico said to his assistant that Bandit was "just like those Secret Service men, you know, when you try to get them to look away for a moment so you can sneak by and get a picture of the President, and nothing doing, you can't distract them."

Enrico was saying this in admiration, but it is not a trait that everyone admires, Bandit's hardness, or the hardness of hard dogs in general; I have heard a number of breeders say, "You can have those hard Airedales [or Shepherds or Rotties or Bouviers or whatever]—I cull the aggressive pups out of my litters!" There is a mistake here—hardness is not aggression; a dog may be fairly "sharp," as we say, quick to take offense, but not at all hard, or a dog may be, as many of the bull breed dogs are, as hard as a rock, and as steady as one, and as difficult to arouse with insult or threat as Bandit is difficult to distract.

Bandit is not as quick as many Shepherds are to alert on What Does Not Belong, or rather, he doesn't alert as pointedly, but he is as serious about it as any Shepherd. I don't know if he would have been different if he had been raised in, say, Richmond, Virginia, in the 1930s, when anyone could walk the streets safely at night and therefore had less reason to be so worried about someone from the next neighborhood over.

Neighborhood. Bandit had to be able to recognize the neighborhood around Henry Street in order to recognize what did not belong there—what persons or behaviors were Not Part of His Neighborhood. In general, a dog, like a philosopher, has to know that something exists—recognize it, know it again—in order to guard it. Classical philosophy and psychology typically deny to dogs the abilities that make such recognition possible. Some of those denials are thoughtful and important, such as the ones that founded behaviorism, but most such denials are casual, part of our intellectual weather. I am taking the following example at random, or rather for convenience—it comes from philosopher Richard Rorty and is the one nearest my keyboard at the moment and will do as well as any:

Human beings who have been socialized—socialized in any language, any culture—do share a capacity which other animals lack. They can be given a special kind of pain: they can all be humiliated by the forcible tearing down of the particular structures of language and belief in which they were socialized (or which they pride themselves on having formed for themselves). More specifically, they can be used, as animals cannot, to gratify O'Brien's wish [in Orwell's *1984*] to "tear human minds to pieces and put them together again in new shapes of your own choosing."

This just isn't so. You can teach a dog to try hard to do something well—that is, teach a structure of thought that is linguistic in that the concept of "doing well" in the dog's world depends just as much on the inventiveness of discourse as it does in our world—and then deprive the dog of the meaningful order he or she expects as a result of having a certain way of thinking and of thinking in that way. If the dog is a very serious dog indeed, you can do this by locking him up in the pound for six weeks and responding to him as though he were vicious. Evidence of the collapse of the scaffold of meaning that a dog no less than a human can mistake for solid ground might come in the form, for instance, of the dog's, for the first time in his life, peeing on the porch upon his return home, in a situation in which "home" is no longer a fully available idea.

You can teach a dog to retrieve, and then laugh at him for trying to retrieve well. Dogs have a lot of heart, but it is as possible to make a mockery of a dog's beliefs as it is of a person's, and though the methods are not always the same, they overlap. It is curious that Professor Rorty should choose the capacity for humiliation to distinguish man from "animals"—as though we were ennobled by our ability to have bad feelings. But nobility—Bandit's nobility, for instance—consists not in bad feelings but in the ability to respond to opportunities for imaginative reconstruction. After six weeks in the pound, Bandit peed on the porch on Henry Street. After two weeks at Silver Trails, in training, he would wait until I arrived in the morning and took him to the exercise pen to pee. It is meaning itself—

social, domestic meaning, the meaning of the personal dignity possible in, say, keeping yourself clean—that is meaningful to Bandit. This is a power, not to be underestimated, and the power that brought him to such a point of confusion that he would pee on the porch on Henry Street is also a power not to be underestimated.

It is the state that so humiliated Bandit, but of course Bandit does not know that the state exists. A dog can know what a neighborhood is, a village, a household—these are human social groupings that a dog can know and guard. The ideal city that Socrates teased out of a difficult conversation was also a state, but it was to have 5,004 inhabitants, and a village of 5,004 people is a physical and social object a dog can understand. There were about 5,000 people at the University of California at Riverside during the period when I studied and taught there, and had my dogs with me, and they all learned what its boundaries were, both physical and social. In the late sixties, I had a German Shepherd, for instance, who alerted on FBI agents on campus, knowing that they were not part of that scene. A dog's alerts are not infallible, and they are *for that reason* meaningful in the way language is—a dog alerts on something that is at odds with the meaning structures by which she lives, and does this, as we do, sometimes nobly, sometimes idiotically, and in error and confusion.

An interesting thing is that dogs, while they can learn something that overlaps my concept of "Yale" or "University of California at Riverside" quite closely, cannot learn to recognize uniforms, despite the best efforts of numerous armies and police departments. That is, a dog cannot be "trained" to be hostile toward anyone wearing the wrong uniform, friendly toward anyone wearing the right one; a dog always beholds you, not your gown, and if the dog is mistaken, it is about you and not your clothing. Hence a dog can be loyal but not patriotic, because a dog does not respond to uniforms, flags, other memoranda of social meanings abstracted from persons. You don't find a dog, ever, going about trying to make the world safe for democracy, because doing that requires an ability to streamline concepts by means of writing. You can't wave a flag for a dog, you can't teach Bandit respect for the authority of a Canine Control officer's uniform. You can't even teach him "respect" by giving him an electric shock every time he tries to make friends with someone wearing a certain uniform. If he generalizes, it will be to something the persons wearing the uniform have in common, such as gender, or a particular aftershave lotion, or the particular wool blend of the uniform, but not to the uniform itself, because the uniform itself is a notation, and you cannot leave a note for a dog.

Hence the gap between a neighborhood or a village and the state is vast, and Bandit cannot guard the state, which may explain the state's hostility to him, and before that the church's frequent hostility toward various kinds of animals. A dog cannot be tricked into believing that there is order, government, where there is none; a dog depends on what a dog knows, and Socrates says, gaily but not lightly, that this should be some cause for us to wonder in the creature.

But there is a state the founding of which is celebrated in the form of a statue of a pit bull, or bulldog in the generic sense. That state is no pastoral dream, but a long series of realities woven together from the time of Livy with some of the most exquisite memoranda of statehood our kind has been capable of. I do not mean Athens—democracy is a notation of the idea of neighborhood, which is in turn, as Derrida has been saying lately, instituted as friendship. Therefore, democracy is the only form of human political organization a dog can participate in. But it was not a democracy that claimed one of the finest pieces of animal sculpture in the world as if it were a statue of a Founder—it was Rome.

EIGHT ························

The Pit Bull
Who Founded Rome

"Aslan is a lion—the Lion, the great lion."
"Ooh!" said Susan. "Is he—quite safe?"
"Safe?" said Mr. Beaver. "Don't you hear what Mrs.
Beaver tells you? Who said anything about safe? 'Course he
isn't safe. But he's good. He's the King, I tell you."

—C. S. LEWIS, *The Lion, the Witch and the Wardrobe*

SHORTLY AFTER I picked Bandit up for training, a friend sent me a postcard from Rome. The card had a photograph of the Capitoline Wolf on it, the wolf that Livy tells us founded Rome when she gave suck to Romulus and Remus. The figure of the dam is Etruscan, as early as the fifth or sixth century B.C., according to the authorities.

My friend had written on the back of the card, "That there is no wolf. Rome was founded by a *bulldog,* and now her history makes sense!"

And he was right, about the statue at least. I do not know whether or not Rome's history makes sense.

My friend is a true bulldog fancier and so did not mean the breed with the short snout and the breathing problems that almost invariably requires a cesarean to whelp. He meant, in his first ebullience, the American Pit Bull Terrier, but probably calmed down and recalled that the pit bull is but the latest (and probably most glorious) of the bull breeds. These include the mastiff who would have accompanied King Arthur when he went out a-riding, the ubiquitous heraldic dogs of Western art, and the modern (English) bull terrier.

I should say here that bulldog fanciers are not the only ones making claims on the Capitoline figure. I have a friend who breeds Rottweilers and insists the figure is a Rottweiler. I have

174

The Capitoline Wolf (THE BETTMANN ARCHIVE).

another friend who breeds Boxers and has his own ideas. The competition among dog fanciers for the proto dog, the archetypal dog, is full of strenuous rhetoric, but the bottom line here is that my friend was right: That there is a bulldog. It was a bulldog who founded Rome.

Consider, first, that the expression on the face of the so-called wolf, with the raised, worried eyebrows, is quite plainly one of largesse and concern, an expression typical of a responsible sort of domestic dog. It is the expression that characterizes the dog drawn by James Thurber, part Bloodhound and part pit bull (that is, in Thurber's day, American bull terrier, none of your English bulls). This dog, according to Thurber himself, represented civilization and decency. His dog's eyebrows are often raised worriedly in response to the alarming antics of his human characters.

If you found a stray who looked like the Capitoline figure,

you could take her into the best bulldog circles without fear of ridicule. I have seen her cousins quite frequently in the show ring and being confiscated by the dogcatcher on television.

I did some research to find out what art history could tell me about this figure, and the answer so far is not much. One writer notes that some authorities have claimed the figure is a lion, and that there has been debate on this point. This caused me considerable confusion: How could people look at what is obviously, archetypally, a dog and debate whether it is a lion or a wolf?

Another art authority notes that the "snarling expression" is more doglike than wolflike. "Snarling expression"? This confused me even more. It is true that the lady's teeth are showing, but that is because it is a hot day—it is hot in Rome—and she is panting to stay cool. Her panting coupled with her posture suggests that she may have just exerted herself, perhaps moving her puppies to a safer place or else herding her owner's human puppies out of the way of a passing chariot.

When I show a photograph of the figure to people who are sensitive to visual images—an artist friend of mine, a filmmaker, and so on—and ask them, "What's that?" they say, "Why, that's Annie, of course!" Annie is my bulldog—that is, my pit bull.

I am not, of course, suggesting that the dog who represents the founding of Rome is an American Pit Bull Terrier. I am perfectly ready to acknowledge that Rome is older than the United States. What I am saying is that the breed of dog registered with the United Kennel Club and the American Dog Breeders Association as an American Pit Bull Terrier, and with the American Kennel Club as an American Staffordshire Terrier, is the latest incarnation of an ancient and noble type of dog.

When I proposed the notion that Rome was founded by a pit bull to some of my friends, they reacted with exasperation. We have the authority of the story as given in Livy, and that ought to settle it. But some said, "Well, yes. It's sort of as though there were a statue of the cherry tree George Washington cut down, and some botanist came along and said, 'But that's an apple tree!'" It is not exactly like that, though, because both cherry and apple trees are domestic species, and wolves are not domestic, so the difference to the allegory is immense.

The Capitoline animal is a bulldog, with cropped ears no less. The cropped ears suggest one of two things—that she was of a fighting breed or, somewhat less strongly, that even two and a half thousand years ago people were cropping the ears of guard breeds such as bulldogs and Great Danes and Dobies, to make them look more impressive. In any case, no artist is going to accidentally render such an exquisitely true bulldog. The statue is evidence that there was at least one breed of dog related to our pit bull that was held in quite a bit of reverence five centuries before the birth of Christ. How she came to be labeled a wolf I have no idea. It drives me nuts. How *could* anyone think that is a wolf?

How *could* anyone think that Bandit is a wolf, or that a wolf is Bandit? What is going on here? What *is* civilization?

Bulldogs of one sort and another have been held in reverence for quite some time. On my wall is a poster of some fountain statuary featuring canine figures typical in Italian art. Like Andrea da Firenze's fourteenth-century fresco *Dominicanni,* which predates by a couple of centuries the first modern versions of breed grouping and history, the poster shows the progression of type from bulldog to gazehound. The pit bulls are rendered with great care and feeling, as are the dogs that look like our modern greyhound.

Da Firenze's fresco was made at just about the time an interesting change was going on in English: The word "hund," which is generally accepted as the medieval equivalent of our word "dog," the generic, the word that covered everything from Chihuahuas to St. Bernards, began to be replaced by the word "dog" as the generic term.

The word "dog" in medieval English is held to have represented a "formidable race of dogs." Hence "dog" meant a breed of dog, or at least what we would call a kind of dog, as when we say "terrier" or "hound" or "sporting breed," referring to bird dogs. The evidence suggests that this medieval "Dog" was a bulldog or mastiff type of dog—that it was an ancestor of the pit bull, a guard breed, and probably popular with the lower classes.

This evidence is largely literary. The medieval term "hund" was used, customarily, with adjectives such as "noble" or "gentle" (as in "of gentle birth") or "loyal" and so on. That is, the hund was a good dog. The medieval breed "Dog," however, was a bad dog, snarling, attacking, showing its fangs, and so on. So, in English, dogs have from the beginning been bad dogs.

The dogs of the lower classes are customarily seen as ferocious. The Collie, for example, only recently came to have the aristocratic associations made famous in *Lassie Come Home* and in the stories of Albert Payson Terhune. Up to and including the first half of the nineteenth century, the collie was a lowly creature because people who tend sheep were (and are) lowly creatures, which is why the universality of Christ's love is figured in allegories about shepherds. And the collie, like the bulldog, was seen as vicious and as "scarcely capable of education," as one authority puts it. Another authority, William Youatt, writes in 1839 that while even a greyhound would cause no diminution of respectability, a young man with a bulldog would speedily become profligate and debased.

But Queen Victoria became fond of both collies and bulldogs, with the result that these breeds became popular among the upper classes. The Bulldog Club was formed in 1854, almost simultaneously with the founding of the dog show as we know it. And, as is standardly the case when people who have no concept of the work a dog does begin breeding it, both dogs came to resemble in virtually no respect the good, true-hearted working dogs their shepherd and farmer devotees had so carefully loved and bred.

I must digress here, by the way and say that these pre-dog-show collies were *true* collies. That is, this term "collie" is used among people who breed working collies, especially Border Collies, the way "bulldog" is used among educated admirers of the American Pit Bull Terrier, to mean the archetypal kind of dog under discussion. "Collie" is an old Scottish word that means "useful"; the Collies were the dogs who were useful around the farm.

Students of breed history think that the modern collie of Lassie fame got its narrow head through crosses between the old collie and the Borzoi, or Russian Wolfhound. Hence, the aristocratic collie is a mixed breed and not a true collie at all. Also note that the narrow Collie skull, which is held by amateurs to be the result of "inbreeding" or incest, is in fact the result of a cross between two radically distinct and separate gene pools. When I hear that Collies were "ruined" by inbreeding, I don't know what to say. The ones that are ruined were ruined in the way all breeds from time to time get ruined—as a result of their becoming popular with the genteel classes. City slickers. People who have no more idea of what a working dog is than I have of how Wall Street works begin breeding the dogs, and judging the dogs, and writing breed standards for the dogs, and pretty soon you have no dog at all.

The theory that inbreeding causes stupidity and craziness and so on has nothing at all to do with science and a great deal to do with the ways scientific concepts become popular myth. A large part of my childhood was spent in the Deep South, and there I heard the theory that Negroes—one said "Negroes" in those days—were poor and illiterate because of "inbreeding," the lascivious suggestion being that fathers impregnated daughters, and brothers sisters. Another way the "inbreeding" fairy tale comes up is as an explanation of the upper classes. Queen Victoria, it was said, had a hemophiliac child because the royal family was "inbred." This is not true. Victoria's baby was a case of the rare spontaneous mutation of a key gene.

Genetic nonsense is the sort that people have to worry about in this century, and the story goes that Elizabeth II worried about it before deciding to have an heir to the extent of consulting the royal geneticist or some such person to determine whether or not, as a female descendant of Victoria, she could be a carrier of the hemophiliac gene. It was determined that she was not, because on her side of the family the succession had been entirely through the male line, which meant that her chances of having a hemophiliac baby were the same as those of any member of the population, very remote. Common sense could have told her this; even with a slow-developing animal such as *Homo sapiens,* a century is long enough for the presence or absence of a marked trait to become noticeable in a line, though it would take far longer, five or six centuries at least, to *establish* a trait in a line. No one lives long enough to do that, which is the principal reason the programs of the Nazis and the Ku Klux Klan are not only vicious but doomed to failure.

Actually, Elizabeth II is not truly "inbred," but rather "linebred." "Inbreeding" means breeding parent to offspring or sibling to sibling; anything else—cousin to cousin, for example—is linebreeding. Some breeders use inbreeding deliberately, either in order to eliminate undesirable recessive traits—because if you inbreed you can be pretty sure that the pups that don't show the traits also don't carry them—or sometimes in order to preserve a desirable recessive trait.

The good, intelligent, brave, and reliable working collie, the one on whose diligence and good sense the livelihoods of many people still depend, is of course the product of, among other things, inbreeding. Also linebreeding. The same is true of any breed that can do a job of work.

Notice that the horror story about inbreeding is a peculiarly (though not exclusively) American horror story. German horror stories about Dobies in the thirties were also horror stories about breeding, but the idea was that Dobies were of *impure* blood, rather than of as-it-were *too* pure blood, and therefore vicious and unstable, like the Jews. Or so one of my clients told me one time when she was looking around for a dog. She wanted a largish dog, short-coated, easy to train yet protective. I said that she was describing a Dobie, but she wouldn't have it, said that she was still suffering from the effects on her of German propaganda from the thirties, even though she realized that it was all lies.

Donald McCaig, in a wonderful book called *Eminent Dogs, Dangerous Men,* observes that "what the English noticed about their dogs, they attributed to their kings," and also observes that no duke anywhere has ever been as thoughtfully bred as a sheepdog is, to do a job of work. In English tradition of the last couple of centuries, there is some ambivalence about this business of whether or not close breeding is bad. It is bad for the lower classes, good for dukes and kings. Good for Border Collies, bad for pit bulls.

McDowell Lyons, who wrote a great book, *The Dog in Action,* on the relationship between structure and movement and various kinds of work in dogs, tells the story of how he first came to understand the long work of breeding, which is in serious situations the same as the work of living itself, and no toy for foolish suburbanites. Lyons had gone to the Tensas Swamp, in Louisiana, having heard of a wonderful sort of dog used there to round up wild boar—they were just called "hog dogs." He went out with a farmer and some other men, who rode mules. The hog dogs eventually found a wild boar and proceeded to tease and irritate the boar until he began chasing the dogs, who then hightailed it for home, stopping to tease the boar some more if he showed signs of losing interest in killing the hog dogs.

Back at the farm, there was a hog pen, which had solid sides except for a smallish window about three feet above the ground. The dogs ran into the pen, followed by one or more angry hogs who were in turn followed by men on mules. Once the hog was in the pen, the farmers closed and barred the gate, and the dogs escaped by jumping through the window.

Lyons was of course wonderfully impressed with the intelligence of the dogs, and asked the farmer how he trained them.

The farmer says, "You don't train 'em. What you do is, you take yourself one hell of a good hog dog, and breed her to another one hell of a good hog dog. Of course, all the pups don't come out of the swamp. But them that does, is hog dogs."

Now, the farmer's answer was no doubt abbreviated somewhat so that the fool of a city slicker could follow it, but his remarks amount to an account of how real dogs get bred. They are not selected for looks at all, but rather for working ability. Consider, for example, the fact that if a pit bull or a St. Bernard or a Louisiana Catahoula won a serious sheepdog trial, she would be eligible for registration as a Border Collie, or else the Border Collie people would have to stop saying that Border Collies are the only sheepdogs.

Let us return to the bulldog—that is to say, the pit bull. Like

the Border Collie, she was bred for working ability. This means
primarily fighting ability, although it also means the ability to
work cattle and wild boar, and prowess in weight-pulling contests. And fighting ability, as I have said before and will say as
many times as I am asked, does not mean savagery or viciousness at all. Just as a good bird dog is one who alerts on birds
naturally, from birth, and on nothing but birds—a bird dog is
expected to ignore squirrels, woodchucks, and other dogs, and
a Foxhound is a dog who goes after foxes but is unmoved by
deer, raccoon, and lion scent, and a Rhodesian Ridgeback goes
for lion scent and ignores birds—a good fighting dog is one that
wants to fight other dogs and *only* other dogs. Some of them in
my experience don't even fight *all* other dogs, but only dogs
who issue serious challenges, and in some cases only in a pit. I
have, for example, a little bulldog I call Rosie, though her
ADBA registration names her Walsh and Hearne's Irene. Her
mama, Sandy, is one of the gamest fighting dogs in the country,
by general agreement, and Rosie takes after her ma closely
enough that her litter name was Sandy II. Sandy is at the moment housed in a kennel that also contains some feisty Schnau-
zers, Lhasa Apsos, and so on, all of whom issue ferocious
challenges from behind their gates. It came about that Sandy's
caretaker was closing the kennel one evening, not having been
in for several hours during the afternoon, and found Sandy's
door had come off its hooks. The runs there are chain link, but
not commercial grade—they are made from the lightest wire
that is stiff enough to form chain links at all.

Sandy, according to all the myths, should have been rampag-
ing through the kennel, killing dogs right and left. And some
fighting dogs might very well have done just that, not because
of the myths but because their wisdom doesn't always match
their prowess, but Sandy didn't. In fact, Sandy didn't even leave
her run, with dogs a few feet away from her using terrible bad
language.

This sort of thing is mysterious only when one assumes that
there is a single trait referred to by the term "aggression," just
as history gets mysterious when you assume that at any given
moment there is a single town called "Rome." I like to think

that the Capitoline Pit Bull was like Sandy: restrained, a good mother, sensible, and deadly when crossed rather than bent on fighting anything that moves. She looks like Sandy, actually, though she is thinner than Sandy was when I last saw her; like many pit bulls, Sandy is something of a couch potato when there are no epic conflicts at hand.

Since I myself have never fought a dog or seen an organized dogfight, my notions of fighting dogs are based solely on observations of bulldogs in kennel situations, where I see male pit bulls who are perfectly peaceful with the dogs that belong to the kennel—the family or house dogs—and with 99 percent of the dogs who come in for boarding, but who occasionally decide that Something Has to Be Done about a certain dog.

Other pit bulls are, of course, fight-crazy, just as some horses are jump-crazy. This is not to say that fighting is the only thing they can or will do with pleasure, only that the first question is always, "Are we gonna have a fight? Huh, Mom, huh? I wanna fight!" Similarly, I have known Pointers who had to be brought to trial grounds in welded steel crates, they were that eager to get out there and work. For a Pointer, work doesn't even mean picking up the birds, just finding and pointing them.

With Bandit, there were indeed a few discussions about Doing Something About That Dog, though the dog thus singled out was one that the kennel help also had to Do Something About, or at least felt like Doing Something About—the Boxer, say, who had to be put on the end run with an empty run next to him. The sort of dog who says as you pass by, "Go ahead. I dare you. Just *say* something about my mother!" After about ten passes this would get to be too much for Bandit, and he would say, "Leave this to me, Vicki. I'll teach that snot-nosed brat to talk to you that way!" So he had to learn, one evening, that he was in a professional kennel, a business, and the customer is always right. A hard lesson for him, though it didn't take that long, not nearly as long as it took me.

The Capitoline Wolf is not the only instance of a bulldog representing the virtues of a state. England has for a couple of centuries now been best typified in foreign policy as John Bull—

a bulldog—and this identification of national pride with the bulldog slightly predates the appearance of the modern English Bulldog, wobbly and asthmatic (and in most cases admirably good-hearted).

At the beginning of World War I, the American Pit Bull Terrier was the breed that represented America's position on the conflict. He is pictured on a poster of 1914 with a sweet, clear eye, saying, "I'm neutral but I'm not afraid of any of 'em!" Wallace Robinson, who made the painting on which the poster was based, was no doubt an admirer of Teddy Roosevelt's pit bull. The American Pit Bull Terrier appears throughout classical American literature, too, because the dog stood for the courage, loyalty, inventiveness, and lack of upper-class pretension associated with the pioneers, the American woodsmen, and so on. John Steinbeck had a beloved pit bull named Jiggs, Buster Brown's Tige was a pit bull, as was Pete the Pup in the old *Our Gang* comedies. The great humorist James Thurber had as a young man a pit bull named Rex, and his second wife says that he would wake up mourning Rex even as an old man. Throughout his life he developed the gentle, mournful hound that was his hallmark—and that dog was based, as I said, partly on the Bloodhound and partly on the pit bull.

In 1940, Franklin Delano Roosevelt issued a call to the Democrats of Virginia to rally round the White House for the elections, and one answer came from a pit bull named Champion Bud, pride and joy of Arthur "Stubby" Stubbs, a Golden Gloves boxer, who said he didn't know if he got the fightin' instinct from Bud or if it was the other way around. In any case, Bud did not go on killing rampages, but there were two English Bulldogs who came over one day to challenge Bud, as they challenged every dog in the neighborhood. There was a fight, after which the bulldogs forever acknowledged Bud's right to the title, however reluctantly, just as England had to acknowledge America's rights, however reluctantly.

Champion Bud was a singer. When he showed up at the White House in 1940, in response to the President's call, FDR asked him to sing. (Bud had also sung at the Grand Ole Opry, and preferred Stephen Foster tunes; Stubby would accompany him on the banjo.) When I learned about Bud's visit to the White House I was concerned about Fala, FDR's Scottie, though a Scottie can be a tough customer in a fight himself. I called Mr. Stubbs, who, two years ago at least, was still living in Richmond. I asked if he had seen any Scotties at the White House in 1940, and he said, "Oh, well, the President had some sort of little old streetdog with him, but he behaved himself, and Bud didn't bother him."

I was not yet born in 1940. Nonetheless I wax nostalgic for the days when an American president could know something about dogs or, failing that, invite Bud to sing.

Stubby remembered the good old days, of course, when there weren't so many cars and a dog could roam safely, and remarked when he had finished telling what he remembered of Champion Bud, "I don't know what to say about anything these days, except that I sure wish Bud were here." I said, "So do I."

It is true enough that pit bulls grab and hold on—but what they most often grab and refuse to let go of is your heart, not your arm.

Mark Twain, of course, didn't let people stay complacent with their myths, and in *Tom Sawyer* and *Huckleberry Finn* he achieved in great form something he had attempted throughout his writing career—a legend of the great American that made people uneasy. Tom's adventures are spoofs on the American pioneer, who as Twain knew wasn't (couldn't be) the lawabiding, proper, and genteel citizen of Sunday school stories any more than he or she could be the gigantic figure of the American tall tale. In his first story, "The Celebrated Jumping Frog of Calaveras County," he also enjoyed himself making fun of the kind of bragging Americans do. And bragging about their dogs' fighting prowess is one of the things Americans do. It is part of the American tall tale tradition from which Paul Bunyan comes. So in Twain's first published story, which is throughout a story about bragging and placing bets—what I heard someone call a fool's argument—there is that small account of a bull pup named

Andrew Jackson, the great fighting dog, the hind-leg dog who finally lost when he was matched against a dog who had no hind legs. In calling the dog Andrew Jackson, Twain is poking a little fun at reverence for that great human fighting hero.

One of the traits of tales of glory and courage is that they flip over so easily and become tales of horror. During the latter part of the Vietnam War, revulsion at violence began to replace admiration of physical courage as a dominant impulse in this country. It is true enough that not so long ago we had a president who in California in the late sixties was damning the students and others protesting the violence in Vietnam, and that this man's image depended in part on the way his voice and mannerisms echo the gutsy cowboy of American myth, but he was not a true cowboy. It is possible that America has never known where to find the true cowboy, much less his horse, Trigger or Tony the Wonder Horse, or where to find dogs like Rin Tin Tin. Today we have the cop story, and the cop, like the cowboy, is often a lonely fighter for freedom and justice. And the cop, or the stray honest secret agent, must fight corruption in the heart of government just as the cowboy had to fight the evil and dishonest sheriff, but the odds in the modern story really are hopeless, because the scale of the evil is global. It isn't just one corrupt town out in the West that can be straightened out when the Texas Rangers ride in, nor even just the White House and the Kremlin where the moral rot is. It is in the very air, possibly because I am getting older and my eye yellower.

However one reads political or literary history, various forces have finally ousted the American Pit Bull Terrier from his place as the unofficial representative of American virtues. What troubles me is that this ousting coincided with many successful attempts to reimpose decency on Americans, that the images of the pit bull himself were images of decency, and that Hannah Arendt is right to emphasize the Nazi genius for exploiting decency. I think, for instance, of the late sixties, with its many important calls for the ideals of peace and health, and of the fact that the Humane Society of the United States, formed in the early seventies, is the principal source of the anti-pit-bull campaigns of the late eighties. I sometimes think—this is just my opinion—that the nineties will be the decade in which the stupidities of the sixties triumph, and that that triumph will entail in part an exploitation of my own decencies and those of my dogs. I sometimes think that decency is not the only but one foundation for horror.

Some such gloomy theory is called for, because America's dog, the American Pit Bull Terrier, has become Public Enemy Number One, by way of the humane movement, which, I keep saying, doesn't have to tell its stories about viciousness, though it does so now as it was always wont to do.

A recent *Wall Street Journal* carried the front-page headline "An Unlikely Battle Pits Englishmen Against Mad Dogs." The story featured one Chief Inspector Jan Eachus, saying to a captured pit bull named Bella, "See ya in doggy heaven," and adding that the only thing a pit bull won't bite is "a 747 jetliner—if it's in flight." He is a chief inspector, which sounds more impressive to me than "chief Canine Control officer" as a euphemism for humane cop or dogcatcher, but then the British have always had it over us on titles. Mr. Eachus, with his "See ya in doggy heaven" line, is, according to the *Wall Street Journal,* a chief inspector for the Royal Society for the Prevention of Cruelty to Animals.

The article has a description of another dogcatcher,

taking no chances. Standing beside her van in the north England city of Bradford, Pat Harwood dons the latest in canine battle dress. Long blond curls vanish beneath a visored helmet designed for riot control by the North Atlantic Treaty Organization. Hands slip into elbow-length gloves. She cradles a reinforced plastic "Armadillo Tactic Riot Shield" used by police to repel missiles. Her tall frame is enveloped by a zip-up jump suit, lined with chain mesh and heavily padded.

Diana Cooper won't let me read this sort of thing to her over the telephone any longer, but I am not quoting it here just because my feelings need an outlet. I am also quoting it because

I think I know why art historians cannot come to grips with the Capitoline Pit Bull. It is because they read newspapers.

As it happens, careful studies of the statistics at Tufts University, Cornell, the veterinary school at the University of California at Davis, and Washington State University have shown that there is no scientific basis for the fear of pit bulls. Dr. I. Lehr Brisbin at the University of Georgia and Dr. Bonnie Dalzel at the Pennsylvania veterinary school have done anatomical and physiological studies of pit bulls to discover if there is any physical basis for the fear. There is not—the jaws do not lock, for example, physically or scientifically, because there is no bony or muscular mechanism by means of which they can lock.

Pit bulls and other bulldog breeds do seem to have more efficient hugging muscles—the muscles that bring the forearms together—which may be why some pit bulls can climb trees. But cats climb trees, too—tree climbing is not viciousness.

Why am I saying this? To whom do I address myself? To the art historian, perhaps, who gets it all from newspapers, who needs an education in bulldogs in order to understand . . .

Degas, for example. While I was brooding unhappily on how one might untangle the ideas of kindness and viciousness symbolized by the curious belief that Rome was founded by a wolf, I went to a large Degas exhibit at the Metropolitan Museum of Art in New York, and there found a painting called *The Fallen Jockey*. It shows a rider flat on his back, and a horse freaking out. The posture of the jockey is that posture of rapt contemplation familiar to most riders, during which one considers anew the wonders of the sky, a meditation that gives way to the mundane, the bone-by-bone safety check and so on, and rapidly also to a question about whether one is going to be able to catch the sucker before he does himself or someone else an injury.

The horse in Degas's painting is at all angles to nothing in particular, as horses are when the rider falls and the comfortable and crafty order of things has rudely vanished. There are various failures in the saddle that one speaks of as cases of "dropping" the horse, and falling off is the ultimate way of dropping the horse, which is why falling off is frowned on—it is a training

error. When you fall, you precipitately abandon your commitment to the horse, and the horse finds this upsetting and makes
wildly energetic poems on the subject of things falling apart and
the center not holding.

I went through the exhibit with earphones, listening to the
tape guide. About this painting there was a great deal on the
crumpled, broken, lifeless form of the jockey, and the painting
is supposed to be about the finality of death. This passage in the
guide's remarks was of a piece with the whole, which was about
the terrible things Degas was able to see, was obsessed with
seeing. About, in short, the anguish of the artist.

But that jockey isn't dead, no way is he dead. Nor is he
crumpled and broken. He is just suddenly in a position to gain
that perspective on the sky that is one of the visionary building
blocks of the knowledge of riding. Degas would have seen it
hundreds of times, would have known that in a moment the
jockey will begin to stir, trying out his breathing apparatus, and
the moment of celestial insight will be gone except as a memory
of those particular heaven-wide dimensions of the art of riding.

This is a vision you can't get at on purpose. You can't, for
instance, go lie on your back in a meadow and get it, because the
vision comes only from the sharp gaze that occurs when you are
unexpectedly translated from an upright and even lofty posture,
a posture that gives you a view of the ground only—a sweeping
view to be sure, a magnificent view in which speed is an aspect
of the articulation of rock and tree, but still a view of the ground.
You can't see the sky from up there because you *are* the sky.
Then, without the mediation of time or step-by-step gymnas-
tics, you become, all at once and of a suddenness beyond the
analysis of physics, the ground. Now you can see the sky, see
what you once were and will be again.

You also can't get at this vision by, say, studying falling and
planning to fall onto your back. It comes only in the context of
another plan, a transcendent plan of order that sometimes transcends the planner. This whole visionary business is a precipi-
tate, incautious affair, not the sort of thing you want going on
in the Metropolitan.

The main thing is that this jockey is *not dead*. The dark question is, Why is the art historian so eager for him to be dead? What twists of the human mind, what devious horrors of bland intellect are we here confronted with?

The art historian is eager for him to be dead because our species is uncomfortable when art and newspapers tell different stories, and newspapers tend to win out. But Degas knew better than to believe rumors, Tolstoy knew . . .

St. Paul knew. St. Paul, on one account, saw through to the nature of things when on his back in the posture we see in Degas's painting. There is a painting of a fallen St. Paul, or rather of Paul-becoming-St. Standing over Paul is a skewbald horse who, while Paul is rapt and motionless from his collision with Truth, is wondering what in the world Paul is doing down there. For horses the reality and absolute nature of the universe is native habitat, so they don't have to search for it, and are never struck down by vision. They *are* vision, its homeliness, its exercises at the barre, its preoccupation with tack. St. Paul was something of a fat-boy spoiled rich kid, so he might not have known that about horses. I do not know if his riding improved after the fall, nor even just what this scene looks like, because it is in a painting Diana Cooper told me about over the telephone, and she can't remember where she saw it. It occurs to me to wonder if Degas had seen it.

Descriptions of Degas's depiction of a fortunate fall as a meditation on the finality of death cause the bony protuberances over my eyes to drop and thicken, and cause me to mutter about people who don't know the first thing about animals, but of course it isn't the case that art criticism and history would improve if students had to take courses in, say, bird dog training so much as it is the case that there are no courses in learning to recognize where one's own ignorance meets or fails to meet the artist's knowledge. (And I should say quickly here that while I do believe that the artwork can know more than the artist, it doesn't follow from this that the critic does.)

Another case, as I began by saying, is the figure called the Capitoline Wolf, the she-wolf supposedly suckling Romulus and Remus, the one who is tired but goes on because she has promises to keep.

Keeping promises to human beings is a kind of odd thing, unusual in an animal, and found almost exclusively in domestic animals. Whether animals are improved or contaminated by having the ability to keep any promise that is not the animal *lui même*—her own promise of herself to God, the only promise the ostrich makes—that is something we could debate. It is the case, however, that a wolf does not make promises, in somewhat the same way we do not try to marry mountains, most of us. It doesn't occur to a wolf that she might ever have that kind of control over weather and time, so she doesn't do it, but we make promises and then when hell gets in the way of the promise we literally go through hell to keep the promise sometimes, and as often as not get stuck in hell while we are about it, so the capacity to make a promise is the capacity to promise oneself to something besides God.

Pit bulls and many other—though not all—domestic breeds have this capacity. They can promise themselves to an idea, or to a person, just as we can. That is why it is of course the bulldog bitch there in Rome, displaying the truth of the city to anyone who cares to read it, even though few do. The expression on that lady's face—that is the expression of promise in action.

I have said to various people, "That there is no wolf, Rome was founded by a bulldog for crying out loud," and they have said, "This can't be—haven't you read Livy?" Besides, they went on, the sculptor probably had to use a dog for a model, failing a handy or at least a cooperative wolf. But that doesn't begin to explain the effort that went into making that figure a portrait of a dog, and of a very particular sort of dog, at that: the type that has appeared as the old Roman cart dog, the Molossian, the bandog or catch dog, the nineteenth-century bulldog—basically, a short-coated dog that sometimes, especially when used for hunting, is bred for a longer, more "houndy" body of the sort one sees in the Capitoline figure. She does not look like all bulldogs but is, as my friends noted, built very like my own bulldog Annie. Artists don't accidentally render things that well, so whatever is meant by the figure, it isn't what we read about in Livy.

Of course, there are scandalous reproductions of her. When you enter the Sterling Library at Yale, you will see one as you look up, a rather ferocious carving that doesn't actually look much like an animal after whom solid, civilized cities could be figured. This, of course, is not a carving of the Capitoline Pit Bull, nor yet of Livy's wolf, but rather of some professor's wolf, some professor who has, after the fashion set by many thinkers including Bertrand Russell, decided to count the world in front of his or her eyes well lost for the sake of the abstractions by means of which one maps out one's private version of the library. That is well and good—God bless the professor, who is rather too often bent by the load of books she carries to look up at the portals anyway and also has promises to keep—but what does the Capitoline Bulldog tell us? I use the phrase "Capitoline Bulldog" to refer to the actual statue in Rome; the carving at Sterling Library and countless other verbal, painted, and carved rumors about her I call the "Capitoline Wolf." I am told that those rumors are no less slanders of wolves than of dogs, though it is slanderous enough to tell the truth about the training relationship with a wolf, which *is* a somewhat giddy, goofy affair.

The most remarkable thing about the Capitoline Bulldog is that she forms an excellent figure for a civilization, as do the other pit bulls who appear throughout the history of Western art in one ceremonial or heraldic position or another. Helping the Dominicans to guard the gates of heaven, for example, and also in Degas's *At the Races*. Here the bulldog is black, and rides on the carriage with his back to the viewer, and is central to the painting—in the center of it, that is. It isn't impossible that Degas noticed the heraldic dog's ubiquity, and here has the guardian of the palace turn his back on the palace of art, which is to say, the gallery, museum, or heraldic living room Degas would have had more than one occasion to contemplate in detail by 1870. The painting is featured on the cover of the catalogue of the Metropolitan's Degas exhibition. Hence, the pit bull is literally at the center of the Metropolitan's recorded celebration of Degas, but no one is the wiser for it as near as I can make out, which is how it happens that the foundations of civilization are a mystery even though they are not hidden, not secret in *that* sense, not secreted away anywhere.

Tell that to an art historian.

There is another painting that belongs in this list of representations of dogs and horses, a portrait by George Stubbs identified and commented on as a portrait of Lord Pigot of Patshull mounted on a splendidly powerful horse, a pair as misread as the Capitoline Pit Bull. Stubbs was a painter who knew in painful and painstaking detail what correct movement looks like, and he here lets it all out, shows everything he knows about correctness of horse and rider, a correctness that entails great concentration. And there is great concentration on Lord Pigot's face—indeed, he resembles no one so much as the great twentieth-century rider Alois Podjasky. My Stubbs volume repeats some possibly true slanders about Pigot's personal history, says that the painting shows Stubbs's antagonism toward Pigot, and emphasizes how "arrogant" Pigot looks. But Pigot is not arrogant—everything about him turns inward to himself and his concentration on his horse's movement. Stubbs could and did paint carelessly arrogant riders, but Pigot is not one of these. The power expressed in the painting is the power of art, not state—though the painting is, of course, aware that the state can purchase art.

Before anything more can be said about the glories and ambiguities of true human power, a bit more must be said about one idea of power, the power of the game breeds. These include not only the bulldog types, or bull breeds, but also Airedales, Australian Terriers, Cairn Terriers, Jack Russells, and so on. And Shar Peis. The game breeds are deeply tuned in to human beings and have greater inhibitions against biting people even than the herding breeds, in some ways deeper than the inhibitory mechanisms in the working dogs, such as Shepherds, Danes, Dobies, Malamutes, and so on.

Game dogs are bred to be handled closely by human beings

while they are at the pitch of battle fever, whether it's battle with stoats, badgers, lions, or other dogs. You may have seen on TV one of the brief fighting sequences that were aired a great deal, in which two dogs are "rolled." This sequence is brutal. It is not pretty to see one dog holding on to another's face for dear life. But an important detail that was never mentioned is that the camera crews and the people handling the warriors were perfectly safe. The handlers have their hands at some points actually in their dogs' mouths.

Early-nineteenth-century engravings designed to show how brutal dogfighting is also show inadvertently how safe the dogs are to handle. You typically see a pit about two and a half feet deep, with two dogs fighting and three or four men—one handler for each dog, and one or two judges or referees. The spectators crowd closely around the pit, and seven or eight of them are holding dogs who are excited about the fighting. The excited dogs are held in people's arms, restrained without leashes or collars. It is not pretty, but it does show that there is little to fear from a pit bull from a fighting line. For one thing, the practical exigencies of handling the dogs require that they be very amiable toward humans. And there is also a tradition in dogfighting circles according to which a dog who is dangerous to humans is a coward in the pit. I have no way of knowing if this is true, but it is of course connected with the tradition of the American hero that the pit bull represents. In the war movie or the cowboy movie, when the villain is seen hurting a child, a woman, or an innocent man, you know that he's a bully and a coward.

I do not like dogfights, do not know how I can emphasize that strongly enough—this is not an *apologia* for dogfighting. But I cannot see that in this or any other case we can find a foundation for admiration, for a fully ethical response to the world, that at once turns toward the virtues we yearn for and away from the brutality we abhor. When you no longer breed game dogs for true fighting virtues, you also leave off breeding them for heart, loyalty, and even gentleness, since what is gentle in dogs accompanies what is stalwart in them, and stalwartness is not always a soft virtue. It is as though virtues themselves were morally neutral, and as though it were extremely important not to make a mistake about this. In 1988 I was worried enough about the presidential elections, but I became much more worried when George Bush, announcing that he had selected Quayle as his running mate, said that Dukakis would now have "a couple of pit bulls" to deal with. I have no faith in Bush's insights into dogs, so I worried that he was perhaps here confessing that he suffered from the Jekyll-Hyde syndrome, that all his talk of a kinder and gentler America was a prolegomena to brutality, not of the sort found in organized dogfighting, but of the sort found in war and tyranny, which, as I keep saying, is a brutality that depends on faculties dogs lack. (I worried also because he didn't seem to realize that a pit bull is not a Republican dog; I do wish our leaders would get their iconography straight.)

I should say something else about the connection between fighting virtues and other kinds of work. The resoluteness of the pit bull style of fighting, which as everyone knows is to grab and not let go rather than to slash Collie or Shepherd or wolf fashion, is a real phenomenon, and it expresses itself in other ways. Once a bulldog has decided to work with you, he or she will gladly die doing the task at hand. Consider Bandit. It turned out that he was interested in doing Up and Off for me, as I have said, so I quickly taught him to jump up onto woodpiles, truck beds, whatever was handy, and even into the waist-high bathtub in the grooming room, on the command "Up!"

One day I was working Bandit out by the barn and the cow pasture, and Charlie asked me, "How do you teach a dog to climb a ladder?"

I actually wasn't thinking too quickly, so instead of keeping a wary eye on Charlie, I went on a bit about how you need to start with easy climbs and build the dog's confidence slowly, and I bragged about an Airedale I had who did a very fine job of climbing a ladder once in Sunnymead, California, in 1974, though of course you need the right equipment, to get the dog used to it, and while I was so immodestly babbling Charlie leaned a *verrry* long aluminum ladder up against the barn so that it led up into the hayloft.

Such is the power of Charlie's presence that without hesitation I sat Bandit in front of the ladder and gave him the old command, "Up!" He began climbing. He is a heavy dog, not at all like a Poodle, and his feet kept slipping, and there were other difficulties, but he kept going up for no other reason than that it was something he and I were doing together. At one point he slipped and his testicles were crushed against one of the rungs, but he recovered and kept on climbing.

My own little pit bull Annie is a comfort-loving dog, like so many of the lady bulldogs. Indeed, when I was beginning her obedience training, the most tempting distraction to work her around was not kitty cats, other dogs, elephants in white spats, parades, or roast beef, but a pillow. If you left her on a Sit-stay near a pillow, she would break her stay and make a mad dash for it. And woe betide if her blanket isn't smooth—talk about the princess and the pea!

Nonetheless, she is good, as I said earlier, with boulders. She is also "good with children." I don't mean by this just that she doesn't bite them—neither does the sofa bite them. I mean that she is *skillful,* competent, good in the sense Nietzsche seems to have had in mind when he congratulated himself on having destroyed the distinction between good and evil without destroying the distinction between good and bad. There are dogs who will not hurt children but do not have the skill Annie has. For instance, babies between one and two years old go through a stage when they continually throw things to the floor. Annie perceives this as the moment to begin the baby's education in dumbbell handling. She will go and get a dumbbell, bring it to the baby, and hold on to it until the baby takes it from her with both hands, one against each end. The baby takes the dumbbell and throws it, and she repeats her return, not resting until the baby is taking it properly.

An important point about Annie's retrieving in these situations is that she is not a natural retriever. For a long time, indeed, she hated retrieving. She never chased sticks or balls as a puppy—this is not a case of the obsessed Golden Retriever, for example. What she is obsessed with is the education of the young—I can see the Capitoline Pit Bull patiently putting young Romulus and Remus through their paces in just this way. It would be well-nigh impossible to get Annie retrieving in the field as Labs and Goldens do, but I didn't have to do anything to get her putting all her heart into teaching babies the foundations of nobility. One of the obdurate facts about training is that you cannot get an animal to perform reliably something completely alien to his or her nature. Ninety-nine percent of training activity is a matter of taking some movement of body or mind that is innate in the creature's heart and formalizing it with command and responsiveness on the trainer's part. This is one reason "disobedient dog" routines are among the most difficult in the circus and movie repertoire; it takes a very skillful performer to be responding to the dog, giving the dog his or her right to that power over the trainer's response, while appearing to the audience to be giving a different sort of command altogether, and to be frustrated with the dog's apparent disobedience.

I do not know whether the bulldog who is mistakenly called a wolf was a fighting dog, a hunting dog, a war dog, a ceremonial (obedience or performance) dog, a guard breed, or a breed used for all of those activities, as the modern pit bull is. But I can think of no better national symbol, for any nation noble enough to remember that it is a figment of human imagination. As James Thurber said at the end of his story about his boyhood friend Rex—who once brought home a chest of drawers—these dogs can strongarm the Angel of Death. And they are game, game the way Mark Twain and Abraham Lincoln and Teddy Roosevelt were game, and of course the way that bulldog of all bulldogs, who even looked like a bulldog, Winston Churchill, was game. That is to say, their gameness is not necessarily reassuring, but it is all we have in the way of reassurance.

One final note about their gameness. There are a lot of pit bulls these days who are licensed therapy dogs. Their stability and resoluteness make them excellent for work with people who might not like a more bouncy, flibbertigibbet sort of dog. When pit bulls set out to provide comfort, they are as resolute as they are when they fight, but what they are resolute about is being gentle. And because they are fearless, they can be gentle with anybody, and that, finally, is the reason so many of their owners are so loyal to them despite harassment, threats, and lost friendships. A lot of human beings are emotional klutzes a great deal of the time, and what the courage of the fighting dog finally comes to is the courage to be gentle, even with as unpredictable and strange a creature as *Homo sapiens*.

Yale University has for around a century now had a Bulldog (English) as its mascot. Not a true bulldog, but the sort that huffs and puffs and has to have cesareans. Handsome Dan is an amiable fellow, and I have nothing against him, but he is hardly up to sustaining the complex and ironic triumphs of *Lux et Veritas*. Yale nonetheless continues, largely because over the portals of the Sterling Library is that carved reproduction of the Capitoline Wolf. The craftsman seems to have tried to take the advice Degas is said to have given to a young artist, about painting what is inside rather than what you can see, and what was inside was rather more of a currish strength than the sort the Capitoline artist envisioned; the carving at Yale, unlike the original, does snarl. Perhaps the art historian who found the "snarling expression" more doglike than wolflike was influenced by that doorway. It's not important; the true nature of strength is as much a secret as anything else.

Nietzsche had various insights. One was that the idea that strength is bad was a brilliant rhetorical move on the part of the weak. Now, Nietzsche speaks with contempt of trainers—he says, virtually spitting, "these animal tamers" when he wants to show how he despises priests—but that is a detail of historical and psychological debris, and indeed one of the few places in his writing that is a kind of genuine foreshadowing of the Third Reich. The idea that training is a matter of coercion, like the idea that pit bulls are vicious, is an idea gleaned from the local equivalent of "60 Minutes" or the *National Enquirer*.

I think that the confusion that leads to the idea that pit bulls are vicious, that animal trainers are sadists, and that the ability to ride a horse well, as celebrated in Stubbs's painting of Pigot, is arrogance, is a confusion between mere power *over* someone or something, and power *to do* something. In the case of horses, say, or Bandit, power *to* is a matter of the power to do something *with* the animal; power *over* is the power to do something *to* the animal. Sometimes I suspect that when poets and animal trainers and pit bulls are seized by the state, the bureaucratic impulse is desire, a desire for the power in question, and impoundment or imprisonment is one way the desire to seize power is expressed.

But power *to* cannot be seized. Confusion on this point is displayed in the long weak misreadings of the wonderful horses of Western art, no doubt because the money to buy horses and to pay horse trainers is often enough obtained by means of power over people, the sort of power that can be seized when the palace is seized. The failure of art history to read horse painting is equal to the failure of the West to conceive of animals as anything but expressions of human will, and thus the failure to conceive of animal and human engaged in a work that, like any other work—painting, for example—can be used to decorate the palace whether or not the horse or the rider or the artist cherishes the king's body politic.

If the Capitoline figure is read as a wolf, as savage and vicious, then it is a weak fantasy of the founding of civilization. If it is read for what it is, a portrait of an animal, a kind of pit bull, whose power, restraint, and beauty are the result of artistry— the art of the breeder, for example—it is a very different kind of thing, with or without the infant Romulus and Remus. She is plainly a domestic animal, for one thing, and the formality of the texture often interpreted as the wolf's "mane" does suggest ceremony, possibly a ceremony of war. However that may be, she is no wimpy, giddy, shivery-chinned wolf but a very great lady of tremendous heart and substance.

And restraint. She has, for example, said nothing all these years, indeed eons, about the slanderous, gossipy misrepresentations of her, such as the carving over the portals of the Sterling

Memorial Library, or Mussolini's childish prattle about the children of the wolf. She must have her reasons for this restraint, so
I hope that you will keep her secret. Civilization was founded in
the composed, compassionate, and steady heart of a pit bull, but
don't tell anyone, particularly not the art historian, for if the
truth is revealed the museums will be torn down.

NINE ···

Beastly Behaviors

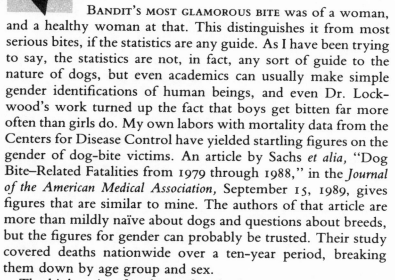

Believe you me, no class of persons ranges so far afield from the cosmic perspective as do small boys. No class of persons embraces so wholeheartedly the first-strike doctrine of let's do it to them just in case somewhere down the line it might enter their head to do something to us.

—COLIN MCENROE, *Swimming Chickens*

BANDIT'S MOST GLAMOROUS BITE was of a woman, and a healthy woman at that. This distinguishes it from most serious bites, if the statistics are any guide. As I have been trying to say, the statistics are not, in fact, any sort of guide to the nature of dogs, but even academics can usually make simple gender identifications of human beings, and even Dr. Lockwood's work turned up the fact that boys get bitten far more often than girls do. My own labors with mortality data from the Centers for Disease Control have yielded startling figures on the gender of dog-bite victims. An article by Sachs *et alia,* "Dog Bite–Related Fatalities from 1979 through 1988," in the *Journal of the American Medical Association,* September 15, 1989, gives figures that are similar to mine. The authors of that article are more than mildly naïve about dogs and questions about breeds, but the figures for gender can probably be trusted. Their study covered deaths nationwide over a ten-year period, breaking them down by age group and sex.

The high ratio of males to females here is striking, and the sample—157 total deaths—is large enough to be statistically significant.

More females than males are killed up to the age of one year (though there are a couple of cases in Alaska where investigation might show more about the perceived worth of female children than about the behavior of dogs), and it may be that until they

Age Group	Males	Females	Total
< 1 mo	4	5	9
1–11 mo	6	10	16
1–4 y	36	20	56
5–9 y	23	6	29
10–29 y	8	1	9
30–49 y	3	2	5
50–69 y	9	8	17
> 69 y	6	10	16
All Age Groups	95	62	157

learn to walk boys and girls are equally likely to get hurt. Also, since girls develop faster, they may be coordinated enough to get into a little more trouble than boys do that early in life. But the numbers here are far too small to interpret. However, between one and four years, the figure is 36 boys to 20 girls. As the children get into grammar school, the figure becomes 23 to 6—almost four times as many boys killed as girls—and the teenage and young adult years show a ratio of eight to one. By age thirty, the boys who are still alive seem to have developed some sense, and the figures settle down until people get to be seventy, at which point more women get killed, either because there are more old women or because old women start wandering around where they shouldn't be, or else because their neighbors feed them to the dogs.

Men are killed by dogs more often than is reasonable, and men handle dogs that kill more often than is reasonable. How do we explain this?

Gender theory has always been a nerve-racking business for me, because whether it was the old gender theory, which is now called sexism, or the new gender theory, which is now called feminism, I keep turning out not to be a woman no matter who is doing the theorizing. I don't mean that I turn out to be a man, exactly, just not a proper sort of woman. Sexism says that women are shy, retiring, gentle, sensible, good at sewing, and interested in feminine activities. The new feminism says that women are not pushy, are gentle, sensible, good at sewing, and interested in feminine activities. Sexism says that women seek their identity through others. Feminism says that women seek their identity through other women, because you can't know what you are or who you are until you have had your consciousness raised and learned that the important thing about Emily Dickinson is that she knew how to fold things away in drawers, as was argued in a recent article about her work by an otherwise sensible person. Sexism says to women, *Cherchez l'homme*. It's all his fault, because you are too powerless for it to be your fault. Feminism says to women, *Cherchez l'homme*. It's all his fault, because you are too powerless for it to be your fault. At least, that's the way it sounds when you hang out around literature, law, history, and so on these days, though there used to be a kind of feminism, which is kind of grotty with age now, that said, as I recall, that women could do whatever they wanted to do, that whether or not childbirth was divine punishment was not a matter for magistrates to propound on.

An animal trainer, however, ends up eventually involved with gender if not gender theory. The ratio of women to men hanging out around a kennel or a stable is as unbalanced as the ratio of men to women either getting killed or having their dogs kill people in the statistics I cite above. It is said that women are more nurturing, more motherly, than men, and that is why they do well with animals, but that would mean that when Olympic competitors Kathy Kustner and Leslie Burr ride a powerful and trappy Grand Prix course they are in a motherly mood, and for that matter that William Steinkraus, the first American to win the gold in stadium jumping, and Hans Winkler, winner of five gold medals in the same event, are motherly sorts, which doesn't seem entirely consistent with what one knows about Olympic contests.

Since I am a woman, and since I came of age in a period when men did all the talking, to me and at me, about what my gender is like, it has usually been men rather than women who prompted me to produce gender theories. So it is largely men who deserve the credit as well as the blame for prompting me here to consider men's relationships with animals.

What is it about men?

After a couple of decades of being a woman, I came to think that men are afraid of dogs and horses. My evidence was that I couldn't get them to come riding or tracking with me. Always they wanted to do dinner and whatnot instead.

They are afraid of horses, I decided, because they can't understand horses and what horses mean to be saying to them, or at least they can't prove what horses have in mind, not in the way you can prove Morley's Theorem. With theorems, it often turns out that you can prove, step by step, that they are true. You prove animals differently, not step by step, but more the way you prove people or poems, by first believing them and then coming to have knowledge of them, rather than by deducing them.

The whole of actuality is, as it happens, logically impossible, but the logician in us more easily grants the existence and nature of some things than of others. Teacups and tables and tenure, for example, are readily accepted, but not the rationality of other minds.

Some will grant tentatively that human minds exist, or at least that minds properly tutored in logic exist, but become agitated at the suggestion of any other kind of mind—one tutored in poetry, for example, or weaponry. We call people who are good at doubt scientists and philosophers, often, and science and philosophy and logic are ignorant of a great deal because they are so good at ignoring so much. That isn't all bad—concentration on your work and ignoring distractions is a wonderful thing—but what I have in mind is that men, or at least some bits of the mind traditionally associated with men, don't seem to notice very much about animals, and jump to conclusions. The jumped-to conclusions that occasion my thinking about this concern pit bulls, but on almost any topic you can find human beings loudly jumping to conclusions and failing in their hurry to notice the sort of detail that never escapes a dog's attention.

For example: I was once involved in a panel discussion at which the idea was voiced and elaborated that riding horses was a good way for girls to prepare for marriage because it gave them practice controlling something powerful and dangerous between their legs. I thought, and at enormous risk of self-exposure said, that controlling something powerful and dangerous between my legs didn't characterize either marriage or horsemanship as I had experienced them. It is true that some activities that fall under the heading "sex" can be dangerous, but before AIDS it was the thing the man sometimes had in his hand, and not the thing between his legs, that was worrisome. And there are some differences between husbands and horses that I thought worthy of consideration, including the fact that in the case of husbands direct mutual genital contact is to the point, whereas it interferes with horsemanship. I don't doubt that it is possible, only that it is horsemanship.

The persons propounding the P&D Between Your Legs theory were both male shrinks, and Lord knows what they made of me, given their experience of horses and other things between their legs.

I am sorry to speak so crudely. There are many men of subtle and strong hearts and intellects who quite easily distinguish between horses and penises, and for that matter between heat-seeking missiles and dragons, but they don't all, as I realized one day when I was youngish, while listening to a lecture in which it was explained that Raphael's St. George was riding the good penis and killing the bad one. The bad one, like the good one, was supposed to be a universally understood phenomenon. None of the boys in the class wanted to talk about it afterward, so I never found out about the Good Penis and the Bad Penis, but I do know that *horses* are not universally understood. There isn't even all that much awareness around and about that there is such a thing as understanding horses as distinct from penises, dragons, kings, rifles, and motor cars. (Raphael, by the way, did quite well, as near as I can tell, at distinguishing between horses and dragons.)

Women are capable of this sort of ignorance, of course, capable of ignoring whatever or whoever cannot prove itself, including the opposite sex and horses. In fact, the person at that panel who was angriest with me for denying that horses prepare girls for marriage (what an idea that is, anyhow—preparing girls for marriage!) was a woman. But I am not the first to note that it is in activities associated with men—politics, murder, rape, war, skepticism, and behaviorism—that one finds logical terror and logically founded ignorance most richly displayed. I do not believe that this is particularly a function of social conditioning, either, because I have been around little boys and little girls, and I learned that they are different from each other and that they can't be brainwashed, they won't sit still for it, which is why they usually don't start going to school until they are five or six. You can't do all that much brainwashing with them even at that age, but you can teach them to sit still, some of them.

The thing is that as a trainer I have come to suspect and every so often to believe that certain kinds of failures to understand animals—certain kinds of dog blindness, like certain other eye problems—probably have something to do with brain damage caused by testosterone. (A companion piece to this one, on the brain damage caused by estrogen, will appear under separate cover, and under a pseudonym. Some of the idiocies of women are too crude even for me in my present mood to discuss.)

There are different "proofs." The word comes from the Latin *probare,* to prove in the way you prove, test, a gold coin for genuineness. But as Stanley Cavell has undismissably shown, not everything is open to this sort of proof. There is a limit, for example, to what you can prove to yourself about the love of women through probing, a point that greatly troubled Othello. Women also suffer when in the grip of the knowledge that they can't probe-prove someone's loyalty, but are somewhat more open to suggestions such as "Why don't you ring up and ask?" Just as they are more likely to ask directions while driving. And in my experience women are more open than men are to the idea that getting to know Bandit would be a good way to find out what he is like. During his case the *Hartford Courant* reported that Vincent Majchier, assistant commissioner of agriculture, said he wondered how Judge Dean was going to decide whether Bandit had been "retrained." "Is he going to jump into the cage with him? I know *I* wouldn't."

I don't know whether or not Majchier said that, of course, only that the *Courant* said he said it, but the point is that that image—"jumping into the cage with Bandit"—appeared often in discussions of the case, and it was always a man who had the idea that that is what you would do, jump into the cage.

And that is what small boys do with dogs, they jump at them. A typical scenario goes like this. The small boy is brought by his grandmother into the dog's presence. The boy stiffens, hides behind a chair or Grandma's coat, peers at the dog from an upside-down position, darts back and forth if the dog does something alarming such as wag her tail or pant, and then: jumps straight at the dog and pokes his finger into her eye. Or waits until the dog is asleep and then creeps up and blows in her ear.

And gets snapped at, once in a while has the skin broken.

Once in a long while needs stitches.

Once in a very, very long while dies.

Now, some small boys, after getting bitten or snapped at, will report in later years, "So that's how I learned that you don't do that to dogs." Others grow up and become dogcatchers who carry snare poles in sweating palms. For the moment, the important fact about a snare pole is that it is a pole, and that it is often used the way small boys use their fingers—it is poked at dogs.

It is, in short, a weapon, and it makes dogs nervous.

Men and fear of animals. I have heard some dog wardens and the like talk energetically about how their palms sweat when they approach certain breeds of dog. I do not hear women talk that way, from which I do not conclude that women are never afraid of dogs, only that "fear" is a very vague term that probably covers a variety of states of mind and body, and that there is some sort of fear, the sort allegorized endlessly in movies about the martial arts that don't have more than twenty words of dialogue in them, that is compelling to the imaginations of more men than women.

The mysteries of proof (I don't mean in mathematics, where seeing a proof fall out is a high pleasure) and the sweatiness of the demand for proof have been of overwhelming importance to my life in two sorts of situation. One has been personal; I have been in Desdemona's position, trying to prove that I didn't do or want to do something. I came to understand a fair amount of what was going on from reading Stanley Cavell's towering discussions of Shakespeare, but neither Cavell nor Shakespeare taught me how to understand Desdemona's stupidity. The jealous lover brings his charge to the woman, she says it isn't true. He says she can't prove it isn't true. She displays submission or attempts to enwrap him softly in her arms, and he says that her ability to do that after her betrayal just shows how corrupt and false she is. The other situations have been, or often seemed to be, logically identical. Someone says that a dog or a breed of dog is vicious. The dog owner denies it: "Lulu is a sweetheart." Adds details about how she sleeps with the baby or cuddles the kittens or keeps dotty Aunt Martha company. This just goes to show how really dangerous Lulu is, because she can turn on you at any moment, after years of appearing to be a docile family pet.

So what do you say after you say that it isn't true, Lulu is a sweetheart? How do you prove your dog isn't a monster? (How do you prove you aren't a Communist or a witch or a cunningly designed robot? How do you prove you aren't at heart a rapist?)

Well, you can't, of course. What is more deeply unclear to me is the kind of occasion that gives rise to such a demand. I don't mean that I don't understand why serious dog bites are investigated—I have investigated quite a few myself. What is not clear is the occasion for the creation of the mysterious category Vicious Dog or Femme Fatale or Vicious Chauvinist. The (merely) political occasions for such rhetoric are often clear enough; what is not clear is why there should exist such rhetoric in the first place, but since it is not a kind of thinking dogs are capable of, any more than they are capable of uniform recognition, and since most (not all) human concepts that are part of political thinking and imagination are also beyond dogs and, so far as I know, other animals, I have begun to suspect that the ability to conceive of monsters and the ability to conceive of the state are aspects of the same faculty.

The poet Robert Duncan and others have suggested that manhood and womanhood are sociological constructs, gender-specific pictures of thought and behavior that arise in the hurly-burly of social history. This is not to deny the reality of manhood and womanhood, I don't think, or at least of men and women, but in Duncan's work manhood and womanhood appear as weak imaginative constructs with which one struggles imaginatively for the sake of poetic truth. A more recent discourse might claim that manhood and womanhood are political or ideological inventions. There is a great deal to that, as there is to the idea that humanity is a political and ideological invention, though exactly what there is to it must be tempered by the fact—the *fact*—that males and females of virtually all species are, in general, different from each other, and can recognize the differences between males and females of their own and other species. Animals seem to do so roughly as people do, through long habits of observation. Like people, they are sometimes fooled. As a further note, there are some species and some breeds in which the differences are less pronounced than in others. It is even possible in a given line to select for greater or lesser differences between the sexes, so that you might hear that in Edge-cliff Briar Hounds the females are very doggy. (There are, by the way, breeds in which the females are usually more athletic than the males, such as Irish Wolfhounds.)

And I believe that there are tendencies in, for example, writing, that are gender-specific, though not immutably so. There is prose of a subtle intelligence, a sharply controlled and modulated syntax, that seems more likely to be something a Eudora Welty or a Jane Austen will be triumphant with, and there is a roaring sprawl (I do not mean an uncontrolled sprawl) that a Joyce or a Mark Twain is more likely to astonish us with. When Virginia Woolf said she liked the subtlety of women's minds, she was not talking of something fabricated from an ideology.

But those are the glories of gender, and are not what puzzles me. What puzzles me are the gender differences between animals and people. Consider, for instance, that a bitch never needs to learn that she can say no if she isn't in the mood, and does not fake orgasm, is immune to any attempts to convince her that she should or should not. Nor does she read magazine articles about how to get herself into the mood if she isn't.

And I have never seen a stallion or a dog commit rape. I have seen dogs and horses pester mares and bitches unmercifully, but have never seen them have their feelings hurt when they were turned down. I have seen something like this:

In the period when the female is becoming interesting to the male but is herself indifferent to the arrows of Eros, he makes a proper nuisance of himself, jumping about, pleading, poking, pawing at her, or dashing around splendidly with his hooves high, his nostrils flaring, and his voice reverberating, in the case of horses. And the mare says, "Yuck! Forget it!" while turning her hind end dangerously and rejectingly rather than invitingly in his direction. In the case of dogs, the female often makes a horribly ugly noise, snarling at him, *Gwangetouttahereyouretooblameduuuuuugly!* She punctuates these points with her fine, white, efficient teeth. He leaves for a while, feeling sorry for himself, and then he thinks, "Time has passed. Maybe she's ready by now." All of half a minute may have gone by, so she snarls and snaps again, and again he tumbles end over end. He doesn't eat, is untrustworthy with the other males, and all the rest of it.

But here is what does not happen. He doesn't start feeling guilty and unworthy so that when the glorious time of her readiness is at hand she has to hunt him up and explain things to him, soothe his ego and all. And he does not rape her. Perhaps he would if he could think of it, but it seems that he cannot think of it. He accepts her no, for a minute, sometimes longer. He has to be told over and over again, but each time he accepts it.

For her part, she doesn't tease. Nor does she worry whether or not she will be able to "hold" him if she doesn't "give him what he wants." She does not weep and moan and call the police or the dean's office when he is pestiferating her.

And he doesn't use violence to object to her economic management. He doesn't feel that his manhood has been compromised. He does not construct wonderful logics according to which her apparent distraction and indifference are signs that she really wants him. Nor have I ever known a male dog to get so confused that he thinks she will like being hurt physically when she has said otherwise.

I don't mean that animals are mild and gentle when in the grip of eros, only that certain aspects of human eros do seem to be a function of conceptual faculties that are missing in animals, or at least missing from pit bulls, say, and Airedales and Appaloosas.

No animal ever demands of another that he or she prove that s/he is not unfaithful, not a monster, not a robot, not a Martian, not a Communist. There are some inferential processes that animals engage in—these are easiest to observe in predators— but animals do not infer or reason their way to knowledge of the nature of another animal. Animals, on the whole, read each other directly rather than using inference. They are not infallible, mind you, but they read directly, and as I said in connection with police dogs, there are some kinds of observation they are better at than people are, because inference as well as interpretation of symbols is not part of their conceptual equipment.

Inference is relatively rare among animals, and madness is almost unheard of. Animals, unlike people, are incapable of being commanded by reason and/or logic, and are therefore also incapable of being *maddened* by logic. Cavell has shown not only that Othello's reason was choked by "his sumptuous capacity for trope" but also that his madness consisted in his knowing too much for his reason, rather than too little. I do not know of a discussion of Cavell that adequately acknowledges the importance and force of the seamless integrity of the philosophical work that led him to the discovery of this conjunction of two human faculties that are both highly prized but usually given their prizes in separate halls on campus: reason and imagination.

One of Cavell's accomplishments has been to show us reason and imagination collaborating against sanity, and in Shakespeare doing so so often at moments when the major characters are tilted into political and erotic crime or else political and erotic happiness on the same fulcrum, the fulcrum of intelligence running away with itself.

I have never heard anyone intelligent go on at any length

about the viciousness of dogs, at least not in the presence of a
nice one, so it is not exactly the case that the horror stories about
Bandit are the product of what I mean by intelligence, which is
a fine thing in men, women, and dogs, always, but perhaps it
would be accurate to say that if anything is captured by the idea
of "IQ," then Bandit is, as we all are, victims of aspects of IQ.
Not of inference itself, of deduction or induction, so much as of
structures of thought that mimic reason herself the way fear can
mimic courage, perhaps, or mania can mimic genuine passion
—if you are willing to go along with me here in thinking passion, courage, and intelligence to be good things, though not
always all that safe. (Did Socrates ever suggest that safety was
the good? Safety may leave room for the good, but is not itself
good.)

I hasten to say that I am not commending beastly behaviors
to anyone, largely because so few human beings are capable of,
say, the exquisite balance a Border Collie can have on her sheep,
or the sense of duty of a scout or sentry dog, that I might as well
be commending musical virtuosity to the race at large. Also, as
I have already said, we traded some of our exquisite animal
awareness for some of our exquisite human abilities, and once
that has happened it is our fate to return to awareness through
language, if at all. In the case of our awareness of animals, there
is no agreement about what the ground rules might be for the
language or languages in question. In practice, discussions of
animals often are discussions of mind and language, and thus
become discussions of the just and the unjust, the good and the
bad, the honorable and the dishonorable, as though a discussion
of the nature of animals were *always* a discussion of morality and
could not be science. This is plainly wrong, in one sense; there
are animal sciences, veterinary schools, and there are results
obtained in both General Learning Theory and cognitive psychology that are indubitably science. Still, the best knowledge
of animals is often embodied in art and literature—disputes between scientists and trainers about the justice of anthromopor-
phic expressions parallel philosophy's ancient agon with poetry
for more than one reason.

You sometimes hear it said that as a science psychology "has not grown up yet." I used to think that meant that it should at least learn to mind its manners, especially in conversation with the ancient and long-tested arts of training, and that psychology's immaturity explained the testiness that characterized so many discussions of, say, Collie consciousness. But I was eventually told that wasn't what was meant, that the trouble was that psychology hadn't become like chemistry and physics yet, hadn't become "hard." Examples of success as a science were, mysteriously, bombs and plastics and airplanes more often than they were penicillin, which suggested that war was a good test of a science, but in that case horsemanship and dog training ought to be sciences, I ruminated, since the knowledge of them had a great deal to do with success in war. In the case of dogs, it still has something to do with it, and the word was that when we engaged in that drug raid in Panama we shot all of the Panamanian defense dogs, *in their kennels,* including Noriega's personal dog, Zap. Showing our technological courage, I suppose.

However, along about the time we were getting ready to do that, I began thinking about some differences between psychology and physics, and about the fact that what I should have noticed about physics' reputation was not that it had to do with the elevation of bombs over either penicillin or the understanding of a good scout dog's scent work, but rather that it had to do with bombs rather than language, metallics rather than poetics. And I should have noticed how odd it is that physics should have such a reputation, since the uncertainty principle, the (relatively) peaceful coexistence of quantum and wave mechanics, the unseemly joyousness animating a physicist who is telling you about the divinely capricious behaviors of the subatomic world and what is called Our Expanding Universe on television—all of these suggested to me that physicists were more like poets than anything else. Not because physics is inexact (not because of what we mean when we say that medicine is an art) but rather because of a really astounding degree of both poetic and philosophical sophistication that seemed to be at the heart of the difficulties of physics. And books have appeared under titles such as *The Unreasonable Success of Mathematics in the Sciences,* arguing that Space, Time, Matter, and Number are metaphors; the philosopher Nancy Cartwright wrote a book called *How the Laws of Physics Lie,* which discusses, among other things, the gap between Maxwell's equations and the equations used to describe any (actual) laser. When I heard her deliver some of the material in that book, it had not yet become fashionable to use the word "story" in place of words such as "theory" or "account" or "equation," and I thought that *How Physics Tells Stories* might have been a better title. But replacing "story" with "theory" is not enough by itself to confer literary sophistication on a discipline, any more than being able to write $E = mc^2$ on the blackboard confers on one an understanding of Einstein's thought.

Physics, as Cartwright shows, must fudge Maxwell's equations in order to come up with a viable mathematical description of an actual laser. Psychology, however, has so far nothing of the integrity of Maxwell's equations, nothing that can be "fudged" in order to produce a viable description of any given animal. Literature and art, including the trainer's art, are still the truest pictures and models we have. Freud said the poets anticipated everything he had to say, but the psychologists who pronounce so noisily on the nature of dogs do not know how to read the poets, and do not know what goes into getting a dog to come when called.

I found myself brooding about psychology a great deal during the pit bull wars, largely because it was generally people who signed their letters "Ph.D. in Psychology" who wrote or testified in court the most bizarrely.

In Atlanta, Georgia, a black man named Hayward Turnipseed became the first person convicted of a felony—manslaughter —in the pit bull wars. A child had opened the gate to his backyard, where he kept his three pit bulls (or alleged pit bulls), and was attacked and died of his wounds. In order to prove manslaughter, it was necessary to prove that the defendant had prior knowledge of the dogs' potentially lethal nature and had acted with and on that knowledge. This was not at that point hard— all one had to do was say "pit bull" and "locking jaws" a few times. A further twist was provided by the experts, Drs. Lockwood and Wright, who made dolls that "resembled the victim," and tossed the dolls to the dogs in the case, who of course chewed on the dolls, which established not only that the dogs were vicious, but that they hated the child. According to an HSUS newsletter, this testimony was central in sentencing the dogs' owner to prison for fifteen years.

This is enough to give psychology a bad name, as the behavior of ecclesiastical courts in earlier times was enough to give religion a bad name. Over the years, I have had many occasions to curse psychology, since most of the superstitions that prevent people from doing a decent job of getting along with their dogs are studded with Freudian and/or behaviorist terms. This is not so bad so long as the superstitions are kept within the walls of the academy, but sometimes people with degrees in psychology set themselves up as dog trainers. Their shingles usually say something like "Animal Behaviorist." In my experience most (though far from all) of the people who do this are male and in no way resemble the real scientists for whom I have enormous respect, and who are not to be blamed for the fact that their degree certificates have the word "psychology" on them.

When a Ph.D. in psychology is available for consultation to troubled dog owners, what can happen is this: You call the man with the Ph.D. and say your dog is biting people, or stealing your seven-year-old daughter's lunch, or peeing on the furniture. He says to make an appointment, and you do, and you may even be told to bring Fido with you if the psychologist isn't too afraid of the dog from your account. He diagnoses the misbehavior and recommends a course of action, often involving liver treats or a muzzle or tin cans or mounting behaviors or other magical objects and rituals. If, for example, Fido is okay with the family but gets growly and snappy with strangers, the so-called expert will suggest rattling tin cans at Fido when he growls and giving him a treat when he stops growling. Having tin cans rattled at one is annoying in general, and especially annoying when it is done threateningly. The treat is usually timed in such a way as to create in Fido's mind the idea that his growling at the tin cans has an effect on the world—it produces a treat. The problem becomes much worse, and Fido is put down. Humanely, of course. The psychologist has earned his fee if he comes up with a diagnosis of the biting, then, presumably because the triumph of science is explanation. The dog trainer, on the other hand, must take the story he or she is handed and change it, *do* something about the bite, which is why dog training is more a literary than a scientific discipline.

Or this sort of thing can happen: A dog growls and snaps when a stranger tries to touch him. A "psychologist" or "dog trainer," infected with the terms of psychology, says the word "desensitization." Recommends that the dog be muzzled and that people come and pet the dog until s/he "gets used to it." The dog, especially if muzzled on his or her own property, is enraged by being restrained in this fashion. A dog's respiration is almost entirely dependent on the passage of air through the mouth, so a muzzle creates panic and is counterindicated except in an emergency, and is never a training device *except in attack dog training*. Even with a muzzle, an angry and frightened dog can make some extremely horrible sounds. These will cause the amateur who has been asked to "get the dog used to being petted" to jerk his or her hand back. The dog's suspicions about both the muzzle and the petter are confirmed by this confused behavior, and the problem escalates. The dog has learned, among other things, that screaming in rage will make an intruder go away; the dog is in fact being agitated. If the owner cannot bear to have the dog put down and either does not know that there is a real dog trainer in the neighborhood, or else believes that the real dog trainer is "cruel," the dog is liable to bite someone eventually.

Of course, the "psychologists" I am here slandering are the snake-oil salesmen of that world, just as the "dog trainers" a psychologist is likely to know about, perhaps from watching television, are usually the snake-oil salesmen of my world. What

I want to bring into relief and get relief from is the appalling success, whether as a device to encourage people to send funds to dubious "charities" or else as a bit of illicit salesmanship, of anything that has the look of a diagnosis. The current occasion for my slander is all the death and tasteless ramblings I have had to witness and bear witness to, and in particular the sleazy co-operation between false science, false theology, and false charity that not only manifests itself as rantings about the horrors of a child's scarred face, but also as *the scars themselves*. That is, some people get bitten because of the advice given out by "animal behaviorists."

And if there is anything to the statistics, both the victim and the owner of the dog are likely to be male in the case of a serious dog bite. I have not forgotten that I was going to try to explain why men get bitten and have dogs that bite more often than women do.

It is words, morbid attachments to certain *words,* that sponsor and finance a great deal of the behavior I have been describing. In some cases "desensitization" is the word in question; in the case of the phone calls I got during the height of the newspaper coverage of the so-called vicious-dog problem, "syndrome" was one of the words that sent a lot of dogs to the pound and to their deaths. And it is my sense, not so much that men are more likely than women to want so desperately to get a fix on things that they will paralyze the world with a diagnosis, like an entomologist mounting a bug, as that there is something mas-culine about that fixing, something blunt and impatient, some-thing that darts back and forth and then leaps forward into the headlights of the oncoming Word, or dog. I have statistics to back me up: Girls are better at verbal skills than boys are, es-pecially in the age groups that lose the most numbers of boys to dog attacks. Boys may be less likely to know what to say to a dog, or even to have the idea that saying something rather than leaping forward with a chubby finger, or in later years a snare pole, is an option.

Which would not be to say, however, that femininity is pref-erable to masculinity. The generous gratitude Bandit radiated with every move I made to teach him something new is distinctly masculine, and I have a general sense of stallions and dogs as more buoyantly forgiving than mares and bitches are of a handler's incoherence or injustice. Gender of all descriptions, and divided up in any way you like, including in the dull-hearted ways we indicate with clumsy terms such as "homosexual" and "heterosexual" (as if it should mean more that Eros has an object shaped like *this* rather than *that* than that Eros exists), is at once so powerful, so subtle and so fecund a force of blessing, thought, dance, life, that one should mostly remain silent in the face of it, and I would be silent about gender, along with much else, were it not for those pesky statistics.

Besides, my puny attempts to brood about such paltry facts as the success of women in animal work, which, like the success of mathematics in the sciences, is still a major mystery, have been eclipsed by one of the most exuberant contributions to gender discussion ever written. This is David Rosenberg and Harold Bloom's *The Book of J,* a new interpretation and translation of those portions of Genesis, Exodus, Numbers, and Deuteronomy ascribed by biblical scholars to an unknown author called J. Bloom here gives us the "fiction" that J was a woman. He never exactly says, "I believe that J was a woman because she . . ." except in some rare instances, as when he points out that the creation of Eve occupies six times more space than the creation of Adam in J's account, and that there are no heroes in J's text, only heroines. What Bloom continually attributes to J, without being, as I have been and will be, uncomfortably explicit with his gender claims, is sublety and irony.

And, of course, he gives her what is for Westerners the first Word, the beginning, Genesis, Bereshith. Reading Bloom's commentary and Rosenberg's translation, I found myself persuaded that the whole business about Adam and Eve and Yahweh and Moses and so on makes more sense if you hear those narratives in the voice of a woman, a woman of far more literary poise and insouciance than mine, an aristocratic woman, one who can perform the literary equivalent of remaining calm when the cobra crawls over her foot so as not to disrupt the diplomatic dinner.

And it is a man, Harold Bloom, commending this ironic, controlled, powerful voice to us.

But it is not my goal in this chapter to celebrate gender. It is to do something more petty, to wonder what it is about men, why they become so often at puberty unable to ride horses, why adolescent boys lose their skills in the saddle at just the age when their sisters are grabbing hold of riding with a mature intellectual and imaginative passion.

I keep thinking: Men are afraid of horses. They are afraid of horses because neither their professional integrity nor logic will take them to a horse, and because they do not know how to turn, deflect, a horse's fear or rage. If Dobbin says, "You'd better get off right now, because I am going to kill you, wrangler!" you don't of course ignore this, but it is possible to say, "Oh, I don't think you really want to do that. Why don't we try something else?" (Just as Moses' wife said to Yahweh when Yahweh was intent on killing Moses.) As it happens, a talented young male rider can be as formidably equipped with equestrian tact as anyone, but in the general run of things in the middle and upper classes in this country, it is the young women who are more likely than the young men to come up with a tactful rather than a frightened response, and when they become foolish about this later—silliness is a feminine failing—they will say that they knew the horse had good intentions all along.

For centuries, unable to prove Dobbin's good intentions, men have instead proven their courage on horseback. The attitude in question is given nicely in Will Rogers's remark, "There ain't no horse that cain't be rode, and there ain't no man that cain't be throwed." In the (not always despicable) macho dream it *is* an act of courage to ride horses, and this *proves* something, but not something about the horse, at least not for poor riders; the records of the great horsemen show that the better a rider someone is, the more likely they are to attribute success to the horse.

I do not mean that it is despicable to be afraid of horses—they are large, swift, given to sudden visions. But the idea of proving one's courage on horseback, whatever one's gender, is very strange, surpassingly strange. Horses are not all that dangerous, so if you want to make them dangerous you have to work at it, by having a bunch of uneducated colts and fillies slamming around a track at a high gallop, or locating horses who like to buck and coming up with devices that will discourage the horse's natural tendency to be a noble, cooperative sort.

And these are boyish ideas in general, which is *not* to say that women are "good with animals." Their performance is on the whole poor to fair to middling, like that of men. But men are much more often than women *hopeless* with animals.

Among the "investigations" of Bandit was one that occurred after a journalist reported that he saw Bandit try to bite me. Bandit hadn't tried to bite me, as I reported in an affidavit to Canine Control, though it wasn't anyone's business but mine if he had, I thought, since I was the professional Dangerous Dog Handler here. Anyhow, Canine Control officer Maureen Griffin was dispatched to investigate. I called Barbara, the kennel manager, to tell her this officer would be coming. Barbara said, "Oh, good. A woman. She'll do a reasonable report, because women aren't afraid of dogs."

"Afraid of dogs?"

Barbara said, "For goodness' sake, haven't you noticed what a hard time you have finding good male kennel hands? The men are stronger, but they screw up because they're afraid. If a woman goes into a run to do something, pick up a feed dish or whatever, and the dog charges the gate, she just shoves him back and says to Cut It Out! A man will jump back, so that the dog gets loose and maybe gets into a fight or escapes altogether to go on an incredible journey. And the man says, 'That sucker tried to bite me!' Men can't control their animals because they're afraid of them—everyone knows that!"

Counterexamples came to mind, of course: on the one hand, most of the great dog and horse trainers of my experience, on the other, Pat Harwood in her riot gear. But the statistics also came to mind: 27 out of 28 dog-attack-related fatalities over a three-year period were caused by dogs owned and/or handled by men, according to HSUS figures, and the majority of bite victims are male, according to every study I know of that breaks down victims by gender.

The ultimate model of an activity that is at once unquestionably intelligent and intellectual and that also seems to divide the sexes is mathematics. The maleness of a mathematics department is explained either in terms of an allegedly greater male ability in mathematics, or in terms of sex-role stereotyping. You know the sort of thing: "As boys learn their sex roles, they identify with the notion that they should excel at mathematics. Girls . . . learn that mathematical ability is unfeminine," in the words of Diane F. Halpern's *Sex Differences in Cognitive Abilities*. (But logician Ruth Marcus reports that there are feminists who argue that logic and physics are "phallic," and that therefore women who go into those fields sell out, or buy out, or something. They used to be unfeminine, now they are unfeminist.)

MIT mathematician Gian-Carlo Rota said to me one time that he thought both positions were ridiculous. "There are plenty of women with all the talent for math anyone could want," he said. "But women leave math when they discover that you can't do it without sustaining world-class illusions, such as the belief that grips one while one is working on a very difficult paper on a very obscure corner of a difficult subject, that here, at last, everything will be settled once and for all." Interestingly, he doesn't talk about the desire to excel, at math or anything else, as the point—he doesn't mention competitiveness.

I could argue with Gian-Carlo and say that his notion is just the tired old idea that women are more in touch with nature or reality or whatever—that women are nice, and men are glorious. Crazy, but glorious. I do not know, having never been accused of womanly virtues, and knowing no women who gave up mathematics at the level he is talking about—he does not have in mind girls and young women doing poorly in high school or undergraduate courses. And I do not believe that in mathematics or anywhere else we have so much as *begun* to plumb the gender-related confusions and bafflements that are embodied as wastes of talent and spirit. Economics, brutally imposed role models, and major and minor slights and discounts plague the spirits of women and men both, often differently, and all have their place in the encyclopedia of explanations. But the arresting idea in what Rota says is that there is something askew about the faculties that lead to greatness in mathematics. Rota calls it "illusion."

But illusions are necessary to any quest, because knowledge is so limited, so I want to give Gian-Carlo his say here while noting that perhaps some illusions are more flexible than others. (And that the evidence on what women might achieve in mathematics were mathematics to become more reasonable is not yet in.)

Rota identifies the illusions necessary to mathematics with the faith that sustains a friend of his who is a priest. Women refuse such illusions or, say, don't care about them, are able to remain relatively calm in the face of the fact that there are issues that won't be settled once and for all, such as the exact nature of the universe or exactly what Daffodil means when she cocks her head and sticks her tongue out at you. I do not mean that women working with animals are satisfied with oversimplified or partial theories of animals, only that their minds are complex enough to sustain their contact with what they *do* know while noting also where their knowledge of Daffodil leaves off.

Hence it was a man, Descartes, who denied that animals have any sensations at all. He was buttressed by the church. B. F. Skinner, buttressed by the National Science Foundation, denied that knowledge of internal mental events is needed for the explanation of behavior. Donald Davidson, billed at one point as "Top Philosopher" in the *New York Review of Books,* proposes that the behavior of animals is like the behavior of a heat-seeking missile. It *looks* purposive when a dog chases a cat up a tree, but isn't really, because dogs do not have the conceptual apparatus required to chase cats up trees. That is to say, they haven't had any taxonomy courses. So another way to interpret the statistics about men's dogs getting into trouble might be this: Men are maddened, or diminished, by their logical powers. Bothered by the possibility—nay, the certainty—that a dog isn't thinking exactly what they are thinking about cats and trees, they often end up with dead cats, because they don't say to Fido, "Leave the cats alone!"

The maddened logician can't say, "Leave the cats alone!" because he lacks the *intellectual* apparatus required. Men say over and over again that their failure to prove that animals have minds is a sufficient reason for denying that they do. They say that instead of saying, "Leave the cats alone!" with the result that Fido becomes unmanageable. The unmanageability becomes intolerable at about age two, apparently—that is the average age of dogs brought into pounds for destruction by frantic owners.

The logical lunatic in any of us can't talk, doesn't know how to say, "Leave the kitty alone!" and further doesn't know how to say, "Let's find something else to do"; and it is more often men than women who are so flawlessly logical that they can't talk to Fido about kitty's rights around the house and yard, or so the data suggests. This is the aspect of intellect that prompted Wallace Stevens to say that one feels a "blank uneasiness" in the face of it, and to say that revolution is an affair of logical lunatics.

When a woman says, "He won't *talk* to me!" she has in mind something more alarming than his failure to talk as much as she does. One sort of advice often given is that this is okay, really. Men have so many other fine qualities, and if he is coming home at night and taking out the garbage then he must love you.

But she didn't say, "He doesn't love me." She said, "He won't talk to me."

And do we want people holding public office who find it so hard to say, "Leave the cats alone!" or anything at all, really, people who kill more easily than they talk? So easily! The *crime passionelle,* the crime that seems to the lunatic the only logical response—which is what witch hunts, Spanish Inquisitions, Stalinist purges, racial assaults, and quotas (the old sort, the ones that limited the number of Jewish students at Yale, for example) are all large-scale instances of—is regarded as something that the man can't help. Boys will be boys. Men have trouble getting in touch with their feelings or, alternatively, can't control their feelings, as in cases of rape. Bad enough, but do we want to allow people who can deny the emotions of others impeccably but can't control their own to be taught math and physics and chemistry and engineering and other subjects that yield technologically advanced ways of doubting the rationality of other minds, whether human or animal?

Love them, but don't give them the keys to the Pentagon, for goodness' sake! (I am not suggesting that women are not ferocious, mind you. Nor do I have any data handy to back up my idea that men are the emotional sex, the ones for whom the distinction between fact and feeling is a problem, but that is neither here nor there.)

I was on Orange Street in New Haven one day, chatting up a mounted cop who was at the moment protecting children as they left school. Protecting them from, of course, male *Homo sapiens*. As he talked to me about the various problems at that corner, I thought about Wallace Stevens's lines about the logical lunatic, the "lunatic of one idea," who "would have all the people live, work, suffer and die in that idea / In a world of ideas." The lunatic who would "not be aware of the clouds." Or the cat or the dog. So I proposed modestly that we should just corral young males until they reached the age of reason. He didn't say that would be unkind or unfair, he just said, "Jesus, do you know what kind of problems we would have then? At least this way some of them eventually learn *something!*"

Of course, there is no reason but fear disguised as logic to ban any breed of dog or human being. Which probably means that there is no reason but fear disguised as logic to disenfranchise men, and that data or no data, men no less than women or dogs touch us completely and only with who and what they are; this is everyone's claim to respect as well as everyone's offense. Though we might, as the mounted cop went on to say about boys, do a better job of educating them. He meant, for instance, that we have to spend more time telling them not to poke dogs and horses, so that they don't get into so much trouble.

What I have been talking about here are traits of the human mind that are conferred, I believe, not by our status as primates or predators or instances of this or that gender, but by *language*. The professor who saw good and bad penises where Raphael saw a horse and a dragon was able so grossly to mistake the subject of the painting because he was a master of the grammar that enables you to equate horses with dragons with spears in part because you can replace one noun with another in a sentence. This is not something a horse or a dog can do. We have traded awareness for language, I have said. We know or fail to know the world through what we say about it. It is our fate, then, to have to return to awareness through language, but what can that mean? It can mean philosophy and poetry, and it may even mean psychology and linguistics, when those disciplines manage to be as sophisticated as poetry is.

There is sometimes talk of poets as the unacknowledged legislators of the world. There are also refusals of this idea—Yeats saying that poets have no gift to set a statesman right, Auden saying that poetry makes nothing happen. It is a common mistake, not Yeats's mistake, of course, to expect that because it is so often language that has gone wrong—as in racist and sexist grammars, or in what has happened to the term "pit bull"—rules must be made about language. These sometimes come as censorship, or descriptions (and punishments) of treasonous speech, or as the false pedagogy of what is wrongly called feminism that establishes pieties about what women may or may not be and say, pieties that are as rigid as what was originally forbidden to women.

And sometimes there is the demand for "women's poetry" or "black poetry" or politically correct verses about how sweet the animals are, or how deserving, so it is not always easy to distinguish between what you read in books of verse and in fundraising pamphlets for animal rights organizations.

We have traded awareness for language, and because poetry is in some ways the ultimate instance of language, or perhaps our second inheritance of language, it is tempting to say that it is poetry that must return the world to us. This cannot happen. On my desk at the moment are two appeals to contribute to anthologies, the proceeds from which will go to "help animals." This I will not do, any more than I would contribute to women's collections even as I smarted from the reality of sexism.

A poem, unlike Bandit, can be aware of the state. A poem can even think about the state. But poetry is like Bandit in that it has no power over the state, and because it has no power over the state it has no allegiance to the state, at least not under the conception of the state invoked by the word "democracy," a conception that creates the fiction of the state obeying its citizens (through the vote) as well as of citizens obeying the fictions of the state.

So when I say it is our fate to return to awareness through language, I am not issuing a call to poets, or any sort of call at all.

One evening at a dinner party I was told a story about a bust of evil dog merchants. It seems that there was someone in New York who was selling pit bulls to dope dealers, to guard their dope dens. The dogs were "trained to kill," in particular by being given smaller dogs to tear apart.

As it happens, "killing" is too abstract a concept for dogs to master, and you can't train them to do it. I thought of this, and of Dickens at this point, because Bill Sykes's dog in *Oliver Twist* is an artifact of RSPCA propaganda about evil fighting dogs and their owners and dope dens and the like, and it is one of the most amazing facts about Dickens's genius and thus perhaps about the genius and idiocy of the English that he got all that stuff from newspapers.

Indeed, Bill Sykes's dog, who has no name, is a killer dog who belongs to an evil ghetto dweller who finally Gets His. This dog marks the moment when literature in English begins fully to discover the dog as citizen: Sykes's dog shares his master's citizenship, or lack thereof, and his fate—during the chase scene, he stays loyally with his master, and falls to his death hard on the heels of his master. The dog is at once the victim of social ills and, in his irrational snarliness, the incarnation of them. As a character, he is remarkably close to many of the fanciful versions of dogs I have been questioned about on the stand—as when I had to explain to a district attorney that the social class of the owner, even if the owner was tattooed, did not affect the genes of the dog. Not too much later, in *Hard Times*, Dickens would give us Merrylegs and other dog heros; Merrylegs is the moral center of that novel, missing throughout the bulk of its hard, black narrative.

Our social consciences make liars of us all. A dog's love, by contrast, is not the sort of thing that can make him into a killer, whether he loves St. Francis or Bill Sykes, and not only because dogs aren't intellectual enough to manage the concept "killing," but also because they can't manage that kind of love. Knowing this sort of thing sometimes interferes with my education.

For instance, a poet read at Yale one night. He was pretty good, and I was admiring him most of the time until he gave out with two or three lines about a demented Bloodhound. The Bloodhound represented the Ills of Society, or the State, or the Mob, or something of that sort.

Now, there is no such thing as a demented Bloodhound, although it used to be that scientists and newspapers said there was, which annoyed James Thurber, so even though Bloodhounds are pretty much left alone these days (except in North Bergen, New Jersey, and a few other municipalities that proposed and in some instances passed laws declaring that many breeds, including Bloodhounds, are "pit bulls"), I lost sympathy with the poet. He did a lot of impressive stuff, but I lost sympathy with him.

In fact, then and there I lost sympathy with a lot of verse writers, and quite suddenly stopped believing the things they have said.

They get it all from newspapers.

After a bit, I started believing what novelists and verse writers and even the occasional philosopher has to say again, but tentatively, especially when the topic is something familiar to us all, such as dogs or men or women.

I would have explained this to my dinner companion, but he was a dentist from Poughkeepsie, so I had to keep trying to hide my disreputable teeth from him, in case he got professional. He had his story from the news, and as an experiment I decided to believe it. Believing it, I was immediately indignant on the dope dealers' behalf, because they were probably charged a lot of money for these dogs, and a dog that is into fisticuffs with other dogs, whether or not he or she comes from a fighting-dog puppy mill, if there were such a thing, is nearly useless for guard work.

Of course, the dope dealer I am talking about, if he is a Connecticut resident, is black and lives in an unheated tenement in North Hartford and drives a stretch limousine and standardly bets $250,000 to $300,000 on a single dogfight. I do not know why he does not pay his heating bills—probably because he winters in Florida.

I asked my dinner companion if the dog peddlers had been pinched under the truth-in-advertising laws. What was fairly obvious to me was that the dope dealers who bought the dogs wanted justice, since that is what is being sold in a protection dog, or for that matter any dog. A good dog is not only the only love money can buy, she is the only justice money can buy.

That wasn't the right thing to say. The right thing would have been to launch into a round of "Ain't It Awful," going on at length not only about scuzzy evil dogfighters but while I was at it dope dealers, vicious teenagers, and so on. And, having no television, I forget that since I own pit bulls the right thing to do at the end of the round of "Ain't It Awful" about the dope dealers is to say with a careless laugh that my own dogs are wimps.

"Wimp" was for a while a term of praise certain desperate pit bull owners learned to apply to their dogs on television and while talking to *Sports Illustrated*. Its opposite wasn't "tough" but "killer." Popular lore had it that it was all in how a dog is handled whether s/he grows up a wimp or a killer.

Since neither of these terms refers to any real dog I have ever met, I don't know quite what they mean, but I understand the *use* of the term "killer" in the story I was told. It means a thing dogs can be trained to do, like heeling and sitting and fetching Frisbees. A trained killer, then, kills whatever you point it at— children, politicians, flies, cows, joy, news stories, weeds, and so on.

The "killer dog" is a relative of the dog who "attacks on command." You may have seen people training dogs to "attack" by having their dogs jump up and bite a padded sleeve. This sort of training is handy if you are ever mugged by someone who is wearing a padded sleeve, but it does make some dogs more obnoxious, always wanting to play and pestering their owners to get out the sleeve, which is more awkward to handle than a tennis ball and more expensive to replace. When "attack on command" is kept under control, however, it is a nice trick, a piece of fancy work. Dogs quite properly regard it as a form of play, and would be as astonished to learn that you thought you were teaching war work as a Bloodhound taught to chase balls would be astonished to learn that the human being thought this was part of tracking down lost children.

At that dinner, I launched into a lecture on the difference between fighting and dog-siccing, and between aggression toward other dogs and toward humans. My companion said, impatient with my earnestness, "But does all this matter? Does it matter what you call it? After all, *something* terrible was going on. Does it matter, as long as we stop the killing?"

I said, "Do you know what happened to the children last year when thousands of their pets were killed! Do you know about old people, the blind, the disabled, losing their dogs and dying, maddened by shock and grief? Do you know about people coming home to find their pugs, Dobies, Rottweilers, Boxers, and Labrador mixes hanging from trees?" When the grief in question is powerful enough, it is sometimes diagnosed as catatonic schizophrenia. When the presence of a dog elicits a response from the person so diagnosed, dogs are said to be "good for the mentally ill because they are nonthreatening," or some such nonsense, but this is not my experience of the "mentally ill."

I recall a boy, about fifteen, who had been silent in a hospital bed for eight months. His pit bull had been killed in response to a breed ban in his town some thirteen months prior to my visit. I was there with a friend, a good amateur dog trainer, who had with him a pit bull marked somewhat as the boy's dog had been marked, a licensed therapy dog. The boy spoke when we came into his room—to the dog. Then he spoke to me and to the dog's owner, asking for another dog like his dog. This story does not end well; the request was duly diagnosed—and denied. It was more important for him to learn to relate to people, or at least to socially acceptable dogs; a ferocious dog like the one he had lost would be bad for his mental balance. So he gave up trying to talk, and I cannot talk for him. We invent both monsters and diseases to distract us from the real nature of our ills, both the ones that are explicable and the ones that are not.

I told this story at dinner. My companion's eyes glazed a bit, because I was now preaching, just like those earnest women you sometimes run into at dinners. And I was forgetting to cover my teeth and they were being given professional scrutiny. I went on nonetheless, about the letters I get, about the young boys whose best pal, named Ollie or Jessie or whatever, is killed by the deliberate action of parents or other authorities, who then locks himself in his room for a while and is next seen buying cocaine. Sometimes these stories are told me by the central characters, who write, "I am now thirty-seven and I finally straightened myself out a couple of years ago." But sometimes they are written by teachers or brothers and sisters, who tell me about the fatal overdose.

I finished breathlessly, saying, "Yes, it is just as you say. So long as we stop the killing."

My companion was not unsympathetic—that's how he put it: "I am not unsympathetic." He may have meant my teeth, but I doubt it; dentists are never sympathetic about my teeth. Then he said, "But what about those punks and dope dealers who come up to you with pit bulls on chains?"

So I thought I'd better find out about people who come up to you with their pit bulls on chains. A few days later I found myself a poor urban neighborhood, and I walked about, waiting to be accosted. I stayed in the vicinity of one corner in particular, because it was a hot day and the woman at the small market was kind to me when I held the door of her cold box open for five minutes, trying to decide which soda to buy, unlike the man in the store further down, where there was a deli bar and a great deal of scowling efficiency. Nothing happened except that my feet, which are flat, began to hurt from walking on pavement.

I did see a young man with a short-haired, muscular male dog on a chain lead. The dog weighed about fifty pounds, was a pleasing brindle color with a white blaze, and had ears that looked like ailerons. The chain was probably mandated by local ordinance. For some reason, chains feature prominently in vicious-dog legislation, even though it is hazardous to try to control any dog that weighs more than five pounds with a chain, because when the dog jumps against the chain, the sudden pain is likely to cause the handler to let go, and the dog gets out into traffic and gets run over. If the chain is of any substance, a small dog can't drag it around, so either way chains are useless for walking dogs.

Fido was taking the young man for a walk, in the manner of conscientious dogs everywhere. The young man said, "Sit, sit sit," and "Heel, heel heel," and "Come!" a lot, all of which the dog ignored as he dragged his owner from one leg-lifting station to another. Owners often object to the speed and vigor of their daily walks with their dogs, not realizing the health benefits. Eventually Fido was done with his exercise tour and dragged the rather slight young man, whose hands were evidently bruised from trying to hold on to the chain, back home, tail wagging in satisfaction.

The owner ignored me, which was fortunate. If he had wanted to mug me, he would have had to get rid of the dog first, because it took both hands to hang on to the lead, which meant it would be impossible to handle the dog and a weapon at once. Also, his chances of getting the dog pointed in my direction without a fire hydrant behind me to motivate him were nil.

He reached a doorway that I took to be his, and sat down on the steps, panting. This was evidently a routine with him and Fido, who plumped down beside him and joined him in gazing on passersby while the man fondled him, murmuring the standard sweet nothings in his ear from time to time.

Fido had a wide leather collar around his neck, so that he could pull comfortably on the leash. He would have been even more comfortable in a harness, but well-fitting harnesses are hard to come by, even if you live in a ghetto. (The word "ghetto" comes from the Italian word *borghetto,* which is a diminutive of the word *borgo,* or "settlement outside the city wall." You are more likely to find a good harness maker outside the city wall, in the *borghetto.*)

It may be that you are one day approached by a Ghetto Dweller, or some other sort of Inhabitant, and a pit bull. If this happens, the thing to do is to ask the Dweller the dog's name. The Dweller will promptly say "Fido," because it takes a seasoned professional handler to resist the opportunity to say a dog's beloved Name. When the Dweller says his dog's name proudly, Fido will as likely as not look up at him and wiggle, releasing the pressure on the leash. This will give the Dweller a chance to straighten up and relieve his aching back. It will be a kindness.

And kindness—dear reader! Kindness these days is *everything.*

Of course, I now have to repeat that when Bandit is on duty he is undistractable. He doesn't care about kindness, and he doesn't care how chummily and admiringly you say his name.

But Bandit listens to the lady dogs. When I first brought him from the kennel to my house, I had my good Annie, a sweet but also severely motherly sort of pit bull, and Lucy Belle, a Plott Hound, about fourteen weeks old at the time, in the back of my Jeep. Since I had never had this particular combination of dogs together before, I had tied Bandit to one corner of the Jeep.

Bandit wanted to investigate Lucy. He became nosy with the pretty young pup, and then all of a sudden was expelled into the front seat. He knew better than to get in the front, especially while the car was in motion, and because he was tied short he was having trouble breathing. I told him not to be an idiot, to get in the back seat. He indicated, as plainly as a dog can, that he would if he dared, but that Annie would *yell* at him.

Annie is about two-thirds Bandit's size, and about a fifth his

strength and agility, and he was saying, "But she'll *yell* at me."
I told him that she wouldn't yell if he would mind his manners
and leave the pup alone, and to go ahead and be brave and get
in the back. And behave.

He did, and things were okay, but in the meanwhile another
aspect of Annie was preoccupying him: She has It. She doesn't
have the most glamorous figure in the world, and Lord knows
she has no patience with any of this male ego stuff, but she has
It. (She also enjoys bossing my husband around.) So Bandit set
himself to winning her heart. He began his campaign soon after
the incident with Lucy Belle, again in the Jeep.

That day the back seat of the Jeep was down, and Annie was
riding there and had told Bandit that he had to be in the very
back, in the cargo compartment, because she just couldn't stand
him. He leaped back obediently when she told him to, and we
set off on a one-hour journey.

I glanced back at the dogs in the rearview mirror from time
to time. Within a mile, I saw that Bandit had reached his head
over the seat and, with courtly grace and humility, was licking
what would be Annie's wrist if she had a wrist. She attempted
to be disgusted with this behavior, but Bandit can be surpassingly black tie when he puts his mind to it, which he doesn't
always.

Soon he had reached a paw over and gently pulled her other
forearm toward him for attention, which Annie tolerated in
some confusion, because while she had encountered many forms
of male homage before, this was her first experience of such a
degree of suavity.

He ever so politely paid homage to the line of her neck and
jaw.

She looked at him warily, but with respect.

He laid his chin on top of her head, but not in the hard heavy
way he does with me. Lightly. Reverently.

Shortly thereafter, he was on the seat with her, and she was
no longer yelling at him, and the two of them rode together. For
about thirty miles, Annie rode sitting up, which is not her lazy
habit, but then she relaxed and lay down, and that is how they

have ridden ever since, except when the presence of a puppy inspires Annie to exercise discipline.

I wish I could say that Bandit is always unselfish with the ladies, but he isn't. I wish, I do wish I could say that he keeps his sexuality discreet, but he doesn't. He is a womanizer, a romantic, but not a Don Juan. Annie has It, but she is no femme fatale, even though her gender is evident in every move she makes whether or not she is in heat.

I have said that "killer" is a word dogs cannot master. So is "rapist." And: "politician," "scholar," "poet," "philosopher." Dogs cannot *seduce* each other because they cannot master that concept, whether in the personal, the financial, or the public, social realm, even though when they are honest they are honest on purpose. Wittgenstein captured a great deal when he said that a dog can be neither sincere nor insincere, and he was almost right about that; Annie never worries about the sincerity of Bandit's intentions because in relationship to her as a female the question of his sincerity cannot come up in the way it can come up for humans. It can come up to some extent; hence, his inventive strategy for disarming her in the Jeep when she said, "Oh, you are just like all of the rest of them." She didn't mean by that what a human female would mean, that, for instance, he is "just interested in one thing." Annie knows that but cannot be sophisticated about it because she cannot be naïve about it. It is just that, being as she is a lady of high appeal, she knows a great deal about how annoyingly clumsy the male can be, so what Bandit had to find was, not ways of convincing her that he did not feel amorous, but only that he could be more beautiful, graceful, interesting than she thought he could.

But where dogs flounder in grace sometimes by being clumsy, human males flounder in morality sometimes by being seducers and rapists, and they have that much more to take responsibility for, if only because they know the word "rape," and for the same reason human females have almost that much more responsibility for avoiding the postures of the femme fatale.

Dogs are noble animals, but they are not as noble as we are, because incapable of the infirmities language gives into our imaginative keeping together with our noble minds—and I do not mean that phrase ironically. Annie and Bandit do not know about rape and seduction and so can be neither honest nor dishonest about it, though there are other matters they can calculate in the moral sphere. Our eyes, however, fall open, grasp knowledge of our naked skin, as the poet J, possibly a woman, noted at the very beginning. And, as this same poet noted at the beginning, it was words, the words of the snake, and not Satan disguised as a snake (as the male poet John Milton had it), that gave us our debasement and our nobility. And this woman tells also the story of the Tower of Babel . . . but let me slow down.

The difference between me and Annie is that Annie never does any gender theory. This is not because she does not know that she is naked and so is Bandit, but rather because she is not naked, nor even nude. We lose our heads when we find ourselves and our fellows without clothes, and imagine that a theory of gender by itself is a theory of mind and heart. Frank Intino wanted Bandit castrated, which as it happens doesn't make any difference to the dominance behavior of an adult dog. We keep looking at the wrong end of the animal at the wrong moments, a point Dick Koehler made with typical insouciant force when he responded to Intino's unseemly lust for castration by saying, "Oh, I don't think that will help. It hasn't done me any good at all."

I noticed something about gender when I was training racehorses; subsequent observations of dogs have confirmed me in the beliefs I started to develop.

In the horse world, most of the male horses you run across are geldings because stallions are more of a pain in the neck to keep and handle. The geldings (if gelded early enough) are quieter, and they are also easier than mares are to train and ride. But what I noticed was this: Given two horses of equal talent, who are equally crazy to deal with, *it is easier to reclaim the stallion* (at least it is easier the way I train). The stallion may well be more violent to begin with, may give you a real time of it, but once you have him moving with artistry, symmetry, balance, and power, he gets the point of the exercise faster. Similarly with dogs, both male and female: If they have been neutered young, they are harder to train. Easier to subdue, mind you, but harder to train.

Bandit is a very male sort of male dog. This can get a bit embarrassing, because he becomes aroused in all ways, mental and physical, if I take him out to work after a period of lazing around the house. Not if he is merely taken out to romp, but if he is taken out to work.

This made him very easy to train, and if he is in a period of steady work, his energy expresses itself as devotion to work instead of a rather too literal attempt to embrace the earth. As an intact male dog of enormous power, he is, as I keep saying, indomitable, impossible to subdue. But a wonderful partner in that dance of friendship in which we are no longer naked, no longer as it were concealed behind the illusion of nakedness.

I do not know what gender is, but I suspect that it is not to be understood by peering at genitals, but rather the way Annie and Bandit understand it in each other, through movement and gaze. (And scoldings and other comedies.) I do believe that gender is important, that the fact that "kind" and "gender" are sometimes synonymous, especially when the word "engender" begins to emerge from the word "gender," is also important, and that there is a reason that nobility is never expressed without the resonances of gender. Nor is nobility safe, cuddly.

Bandit, ah Bandit. His gender is so evident. He came back from the pound with his gender and other bits of nobility all out of order, and he peed on the porch, and Mr. Redd whupped him with that switch for a while, and Bandit bit him in the arm, and Mr. Redd, recognizing as no one else did the mistake he had made, said to me at one point, "So he bit me. Fair is fair. There's more man and more backbone to that dog than to any of these folks who want to kill him."

Is gender safe? Of course it isn't safe.

There are people now who are in the full-time business of being kind to animals and who recommend that all dogs and

cats be spayed and neutered and "phased out" so that we can
return to "a more distant, symbiotic relationship" with animals,
in the words of Ingrid Newkirk, cofounder of People for the
Ethical Treatment of Animals. Dr. Michael Fox of the HSUS
says everyone should spay their dog, and that dogs "don't miss
what they don't know about." By which he means, not gender,
but gonads. There are humane societies, more and more of
them, that require that adopted animals be spayed or neutered
before their new owners take them home. This does not diminish the amount of trouble the dog is likely to be by all that
much, but it does diminish the animals. Sometimes spaying or
neutering a dog is a medically correct decision, but the new turn
of events that makes it into a politically correct decision, a matter of good citizenship, is not enhancing the lives of animals or
of citizens.

Mr. Redd and Bandit, both creatures of backbone, of gender,
had it out there on the porch. It would have been better for
everyone if there had been a *real* obedience class available when
Bandit was six months old. A ten-week course taught by my
friend Dick Koehler would have saved untold amounts of
money, time, newsprint, and grief. Failing that, though, both
the dog and the old man remained intact, I would say. They at
least do not have neutered hearts.

Sometimes there are laws, the most recent and notorious of
them in my ken being one passed in San Mateo County, that
punish people with heavy fines for owning intact animals. Spaying and neutering and euthanasia, all of which hurt and diminish
animals, are done in the name of kindness to animals, and sometimes in the name of animal rights.

Bandit's gender would certainly be less offensively visible if
Frank Intino had succeeded in having him neutered. We are
more offensive when naked, too, but what is our nakedness? It
is, I think, just an idea, like the state. In David Rosenberg's
translation of the Book of J, the serpent has promised the
woman that if she eats from the tree in question, "your eyes will
fall open like gods, knowing good and bad." And, immediately
they eat, the eyes of the man and the woman "fall open, grasp

knowledge of their naked skin." Hence, even though Yahweh says that "the earthling sees like one of us, knowing good and bad," the poet does not say that they know good and bad, only that they "grasp knowledge of their naked skin."

Bandit was not neutered literally, but since the agreement of 1988 included the requirement that he be tatooed, I suppose you could say he was symbolically neutered—not that he can read the symbols in question, of course. The veterinarian who did the work made a great point of laying the tattoo large, along his inner stomach and thigh, parallel to his genitals. This was not my regular veterinarian, who is not so given to making decisions about the bodies of my animals without telling me about it, though it does not matter which veterinarian did it, nor what his intentions were. Now, with the mark of the state laid along his belly, Bandit when he rolls on his back, snorting and laughing, looks naked. This touches my mind abusively, and touches the minds of all who look upon him and grasp the knowledge of nakedness. It doesn't, of course, touch Bandit's gender, but like so many other inscriptions, it etches more than itself on the human mind.

Not his nakedness. He looks naked, but is not. My friend Diana Cooper talks about how the fact that pit bulls are "naked" inspires at least some of the vengeful responses to them. But people do not *know* that a dog, even a pit bull, is naked until someone tells them so, thus obscuring awareness of the dog's gender behind the (possibly false and misleading) idea of nakedness.

Yahweh—the way J tells it, Yahweh says to Adam, "Who told you naked is what you are?" Yahweh doesn't say that they are naked; the exchange might be between any dictator and a subject who has stumbled onto what may or may not be a coherent version of a state secret. (For instance: "Who led you to believe that those warheads are armed?") The notion that nakedness is an illusion that sustains the state is not new, I don't think; I am just ruminating on it. Ruminating on how many people I have heard say, after a holiday in an isolated place during fine weather, that it becomes hard to remember to put clothes on when you go outside.

If Harold Bloom is right, J's account of the birth of the state (soon Cain has a son who is "a city lad") is a woman's ironic account of the birth of one of the illusions about the nature of the political and the divine. Dogs, unlike men and women, cannot grasp the knowledge of nakedness, and cannot grasp the knowledge that there is a state. Nor are they likely to, unless there is another Fall.

TEN ···

Whereas

The righteous man knows his animal, but the tender mercies of the wicked are cruel.

—PROVERBS 12:10

JUSTICE AND THE TRUE NATURE of cynicism—these I wanted to get to, by way of Henry Street, but justice, which I rashly associate with happiness, must wait for the next book. Now, before this book closes, it is time for some more mundane narrative, a list of my grievances against the state—the insertion of a little documentary footage, as it were, which I hate to do since I have to be what Frank Cochran calls literal. But a bare narration of the facts is required, for before I can get to the things Bandit can protect me from, I must get to those things from which he needs me and Frank Cochran to protect him.

That is, the unjust city. Any social order for which Bandit cannot provide protection, whether it be a house or two huddled together in the wilderness or a larger political grouping, is within an unjust city, and may *be* an unjust city.

Nota: Injustice is not a matter of crime. For one thing, injustice is an abstraction and crime is real. My evidence that crime is real is that dogs can understand it, which is how there come to be police dogs. Crime comes from real people, and injustice is an activity of judges and authorities. Injustice comes from flags, and dogs cannot understand flags. The just city need not be crime-free in order to be just. Confusion on this point has led to no end of headaches, including the banishment of the poets from the Republic. Socrates wanted poetry that would encourage children to be kind to each other, so that they wouldn't perpetrate crimes. But justice consists, not in freedom from crime, but in a just response to crime. And poetic justice, inci-

240

dentally, consists in a just, an exact, response to poetry rather
than in laws about poetry. A dog can help you take care of crime
pure and simple, also assault from outside the city, just as a dog
trainer can help you take care of a dog in a confused relationship
to the world. A poet can help you take care of confusion pure
and simple, and of bits of language that are in a confused relationship to the world, but both dogs and poets are useless against
injustice.

Consider, for instance, one case of injustice, or what I think
of as injustice, the Uniform Administrative Procedures Act. At
the hearing on February 8, 1988, the hearing at which Judge
Dean decreed that I could train Bandit, there was a great deal of
argument about the Uniform Administrative Procedures Act,
which I think could be construed to say that Mr. Redd had no
right to appeal Agriculture's disposal order because Agriculture
is an administrative body and the courts are not supposed to
interfere in administration. Perhaps that isn't what it said, that
Mr. Redd had no rights in the matter, but it *sounded* like that was
what it said. I am told there have been a number of unsuccessful
attempts to have the act declared unconstitutional. I do not
pretend to understand the legal reasoning in question, or
whether there is any reasoning in question, but there are a couple of things that are fairly clear to me. One is this: Canine
Control officers in Connecticut are allowed to carry sidearms,
from which it must follow that they can use them. Also, Canine
Control officers and dog wardens and the like may issue disposal orders and orders such as the one that required Mr. Redd
to build the fence. And the Uniform Administrative Procedures
Act is what permits this to go on, what forces you to argue
about whether or not you so much as may appeal the action of
a dogcatcher.

This all seems fairly serious to me—sidearms and disposal
orders and the like—and I can't help but think there should
automatically be the right to appeal the action of an armed official. Of course, I probably do not understand the legal intricacies, being just a dog trainer. I began to have the idea, however,
that the powers protected by this act are sort of like the king's

body politic in medieval law, as opposed to his body natural. His body politic, which of course went about everywhere with and shared the actions of his body natural, was held to be infallible. This is not the sort of thing a dog would ever understand, but it is the sort of thing that can kill you and your dog.

When I speak of the state I mean, mostly, Frank Intino; like my dogs, I lose track of the abstractions and remember persons instead. Evidence of Frank Intino's actions sometimes came to me by way of communications from the commissioner of agriculture, or from the *Stamford Advocate* or various (armed) Canine Control officers. In the course of the Bandit case many other persons behaved annoyingly—the governor, the commissioner, various Canine Control officers who report to Intino, Intino's attorney, AAG Robert Teitleman, the city attorney for the town of Stamford, representatives of the *Stamford Advocate,* and so on. These persons, however, in the context of the Bandit case, are mere adjuncts to mine enemy.

I mention the detail about the Canine Control officers being armed because Bandit and I were unarmed, and while no weapons were ever drawn against me, there were weapons ready against Bandit when he was arrested, and being unarmed against an armed enemy affects the tone and color and atmosphere of a situation. When you are in such a situation and you cannot figure out what if any right of appeal you have against the people who are armed by the state, it starts to feel conspicuously like war rather than like the orderly business the word "government" suggests. The thing about these weapons is: They get used.

About who had these arms that worried me: Not the cops, or at least not the true cops, but armed bureaucrats, which is what humane cops are, while a true cop is a person mostly abused by the bureaucracy. Of course, it is possible for an ersatz cop who has the bureaucracy's blessing to be relatively intelligent and human, so long as his or her boss doesn't find out about it.

Here is what I was dealing with in Frank Intino: A man who testifies strenuously about the Jekyll-Hyde syndrome and other aspects of pit bull viciousness. A Yankee, also—that is to say, a

person from north of the Mason-Dixon Line. This man works
hard to uphold the integrity of disposal orders, and then, while
he is doing this, he tells a film crew that the reason he is in
animal work is because of his background. You might think that
means he had animals when he was growing up, but he didn't,
we know, thanks to the energy of Valerie Humes and to her
documentary, *A Little Vicious*. When Intino referred to his background, he meant his Roman Catholic background. His first
name is Frank, he explained to Valerie, and then went on for a
while about St. Francis of Assisi.

Well, saints start out in unlikely ways, and who am I to say
who is or isn't sanctified—am I the Pope? But it is hard enough
dealing with the bureaucracy without having St. Francis thrown
in. Hence I come before the court to plead as follows.

Whereas: Frank Intino has engaged in conduct unbecoming
to St. Francis, I urge that he not be forgiven in this mortal
sphere. I do not urge that he be punished, only that forgiveness
and trust be withheld until all the evidence is in. Bureaucratic
posturing is one thing; allowing the teasing of a helpless animal
is another matter altogether.

Intino's beliefs may be—probably are—consistent with the
idea that he is noble. If he believes that anyone who is around
Bandit when he isn't muzzled is in constant danger of Bandit's
suddenly "turning," then he was, in coming out to the kennel to
tease Bandit, just behaving like one of those fictional detectives
who *knows* that so-and-so is guilty but is frustrated for lack of
proof.

I was not a witness to the teasing. Lillian Bernard was. I will
give the evidence I have when I get to the agitation visit, item 3
on my list of gripes.

Item 1. Having explained to Valerie Humes how he admired
St. Francis, Intino performed an impatient maneuver. The situation was that Bandit was good and caught. It was the spring
of 1988, and I had been working with Bandit for about a month
at Silver Trails, where he had been ordered to reside under Judge
Dean's ruling of February 8. The judge had given Mr. Redd

ninety days to furnish evidence that Bandit was "retrainable." Bandit was making progress on his leash work, though he had not completed it. At the time, Frank Intino was still trying to catch Bandit, or at least catch him out at something. Since Bandit was already, as Judge Dean put it, in the slammer, this had to be done by way of the telephone and the media.

A sort of reporter, in the person of one Peter J. Reilly of the *Stamford Advocate,* visited the kennel on March 17 and watched Bandit not-bite me. The *Advocate* had not been all that friendly to Bandit and Mr. Redd, having seen fit to write editorials urging that the dog be destroyed, but I was trying to stick to a kind of open-house policy for the press, so when Reilly called I agreed to meet him. I am normally not generous with the media, being a little spooky, but I was agreeing to all interview requests because Bandit is photogenic, more so than the bureaucracy, and the case was an image war.

Bandit worked fairly well that day, and the weather was good, so there wasn't much of anything at all to report. Reilly described a curious scene on the front page of the *Advocate:*

> Hearne steps outside with the dog to give him some fresh air. Minutes later, one of the staff members leaves the building, gets into a pickup truck and backs out of the driveway.
>
> Hearne pulls on Bandit's leash to move him out of the path of the truck.
>
> Suddenly the dog bares his teeth and lunges for her arm.
>
> His strong jaws do not break the skin and Hearne pulls her arm away. She quickly has him under control again.

Reilly's account was wrong, especially the part about how Bandit's powerful jaws did not break my skin. It was his teeth that did not break my skin. It is almost always the teeth rather than the jaws, in the case of a living dog, that do or else do not break the skin. In this case, his teeth did not break my skin because he never lunged for me in the first place, a detail I thought significant. It is possible that Reilly misperceived a hand movement. What I am trying to say is that nothing happened, except that one of the kennel hands got into her truck and departed during Reilly's visit.

The trucks at Silver Trails are trained not to go after dogs, I complained fruitlessly to Reilly's editor, and I complained also that the dog had not lunged for me, and was told by a mincing voice that the paper would stick by its reporter. It wasn't clear to me what that had to do with truth.

Still, I thought the news story wasn't too bad. It's not as though you expect truth from a newspaper, after all. And some of the other fanciful ideas in it were rather touching, such as the one about me being a kind of Father Flanagan to pit bulls, and the one about Silver Trails being a home for dogs with no home, although that one might rile the Mercedes and BMW owners who bring their critters in for boarding. The line about the exercise pen being a giant litter box *was* a little strange, even for the news.

Canine Control, however, got excited, oddly, since Canine Control knows quite a bit more than is right about how copy gets into newspapers. They, in the person of someone who said he was Officer Simon—I don't know where Simon had jurisdiction—called me and wanted my side of the "incident." I said that I couldn't say on account of not having read the news story. Simon said that didn't matter, he just wanted my side of the incident. I said what incident. He said the one where Bandit tried to bite me. I said there was no such incident. He said I had to give my side of the story, and I said I had to read the story first to find out what I was giving a side *of*, and he said he was investigating, and I said I would have to call my lawyer, and he said, "Oh, you have to call your lawyer, do you?"

Whatever that meant. At the time I didn't have a lawyer, for it was another incident that finally prompted my retaining Frank Cochran.

Canine Control called the *Advocate*, which then called me and wanted me to comment on the fact that Canine Control was quarantining Bandit and I wouldn't be able to work him for two weeks. The *Hartford Courant* came out and watched Bandit not-bite me for forty-five minutes, as did a state Canine Control officer, to whom I showed my unbitten arms. A couple of TV stations came out, too, so there was Bandit on the evening news, not-biting me.

I submitted a formal—notarized!—statement to Canine Control about how the dog came to not-bite me, as did the kennel manager at Silver Trails, who witnessed the not-bite. And the not-attempted bite. Or the attempted not-bite?

The quarantine of Bandit was, of course, an *objet d'art,* of protest art or at least political art, or maybe bureaucratic art, an art project consisting entirely of its title, meant to Show Hearne, or Silver Trails, or something. There was in fact no quarantine. The *Advocate* asked me to comment on the quarantine, but there wasn't one and couldn't have been one, since Bandit was already confined.

Inspired by the example of Frank Intino, I was tempted to some more mindlessly flip, sarcastic behavior of the sort Frank Cochran keeps warning me against, and before you judge me, ask yourself what you would do in my place. I was tempted to call the *New York Times* and announce that I was putting the Empire State Building on public display during the period of Bandit's quarantine, by way of making a statement about it.

Quarantining an already quarantined dog with St. Francis as your moral authority is, of course, a little bit like summoning the name of Martin Luther King in support of programs to keep them bad niggers in jail so as to make life better for the Responsible Black Citizens.

Item 2. It came to be May 9, 1988, the day we were to return to court with the evidence Judge Dean had given us ninety days to collect. I was armed with Bandit's score on an American Temperament Testing Society test, in the course of which he was presented with neutral strangers, friendly strangers, hidden gunshots, hostile strangers, and other stimuli, and judged in detail on his responses to these. I also had a video of:

Bandit in his bath, Bandit retrieving a dumbbell, Bandit being peaceable with the cows, Bandit in the local pharmacy,

Bandit on the town green. Bandit working side by side with
Annie. Bandit climbing the ladder laid up against the barn
wall, Bandit doing Up and Off on the tractor seat and the
overturned grooming tub. (George didn't like having anything so trashy-looking in a film shot at his kennel, so I will
explain that it was properly installed just as soon as possible.)
Bandit also in Bookhaven, a nice bookstore by Yale, where
he greeted the ladies, observed a mouse, sat winsomely looking out of the display window, climbed a ladder. (It is hard to
think of ways to film a dog not-biting.)

This video, I figured, would annoy the state, but I also figured it would take them a little while to figure out what to do
about it, and that they might not get their act together until the
judge ruled that Bandit was a reformed character and could go
home to Henry Street.

Before the hearing Robert Bello, Mr. Redd's attorney, told
me that we weren't going to present any evidence, that there
was now an agreement with Canine Control to the effect that
Bandit could live if he stayed with me. I protested, since I had
pretty powerful evidence that Bandit was fundamentally sound,
and I thought that we should argue for the truth, to wit: I had
shown that he was trainable, and in showing that, in showing I
could handle him in public, off leash, when everyone else said he
was "uncontrollably aggressive," I had also given pretty powerful evidence that I could be trusted with the task of teaching
Mr. Redd how to handle him and manage his return to Henry
Street, and I said a great deal more. Bello seemed to feel that if
we tried to argue for the truth Bandit would lose his life. He
may have been right.

My experiences were such that I worried a great deal about
the rationality of believing that Canine Control would stick to
both the spirit and the details of any agreement between them
and Bello, and so I asked if the agreement was in writing. Upon
learning that it wasn't, I warned Bello against trusting in it, but
he was confident.

So on May 9 we gathered in the courthouse to report to the

judge that there was an agreement. The video was not entered into evidence, but it was shown on a player in the courthouse. There, Dog Warden Robert Winski and other persons, including some from the press, viewed it.

The next day, Bello reported that he had received in the mail—he reported this in the morning, so the mails were for once quite speedy—a restraint order I was to agree to. It included the requirement that I build a ten-by-ten concrete floor for a commercial-grade chain link run, that Bandit be muzzled and leashed when not in the run, and, most bemusingly, that I replace all the door and window glass on the ground floor of my house with Plexiglas.

I refused, spluttering. Bello said they would kill Bandit if I didn't. I said—well, I hope I said—"No they won't!" I know I said, "I told you not to trust them," and of course no one likes to hear Itoldyouso, so Bello said crankily, "How was *I* supposed to know they wouldn't keep their word?"

This puzzled me. It was obvious during my first five minutes at the hearing of December 10, 1987, that we were not dealing with what dog trainers and cops think of as stand-up guys, but of course a lawyer's world has a different texture from a dog trainer's, and maybe integrity sounds different in government from the way it sounds in animal work and writing.

Or maybe my darker, more paranoid idea was closer, that neither Bello nor the judge realized quite how "political" the vicious dog issue is.

This bit about cement runs and Plexiglas is still in the forgivable range, however, because it was not a direct assault on Bandit, only an assault on my pocketbook.

Item 3. Toward the end of May, I went to California, leaving Bandit at Silver Trails. I was writing a magazine piece about Hollywood animal trainers, and there was beautiful sunshine, a rented car with insurance, I was *learning* things, I was meeting beautiful animals, I was thinking that sometimes work is a way to visit Eden. To drive on beautiful California highways, to climb a one-lane road up a mountain so sweet and clear with fragrance I hummed "That Big Rock Candy Mountain," to arrive at the Animal Actors training compound at 7:00 a.m. in time to watch three baby elephants out for their first stroll of the day in the cool air. Also, to be consulting with friendly editors, to be free of mosquitoes, to have filled three notebooks with observations about chimpanzees and lynxes and bears and hawks and snakes and wolves, such as Sandra, who is a good wolf but who had to be removed from the pack because she was not a just boss, said Hubert Wells in his Hungarian accent. Some accents make people sound as though they know what justice is.

An early traveler to inland Southern California wrote, "The mountains cut the land off from sympathy with the corruptions of the East." Nonsense, of course. The occasion for my story was greed, delusion, righteousness, and the peculiar illusions that for many Hollywood types blur the distinction between image and self.

But it was beautiful. And I didn't have to think about the state of Connecticut, or not until Lillian called.

It turned out that Frank Intino had visited the kennel one afternoon, about three o'clock. The morning shift had gone home, and the evening shift had not yet arrived, so Lillian was alone. I do not know whether Intino knew she would be alone. He wasn't. He was accompanied by one Professor Ginsberg, of the University of Connecticut, and one Alice Trattner, a dog trainer, or said to be.

Lillian never got to testify about that visit, nor did the kennel hand and the client who were also there, but I taped her account and made a transcript of it, which I here reproduce. I have a lot of reasons for not doubting Lillian's veracity, which include her tendency to get the myriad details of life at the kennel right when everyone else's memory has been editing them, as well as her deep honesty.

Late in the afternoon on May 31st, Mr. Intino and two other people, a man and a woman, arrived at the kennel and asked if they could see Bandit.

I informed Mr. Intino that Vicki was out of town, and that no one was supposed to visit while she was gone.

He replied, "I know that, that is why I am here."

I said, "Do you believe that this is fair, with her out of town, to visit Bandit?"

He said, "That is why I wish to see him. I'd like to see how he acts with Vicki not there."

I very reluctantly walked them to the back kennel. Bandit was in the last run at the very end of D Building.

Intino did not come all the way to Bandit's run, but stopped about four runs from Bandit's run on the opposite side of the aisle. The two people with him proceeded on to the run. Bandit was sitting on the floor. They looked at him, and he sat there looking back, and finally the lady asked Mr. Intino, "Do you mind if I do something?"

Mr. Intino said, "Do whatever you want."

She proceeded to clap at him, stamp her feet, and then kick the cage.

I said, "If I had a kennel hand here who did that they would be fired immediately. That is kennel abuse."

Mr. Intino answered with, "That's just what we want to see, how he will react."

At this point Bandit did absolutely nothing but look up at them.

The woman asked if she could go around to the outside of the run and call him from outside. I proceeded around to the outside run with her, and she clapped her hands again.

Bandit proceeded to come through the gate to the outside run, but then turned around and returned inside and sat back down again, as the gentleman was still squatting in the inside aisle and coaxing Bandit through the fence.

At this point the lady came back around and slammed the door to D Building's outside section. Bandit looked up at the door and then returned to watching the man on the floor, who by this time was reaching inside and petting Bandit.

At one point Mr. Intino asked me to put the dog on a leash and take him out of the run. I told him that I would not do that.

He said, "The dog's life may depend on it."

I said to him, "You've got to be kidding. No trainer will

allow anyone to take a dog out of the run when he's in training. Therefore I will not take him out of the run."

Mr. Intino said, "In other words, you're afraid of him."

I said, "No, I'm not. I'll go in there with him if you like, but I am not taking him out of the run."

At this point the man on the floor was still talking to Bandit and scratching him under the chin and around the face. Bandit rolled over offering his belly to be scratched, as he often does when someone is with him.

After the lady slammed the door to D Building she came back into the aisle and said, sort of halfway to the man on the floor and to Intino, "*I* can't get him to show any aggression."

Mr. Intino was at this point still back several runs where he was playing with two little Shih Tzus.

I came to him and said, "Now, if you'd like to meet some nasty dogs, try to put these two dogs in the bathtub. Bandit jumps into the tub all by himself."

Mr. Intino said, "Yes, but their bite isn't like Bandit's. They couldn't kill you, but Bandit could."

Mr. Intino informed me that Vicki, if she got custody of Bandit, would not have him glued to her twenty-four hours a day and that therefore they were trying to find out whether or not the public was safe if Vicki wasn't around him, and that was the reason for this visit.

I said, "Give me a break! A few years ago it was Dobies, and before that Shepherds, and now it's pit bulls."

He said, "Yes, but these little dogs can't kill."

At this point I had a customer come through the back door and I had to leave D building and meet him at the top of the ramp.

I felt very intimidated by the way they were talking and acting around Bandit, and asked my customer who was at the top of the ramp to the runs not to leave, as I was not sure what they might do, or say that Bandit did, if I didn't keep them in sight. So my customer stood and watched while I took care of his wife, who was in the front office.

At this time Stacy, who is my night help, came on duty. I

told her that Mr. Intino was with Bandit, and to get down there and keep an eye on things. She proceeded to the back.

Before I finished with my customer, all four of them were back in the office. . . .

The visit lasted for half an hour at the most.

I assume the cage kicking indicates that, after all, someone read the report in which I described the terror of feet Bandit showed in the Stamford pound. What kind of person says, "Ah, this dog is afraid of being kicked. Let's kick him?" What kind of person thinks that agitating a dog is the same thing as evaluating the dog?

When you kick a dog's cage in an attempt to elicit aggression, you are agitating the dog. You are also attempting to induce something in the dog that some head trainers for police departments in my ken refuse to develop in their police dogs, because it is *too dangerous*. It is too dangerous to treat a police dog the way Frank Intino's "expert" help treated Bandit. Treated Bandit behind my back.

Bandit takes things very seriously, and if he perceives a threat to himself as real he will act on it, but he was not impressed with the seriousness of the behavior being exhibited that afternoon. It is possible that if I had been there and someone had "tested" him by attacking me, they would have gotten to see all the thrilling aggression their hearts may have desired. I do not, by the way, have any idea whether Intino or the people he had with him know what it means to provoke a dog's defense drive. I do not know whether they know that it is wrong. They should know, of course, but this is not Utopia.

Teasing a dog in order to elicit aggression without also training the dog so that it is a matter of work and courage and skill and cooperation with a human partner is a behavior frequently found in adolescent boys. When boys behave that way, they should be told not to. When the chief Canine Control officer of the state of Connecticut, with no interference from either the governor of the state or the commissioner of agriculture, behaves that way, deliberately tries to induce in a dog I am handling behavior and a state of mind that is *too dangerous in a police dog,* he should be told not to, or it starts becoming unclear in what sense there can be said to be a "government." I do not thereby become a "radical," do not thereby become an anarchist—it is not a political theory that is engendered in my breast when this happens, though of course this is the sort of event that makes political theories attractive to people. I just start wondering whether or not there is a government at all.

In my world what Frank Intino did when he came to Silver Trails is criminal. I mean "criminal" metaphorically, of course, but why that word? There was the sneakiness of it—waiting until I was in California, and possibly knowing enough to wait until Lillian was alone at the kennel, or at least until George wasn't there. But sneakiness is nothing—you spit on it and make better preparations next time.

It was the teasing, the agitating, of Bandit that made that visit criminal. Not literally criminal, of course—how can the state commit a crime?—but it felt that way, as though I had been assaulted. Those were just my feelings, of course, the feelings of outrage natural to a trainer who is told that someone has kicked her dog's cage, trying to get him to "show aggression" and calling it an "evaluation." What it felt like to me was something else again.

In here reporting the facts of May 31, 1988, as I have them, I am possibly endangering Silver Trails. Boarding kennels must be licensed in the state of Connecticut. Licensed by Canine Control.

Hence, the evidence I have given comes from what they call a "hostile" witness. A reluctant witness, that is: Lillian Bernard, she who said, "Why not? We have plenty of room." She is reluctant in part because she does not seek limelight or days in court, but also because she is at the mercy of Canine Control. I mention this in case, some time after this book comes out, the state decides that the Bernards have to install expensive changes in their facility in order to stay in business, or otherwise singles them out for special consideration.

It was to try to protect Silver Trails that Frank Cochran and

I decided to subpoena Lillian, in order to have a public record of her fear of reprisal for her testimony. Since she never got a chance to testify, there is unfortunately no record of her reluctance, though I suppose there is a record of the subpoena, which was duly served.

I am not saying Intino would have done anything vengeful, only that Lillian and George thought he might, and worried about it. Also, for the record: They do not know that I am here recording their worries.

And for the record: I wish this chapter to be a record of my concerns. Not of what Intino intended or intends or might someday intend; I do not have knowledge of that. In this chapter my only goal is to list the things I hold against the state of Connecticut. Items 1 and 2 and all of the others are forgivable, just barely, because one can talk to oneself about the extraordinary amount of ignorance involved, the excessive zeal, the way emotions run high in a case like this, and the rest of it.

Item 3, the attempt to agitate Bandit together with the swaggering intimidation of Lillian, is not forgivable.

Item 4. Shortly after this, I got a letter from Kenneth Andersen, commissioner of agriculture and Intino's superior. The letter said that it had "come to his attention" that I had had Bandit out in public, and that this was in violation of a restraint order, and that there would be "further action" if I continued.

There was enclosed a copy of a restraint order. It had been issued to Mr. Redd, not me, the previous year. I had never seen it, and it was of course nonsense, since Judge Dean's order giving me Bandit in training rendered it null.

Nonetheless, these two events—Intino's visit to the kennel and Andersen's letter—were what caused me to get a lawyer. I had had those conversations with Steve Wizner, and had of course worked with Mr. Redd's lawyer, but I was not at this point a party to the case, only a *witness*. And I had not done anything not ordered by the judge.

So I called Frank Cochran, after researching the question of lawyers for a while, and asked him whether or not I needed a lawyer. He is the type who will give an honest answer to such a question, and he said, "Yep. You need a lawyer."

At the next hearing, which was July 29, 1988, I became a party to the case and had, in fact, *two* lawyers there, Frank and his partner Linda Francois.

Item 5. This was just a *dog* case, as the press kept saying apropos the five lawyers, two of them there for Bandit and me, who gathered in the State Office Building on July 29, 1988. There weren't any criminal charges against anyone, and there weren't even any civil charges against Mr. Redd, since even in the Constitution State dogs are allowed to defend themselves and their property, according to Connecticut 22-357, which says that a dog owner is liable for damages to persons or property caused by his dog unless the person whose body or property was damaged, "at the time such damage was sustained, was committing a trespass or other tort, or was teasing, tormenting, or abusing such dog." Since Mrs. Powell was, according to her deposition, committing two torts, if I understand the term, you would think that there shouldn't have been any case at all. However, Connecticut canine law is contradictory, for it also says that the various dogcatchers "may make any order concerning the restraint or disposal of any biting dog as [they deem] necessary." That is how the local dog warden turned out to have the power to order an elderly and poor man to build an expensive fence after a justified bite.

I have referred to "the hearing of July 29, 1988," but there wasn't much of a hearing, though it did go on the whole of a hot day. Present was Dick Koehler, who flew from California to give testimony. However, neither he nor Lillian nor Alice Trattner nor Dr. Ginsberg nor I gave any testimony. The hearing officer that day, as on December 10, 1987, was Vincent Majchier, deputy commissioner of agriculture—the same man who, according to the *Hartford Courant*, wondered how Judge Dean was going to decide if Bandit was any good, thus: "Is he going to jump in the cage with him? I know *I* wouldn't," a remark that, if reported accurately, may have been intended to reveal how vicious Bandit is by showing the effect Bandit had on a courageous man.

Or something—I really don't know anything at all about mine enemy and associates of mine enemy except what my disgust tells me, and disgust is not illumination.

Frank Cochran opened by asking Majchier whether he had opined, as the *Hartford Courant* said he had, that you can't train a five-year-old animal, and asked further that if he had said it would he please disqualify himself as hearing officer, for that showed prejudice. Majchier said news stories weren't evidence, and Robert Bello, picking up the ball admirably, said that the clipping wasn't being entered as evidence, they were just asking if he had said it.

Majchier adjourned the hearing for five minutes that became an hour or two. That's the way that hearing was—adjournments and consultations in the hallway. Majchier smoked furiously and anxiously in the hallway, despite the signs forbidding this. I wanted to, but I don't have the power to adjourn a hearing when things get sticky, so refrained.

Every so often the hearing would reconvene for a few minutes and then be recessed, and continue in the form of negotiations and Moments in the Hallway. I remember with special pleasure Intino with his back to the wall and George shaking his finger in his face. I remember that I left Bandit with Robert, since I had to move around a lot, and that Bandit, while he does not understand the judicial process, does know when people are acting funny, and that he became very anxious whenever I left the room, whining for me to return, so Robert eventually took him outside, where he was quite content to play King of the Mountain on various monumental objects scattered around the State Office Building.

I remember a moment when someone thought it would be a good idea if Intino and I and our respective experts—I was no longer an expert, having become a party to the case—met together. We managed to meet for about one minute and forty-five seconds, as I recall.

Intino opened by shouting, "What do you want, Vicki!"

I asked what *he* wanted. He said he wanted: "Plexiglas!"—the word exploding from his lips like the name of a beloved family member who has been kidnapped. I said he couldn't have it.

He addressed me as "Vicki" and I told him it was "Ms. Hearne" to him.

There wasn't much about any of this that was particularly elevated.

Frank Cochran denies strenuously that he is Irish, but he got a temper from somewhere, and was looking decidedly fiery by the time he came to me to report that Intino wanted Bandit's balls cut off.

Mark Vandenberg stayed the course on that hot, miserable day. So did Dick Koehler, so did George and Lillian, so did Frank Cochran and Linda Francois, so did Robert, outside with Bandit.

So did Valerie Humes's film crew. This was when she captured Intino explaining about his connection with St. Francis.

When it was all over and Bandit and Frank Cochran and I were walking down the long flight of steps, Frank asked that the cameraman show Bandit's intact male apparatus. Frank said, "I accomplished *something* today."

We were in a rather light-headed mood, a celebratory mood, all except for Frank Cochran, who said crankily that he didn't know what all the euphoria was about, since there hadn't been anything remotely like justice. This caught me up short, because of course I hadn't been expecting anything remotely like justice, so was surprised that the lack of it at the end of the hearing had any bearing on anything. I went home to think, not right away but in a day or two, about justice.

The result of that hearing was that the state and I agreed to a variously interpretable set of conditions, including the requirement that Bandit wear a muzzle in public, and a clause saying that the parties would meet after a year and review.

Item 6. Another threat.

At that hearing, I agreed to the restrictions, largely because it would have been very expensive not to. It might have cost money that neither I nor anyone else had for an appeal, and thus might have cost Bandit's life. So I agreed, for instance, to build a chain link run. I did so, though Bandit has never spent any time to speak of in that run. He is too short-haired to be out when it is cold, and there are too many people who would like to hurt him, so I don't leave him anywhere out of the house where I can't see him.

Shortly after construction was finished, Maureen Griffin, Canine Control officer for this region, called to say her boss had asked her to inspect the pen. I said that was fine, but that I was taking a trip to Canada for a couple of days and was rushing to be ready for the plane, and could the inspection happen when I returned? She said fine.

A few minutes later the phone rang, and it was a very upset Frank Intino. He was in a state, as near as I could gather, because I hadn't told his officer to come right over. He said, "The AAG is seriously considering contempt of court." I tried to tell him that the conversation was over, and he just wouldn't stop talking, so I hung up.

And called Frank Cochran. Called him on my other line, because there was less static on it and it was easier to hear. While I was reporting to Cochran, Intino called back. Robert answered, and according to him Intino was very concerned that Robert understand that he, Frank Intino, was the *chief* Canine Control officer for the state of Connecticut.

I got on and Intino said angrily to me that the next time I put him on hold I was to tell him first. I tried to explain that I had hung up, not put him on hold, but he wasn't in a receptive mood. I hung up again.

So there was occasion for Frank Cochran to write a letter to Robert Teitleman, the assistant attorney general who was representing Intino, and explain that Intino did not have the right to harass me, and suggest that Teitleman control his client.

Item—oh, never mind. I probably had all of this coming, having been so spoiled in California. There were humane and animal control officers there, too, of course, but they were what would now, I think, be considered old-fashioned types. Avuncular, or "conservative." The head of Animal Control for Riverside County was a man who could actually train dogs. I don't mean he was a King Arthur among enforcement officers, but he did not believe that might makes right, and he did a hell of a good job training some dogs. He had a splendid working Irish Setter named Apples, and he would no more agitate a defenseless dog or go to another trainer's kennel while the trainer was gone in an attempt to collect evidence so that he could put that trainer's dog down than—well, than I imagine St. Francis himself would. Indeed, he welcomed my activities in his jurisdiction, and regarded encouraging competent trainers as part of his job.

Perhaps I had some awareness that those were the good old days.

A year after the July 29 hearing I called Frank Cochran, and he wrote to the attorney general's office, requesting that the restrictions be lifted. This started another series of letters and events. It came about finally that Maureen Griffin called me and said that her boss wanted to evaluate Bandit. I said fine. She said he wanted to inspect my property, for the Plexiglas and so on. I said that there wasn't any bloody Plexiglas in the case anymore, and sent her a copy of the agreement so that she would know. I also said that the disputed issue was whether or not Bandit would be allowed in public without a muzzle, and that therefore there should be an evaluation in a trying public situation, with witnesses. She said she didn't think Intino would want witnesses. I said that there would be witnesses, that there would be a man there with a video camera, and that the public would be invited.

An evaluation was scheduled for mid-October 1989. There were various acrimonious communications from the AAG's office, and on the afternoon before the scheduled evaluation, it was called off. A protocol could not be agreed on. Disputed points included the location—one proposal from Canine Control was that the dog should be in a local pound, with me out of his sight, hearing, and smell—and the content of the evaluation. Teitleman insisted that there had to be "a little provocation."

I said rather elaborately that I wasn't about to leave my dog at the mercy of people who had already shown a willingness to agitate and tease him, said this at length. Wrote at tedious length about what "agitation" and "provocation" are, pointed out that in most cases the law, and even the agreement of July 29, 1988, allowed a dog the right to bite if provoked.

Pointed out that what I was offering, which was to put Bandit through his paces on the New Haven town green, was a much more severe test of both his temperament and his training than most people with show dogs were willing to subject their dogs to. Teitleman didn't like the idea of my having Bandit do obedience work, saying he didn't want "a dog and pony show," thus revealing that he was no different from 99.999 percent of the literate inhabitants of this nation in having no concept, none, of what obedience is.

Obedience is too tough a concept.

The day before the evaluation, there was a moment when such loud and unseemly sounds were coming from Frank Cochran's office during conversations with the AAG that his partner quietly closed and sealed his door, so that the respectable people in there to have their wills seen to weren't subjected to anything so untoward.

More time went by, more letters. AAG Teitleman responded to one of my proposals for an evaluation protocol by saying that I was stubborn.

Finally, in January of 1990, more than two years after the first hearing at which I was a witness, and two and a half years after the case started, I scheduled my own evaluation, at the kennel, because the muzzle requirement meant that I couldn't do it in public.

I also, for the first time in this case, invited the press. Until then I had always responded when the press called, but did not seek out publicity. However, the press was the only thing I had by way of a forum at this point, since Canine Control was refusing to engage in any sort of review process.

So it was for the edification of the press that on January 11 Bandit once more displayed his obedience skills. Diana Cooper throughout the case had lobbied for civility, and in pursuit of civility she catered this event, serving coffee and scones and strawberries, which Intino scorned along with everything else. According to one reporter, he said he saw "no worthwhile reason" to come, since once a dog has taken to biting, that's it. It's like learning to ride a bicycle, it changes your brain structure, and you never know when it is going to be triggered.

I am not making that up, though I did attempt unsuccessfully to clean up the grammar a little, to work out whether he meant by the last "it" one's brain structure or bike riding. In trying to clean up the grammar I discovered that a concept that consists entirely of grammatical mistakes cannot be restored.

That is what the man said, it's like riding a bicycle, and it gave me this delirious vision of all of those people out there who know how to ride bicycles, in whom the response might be triggered at any moment. In the middle of dinner, say, or during lovemaking or church services or while voting.

I think Intino is on to something. Consider people who know how to read books. You never know when *that* is going to be triggered. Consider people who know how to write books, who often cannot be discouraged by the most earnest advice from their friends. God. Think of people who know how to play bridge or the harpsichord or the bagpipe, and what about all those fathers who go out and teach their sons to *throw* things?

Think of people who know how to pray. Think of it if you dare.

Whereas I think that enough is enough, and that this case should be settled, we propose that one of the following two decisions be made by some Court: Either the restrictions be lifted, or anyone who has learned anything be tattooed to that effect. We propose that Bandit, who has learned to heel and sit and stay and stand and down and come when called and retrieve a wooden dumbbell, be tattooed to that effect. Something tasteful in red.

Intino said that what worries him is that Bandit bit his master, and a dog who has no respect for his master is a danger to the public. Now, his master was beating him—"whupping" him, actually, with a switch—at the time of the bite. So I propose also that all dogs two years of age and older be whupped by their masters, and that the ones who don't fight back be allowed to live, provisionally of course, because you never know with these trigger mechanisms.

Similarly with all children who attain a height of five foot two or more, or a weight of one hundred and thirty pounds, whichever is less. A team of psychologists to be anointed by church and state will decide whether the mother or the father makes the best stand-in for the authority of the state during these safety evaluations.

Some of my friends and acquaintances believe that Bandit's case must have made me an animal rights activist, but it has had the opposite effect, solidifying my conviction that "humaniac" is a technical term important in evaluating political rhetoric and activity, even though it is also a term of mindless abuse.

The other effect it had was to make me feel the need of guardians, a feeling that got out of hand from time to time. At one point Frank Cochran said to me, "Well, he's trying to scare you. Unfortunately, he's succeeding."

So when there is no justice around, a dog is not useful as a guardian. Bandit, one of the most stalwart dogs I have ever known, was unable to guard himself or me in this situation.

I keep remembering those press reports about how the United States, when it went into Panama, killed the Panamanian K-9 corps. Every so often you just have to believe what you read in the newspapers. According to press reports, when the Berlin Wall came down, all of the dogs who had guarded the wall were destroyed because they were too dangerous.

Neither a dog nor a cop can guard the just city if they can't find it. Without justice, or if you prefer with justice in chains, a dog is pretty useless. Without justice, a bite is a bite is a bite, and no true protection, for a dog's bite is not self-defense and not defense of the baby and not defense of the old man. Without justice there is no such thing as order and discipline, because tyranny's mode of prevailing is to declare all individual action and self-defense to be either pathological or treasonous.

However, as I said, the only piece of Intino's behavior that I continue to find unforgivable is the visit on Memorial Day 1988, the visit during which Intino intimidated my dear friend Lillian and allowed Bandit to be teased. His testimony as I have heard it, not only in the Bandit case but in another in which he and I were opposing experts, is riddled with what seem to me to be superstition, emotion parading as reason, and immaturity. That, of course, is just my opinion. I do not exactly see him at his best, any more than he sees me at my best, and superstition and that form of nerves we have in mind when we say "emotions ran high" in a case—fear, that is—these are what we are subject to as human beings. Furthermore, since I cannot make any sense out of what he says, it follows that I do not understand him, and I cannot evaluate, analyze, what I do not understand. Having myself known states of terror induced by faulty grammar, I suspect that I might end up sympathizing deeply with the forces that have led him to testify so strenuously about the "Jekyll-Hyde syndrome," "trigger mechanisms," and the like—these notions express an anxious idea of how the world works, and anxiety is agony. Even that I say hesitantly, because I believe that there are as many kinds of minds and hearts out there as there are faces, and most hearts are mostly true by their own lights. All of those words of his caused me discomfort, annoyed me no end, led me to speculate that maybe testosterone *does* cause brain damage, that maybe people who grow up without pets never understand animals later in life, that maybe the fascists were here. Caused me to reread Plato, and to think about the part of the *Euthyphro* where Socrates says that no one commits a crime voluntarily. Also, sadly, it is probably the case that Frank Intino is as human as you are. As I am.

But he teased my dog. He tried to ~~kill,~~ no, uphold the disposal order on, my dog.

What he says nowadays, or at least what he is quoted as saying in the press, is that he thinks the department was too lenient in this case, and that "what you currently have in Bandit is a well-trained dangerous dog." Of course, he hasn't the foggiest idea what training is, or who Bandit is, so it is not important what he thinks about my dog, only what he *does* about my dog. But I don't know what the word "lenient" means here.

In another case I testified in, it came about that I had hurt my foot, and that the deadline for the submission of written testimony was changed from one week to twenty-four hours. The written testimony mattered since everyone was limited to five minutes at the hearing, and there hadn't been time to produce verbally the statistical information that showed that officialdom of the city in question was either massively incompetent or lying. I called a dog club that was involved in the suit, and asked if I could fax my testimony to them so that they could have their messenger take it over with theirs, explaining that going down to city hall myself was a bit of a burden at the time.

The club officer I was talking to asked quickly whether I had been hurt before or after I testified.

Fear, anger, paranoia—these are the usual responses of anyone involved in a highly publicized animal question. From 1986 through 1990 and beyond, a lot of people who normally regarded any toll call as an event began spending major portions of their budgets on the telephone, talking to strangers around the country who owned pit bulls and were in trouble, whether personally or because they were fighting a local or state breed ban. It was just such a *comfort,* to talk to someone who knew what the situation was, or who knew that pit bulls are just dogs, such a comfort to talk to someone who knew enough to realize that not only was neither the HSUS nor the local humane society going to help one, they were the ones who were trying to ~~kill~~ impound regulate ban spay neuter outlaw one's dog.

Or oneself, for the feeble attempt to fight the problem by repeating the slogan "It's not the dogs, it's the people" backfired badly. Animals and the handling of animals is no more the point now than it was in 1933, when Göring took over the Tiershutz-verein and under its auspices began sending scientists to concentration camps, or in England in the nineteenth century, when RSPCA propaganda was far more effective in consolidating class and national hostilities than in helping animals.

The effect of Bandit's case on me was to rouse my suspicions of any group that claims to be helping animals, not because I doubt that they need help, but because in any case in which I happen to know the details, the animal rights groups seem to be at best—and this is at best—no better than what they are complaining about. I do not know what mixture of idealism, genuine concern for animals, ignorance, hypocrisy, ordinary human carelessness, greed, ambition, or idiocy is involved, but that there is little connection between the activities of the noisier groups and anything that looks to me like help does seem clearer and clearer. It even looks to me like PETA and the HSUS have worked fairly hard to get rid of Annie and Bandit—PETA because all dogs are exploited, the HSUS because pit bulls are vicious. This puts me in apparent opposition to organized kindness to animals. That's where "Love me, love my dog" has gotten me—on the wrong side in a well-nigh global fight to protect the animals. The trouble is that I do not know whether or not there is a right side.

In Missouri a man named Jake Wilder was arrested for dogfighting, and his dogs were seized. He was eighty-seven and could not walk—to the patrol car, for instance—without assistance. The chances of his being at that point an active dogfighter were pretty slim. Humane cops searched his house, without a warrant, and seized magazines, the pedigrees of his dogs, other items, such as his burial agreement. The humane cops in question didn't even have jurisdiction in his county.

A man called me from Utah asking for help in his case. His dogs had been impounded, but since he had thirty-seven dogs and there were no local facilities for holding them, they were impounded on his property. So his property was also impounded, and he wasn't allowed to go there, he said. He was worried because it was summer and he lived in a desert area, and he didn't think the impounders would take the trouble he had to keep his dogs watered and cool. Several of his dogs were killed while he was in custody. This was the sheriff's office working with something he called the "humane society." I asked him which humane society, but like most people he wasn't clear that there are so many different humane societies, and couldn't help much when I pressed to find out whether the group in question was private or public, city or county or state. Whoever they were, they had helicopters and arms.

A Boxer was seized and destroyed while the woman who owned her was walking her on leash, on the streets of Lynn, Massachusetts. In 1990, an elderly Boxer who was standing in his own backyard, behind his fence, was shot and killed by police officers.

In Virginia, a man and a woman got into a domestic dispute. Someone, the woman I believe, called the cops. Her pregnant pit bull was out on the lawn. This dog happened to be an obedience dog—had her Companion Dog title from the United Kennel Club. And was evidently a fairly soft dog, was sitting on the lawn looking worried and puzzled, à la Thurber, when the backup unit arrived and shot her.

The day Frank Intino brought people to the kennel to agitate Bandit, recall that I was at Animal Actors in Thousand Oaks, California, talking with Hubert Wells. He was the head trainer on a film called *Project X,* which was selected by a collection of animal rights advocates, including Bob Barker of "The Price Is Right" and Robert Rush of Los Angeles Animal Regulation, as the occasion for a battle with the American Humane Association over who got the Screen Actors Guild contract to monitor movie animals. As I have said, there are thousands of animal welfare organizations, large and small, and they fight with each other, and sometimes publicity for widely touted horrors is just the visible part of a battle over funds or support or contracts.

Wild animal training isn't the subject of this book, but I should say something about it, and about misconceptions about it. Something very sketchy—there are wonderful books yet to be written about the complicated love, respect, and knowledge that go into good work with wild animals, who do not see the point of human domestic enterprises as readily as dogs and horses. One anthropologist told me that dogs are the nightmare of a chimp researcher's life, because as soon as you show that an ape can do something, someone comes along and shows you that dogs can do that too, and you are right back where you started on the project of demonstrating the intelligence of the great apes. Apes just don't care in the way Bandit cares about human domestic forms. (Elephants are different, or at least Asian elephants are; they are sensitive, sometimes over excitable, and because so large sometimes dangerous, but they are probably best described as domestic animals that happen to be born in the wild.)

The conclusion to be drawn is not that wild animals must therefore be beaten into submission. That is simply impossible. It is possible to have a protracted physical disagreement with an animal, wild or domestic, of course. There was my disagreement with Bandit about correct behavior around cows, for instance. But such disagreements are only possible, and only effective, if the animal accepts and understands the terms of the disagreement in the first place. Otherwise, physical force is just another threat display as far as the animal is concerned, and leads to the animal being out of control.

In the case of chimpanzees, if Jane Goodall is to be believed, threat displays are a fairly ordinary feature of their social life in the wild, and so are violent confrontations. None of this is useful on a movie set.

What *is* useful on a movie set or location? In movie work, the animals are surrounded by film crews that are ignorant about the animals. If a take goes badly, an actor might lose his temper and have a violent little tantrum while sitting five inches from a chimp or a tiger or an attack-trained dog. Further, the work is real work, sometimes a matter of take after take, because the special effects man is not handling the machinery correctly, because the actors are not doing well that day, because a small cloud keeps drifting over the sun at the wrong moment, etc. Or because the animals themselves are not having a good day. Sometimes this may be going on in the open, in the Serengeti, and the animals in question are lions. Or in Joshua Tree, where free-flying vultures are background for a soda pop commercial. (You didn't think those magnificent birds of prey you sometimes see on your TV just happened to be there in the right place the day the commercial was shot, did you?) Or you might be working wolves loose in Canada or Alaska. Places where the only force bringing the animals back to you is their interest in life with you.

When Hubert Wells did the film *Out of Africa,* which involved lions, Robert Redford, and Meryl Streep, it would go like this: His lions Asali and Sudan—and by the way, I have never heard love resonate the way it does when Hubert says "my lions"—would come out and work their scenes, and at the end of the day, Hubert would get into his Land Rover and start the engine, and Asali and Sudan would jump on top, ready to go home.

What creates this bond? What is a bond with, say, lions? Well, it is just what you would expect it to be—a matter of twenty-four-hour-a-day commitment. While I was at Animal Actors, Mark Harden was working with a young chimp named Landrover Smith, who was uncertain about everything. Harden spent weeks and weeks teaching Rover to go for a walk. This entailed, mostly, carrying the chimp around a lot, because he was afraid to walk on his own at first, even holding Harden's hand. (Harden complained a fair amount about restrictions that meant that Rover had had to spend a month in quarantine, with predictable consequences for his confidence.)

So as Hubert and I walked and talked, we would sometimes catch sight of Mark and Rover, Mark setting Rover down, careful to keep hold of his hand, saying, "No, no, there's nothing to be afraid of, that is just a baby elephant, here, you can do it." And sitting Rover on a box and patiently, oh patiently, placing his feet together, saying, "Feet down!" and being overcome with pleasure when Rover put his feet down of his own accord for a second or two.

The thing is, you *cannot fake* the pleasure in question. You have to have the capacity to be continuously awed and pleased by animals, by the way a tiger pads or a martial hawk turns and dips his head. You have to be willing to turn your back on the ordinary comforts of human domesticity, in order to care for the animals—Cheryl Schuaver feeds her elephants every two hours, all day long, and works with them between each feeding—and in order to meet the animals on their terms. In a way, it is a monkish life, almost a religious life, or in any event a life apart from the secular one. Mark Harden, for instance, took Rover into town, to the shopping mall, and walked around with him so that he would learn a number of things—among them, to recognize the fact that there exist people who are not part of his social group and are therefore not to be challenged. (It is important that a chimp relax, not feel threatened, by the presence of the strange people on a camera crew.) Mark had to do this on the chimp's terms, which meant that his very way of walking, his decisions about when to turn, when to stop and let the baby look at something, set him apart from the life around him.

The reason wild animal training mostly goes on at isolated compounds is that it is a separate culture. One morning during my visit, for instance, Cheryl Harris came in for breakfast with Masikio, one of the chimp actors from *Project X.* She brought with her no guns, no thumpers, no equipment at all. The "equipment" consisted of the relationships between everyone and the chimp. When Masikio, or Mouse (*masikio* is Swahili for "mouse," and Mouse has large round ears), walked in, everyone greeted him, Hubert offered him a seat, asked would he like some grapes, and so on.

The amount of time and physical energy expended by trainers and performing animals is impressive, but for me the telling details are the ones that reveal the imaginative work involved. For instance, Virgil, the lead role in *Project X,* was played by a chimp named Willie, who had previously been in a lab, so was socially undeveloped, to put it mildly. Originally a chimp named Arthur had been slated to play Virgil, but it turned out that Willie did best in the screen tests. Virgil is a signing chimp, and Willie is a very fastidious sort of fellow. When he made the sign for "apple," which involves bringing the right fist up to the right cheek and turning it forward, it was not "mumbled" as it was with jolly old Arthur, and as it often is with real signing chimps. Instead, Willie made two distinct and very precise movements, as controlled as a ballerina's.

Willie's love of exact articulations got him the lead, but it also meant that for a while Mark had trouble getting on his wavelength. Mark is, by his own account, more like Arthur, a "hangout" kind of guy, jolly and easygoing. Hence Mark rewarded Arthur in the way that came most naturally to him—horsing around for a while after work was done. And he would horse around with Willie, but Willie's interest in his work just decreased as time went on. Then one day Mark saw that while the horsing around rewarded him, it didn't reward Willie: "I realized that he would say to himself, 'Oh, phooey, now I have to play with Mark.' " What rewarded Willie was just sitting quietly with Mark, not saying anything. This came hard to Mark, who can do almost anything but sit quietly. (There were also problems with Willie and Arthur in the scenes they had to play together. Willie wanted his timing to be exact, wanted to hit his mark with not an inch of leeway, and Arthur just couldn't go from Point A to Point B without throwing in a tap dance or a few card tricks. Arthur's antics would throw Willie's timing off, and Willie would scream at Arthur.)

So the work is a matter of thinking about the animals twenty-seven hours a day. Meditating on each one, going over and over small exchanges with them, until you understand where that particular animal's imaginative and emotional life is and adjust your heart and mind accordingly. It is like this also with dogs and horses if the work is serious, but it is even more so with wild animals, because you have to make larger leaps, longer journeys, in order to find a meeting place with them. And with every leap you make, for a while at least, you leave more and more of your human associates behind. Jack London was given to some sentimentalities about animals, and the movies made from his books falsify things even more, but the central image of the human character who forsakes the comforts of the human world in order to accommodate himself to the animal's world is in fact a true emblem of a central aspect of the life of training, which is given sometimes in words such as "respect." But you do not have to go to Alaska or Gombe to do this. Mark Harden, walking the young chimp in a mall in Southern California, has left his own kind as far behind as any of the heroes and heroines of the wilderness ever did in order to live in the animal's world. Indeed, even with a dog it is harder to do this in a shopping mall than in a game preserve, since the pull on the human partner, the sometimes vigorous distractions, are omnipresent, in your lap, and there is the quite natural and understandable but not always easy to handle resentment of onlookers, as when someone addresses a remark to you and you have to respond first to what the dog or chimp has said rather than to the person.

The reason the public never hears about any of this is that the public does not want to know about it, any more than science does. Most people are bored by the actual details of training, as I have always known, and as I learned again when the press would call and ask about "the actual training details" of working with Bandit. I would start to tell them, and they would interrupt, wanting me to get to the juicy part. So I would say, "Well, one day Bandit wanted to go for the cows and I thumped him on the nose," and they were extremely interested in the nose thumper but bored by the other details, the myriad details, of working with an animal.

Sometimes you have to get tough with a tough animal, but that is no more to the point of things than occasional sharp exchanges between two human friends, both of them people of spirit and energy.

Mark Harden says, "The thing that makes it hard, that most people can't manage, is that you have to give up your interest in their loving you, and learn the disciplines of respect and admiration instead. If you stop respecting them and stop admiring them, you can't go on. Because you will get hurt, it is too dangerous, and the animals will not work for you."

The burden here is like the poet's burden—the imaginative burden of dissolving yourself in order to respond with keen precisions to alien ways of thinking and being. To respond with admiration and respect, always, always. It is a burden that few people have the spiritual courage to shoulder, and that even fewer can do well. It is an even more terrible burden when it is so terribly misunderstood, in an age when people whose lives really can be described as "dedicated to animals" are presented to the public as monsters.

Is there physical force? Yes, sometimes, of course, just as there is between wild animals. But when the trainer is Hubert Wells or Cheryl Harris or Mark Harden, there is no punishment, and there are no threats.

Are there no bad trainers? Of *course* there are bad trainers. But you do not often find them heading the animal work in pictures involving sustained animal action. That work is too difficult for bad trainers.

Some bad trainers, finding that threats and tranquilizers do not work, and perhaps believing that the successful trainers are just better at threats and drug dosages than they are, become anti-trainer activists.

My experience of controversies about Hollywood animals, wild or domestic, is such that I assumed from the very fact that I was hearing from the HSUS and other groups about how cruel Hubert Wells is that he must be an exquisitely good trainer. This is, I suppose, another version of Hearne's Law. I went immediately to see *Project X,* and responded to it by being disgusted with the phony Help the Animals plot line, but bowled over by the quality of the animal work. Especially Willie's work; the reality of his fiercely fastidious soul came through the sleazily sentimental story line. For me, at least. Various humane spokesmen had the opposite response. They were taken by the movie's heartwarming "message" and appalled by the animal work. Of course, I know enough about both people and animals to know that it is not true that you can "get anyone to do anything if you beat them up," in the words of Roger Fouts, an energetic critic of Hubert Wells who has not worked chimps on films, though he did consulting work on the film *Greystoke,* with human actors in chimpanzee suits.

There is such a thing as a beating, and there is such a thing as coercion, but it is not the magic wand it is made out to be in Foucaultian and other humaniac fantasies. A poet's command over language is not the effect of a beating or coercion, and Willie's movements, the young chimp's command over his movements, the concentration and seriousness that made them *his* movements and not Mark Harden's, are not the result of beatings and coercion. The idea that they are is a sadistic fantasy.

The truth is that cruelty is possible, but it is not as effective as intelligence. It may be effective for establishing bureaucratic power over other humans, at least temporarily, but it is useless in animal training. My advice is: If someone starts telling you that cruelty is effective, the wise thing to do is to run–don't-walk away, as fast as you can, holding on to your pocketbook.

I had traveled to California in order to find out more about Animal Actors and to write about the situation for the *Los Angeles Times Magazine*. I was there as a journalist, so one of the people I called about the case was Robert Rush, since it was he who had asked the district attorney's office for I forget how many felony counts against the trainers on *Project X*. Because of his position as head of L.A. Animal Regulation, he is free to ask for a felony indictment and report it to the press. This has a powerful effect on public opinion, whatever the evidence.

The next morning—this was kind of spooky—the phone rang, and a voice said, "Thiiis is Booob BARKER!!!!" I failed to swoon. Was invited to the studio, was invited to Barker's home, mumbled that I already had a date. Perhaps a real investigative reporter would have accepted these invitations and nosed around. I had already done enough work to realize that the current furor about Hollywood training was just a new version of a kind I was familiar with, where the trick is to select some trainer who will be easily remembered because he or she has done major movie work with animals and tell the press a bunch of hooey about that trainer. Whether or not the people speaking the hooey are sincere, I cannot tell you. I wish I could.

I should have nosed around Barker, but as I realize from my thriller reading, I am a failure as an investigative reporter, because I was more interested in the trainers and their animals than in Bob Barker and "The Price Is Right" and local bureaucrats. So I was at Animal Actors that day, the day of Intino's visit, and at the very moment, as near as I can calculate from my notes, that Alice Trattner was kicking Bandit's cage I was listening to Hubert Wells say, "What are they going to do with my animals if they seize them? What are they going to *do?*"

Wells is from Hungary, left there in 1956 for the usual reasons, came to this country, learned English, washed dishes and saved money to buy some animals. He is a worker—in not too much time he was doing a nightclub act involving a hawk, a leopard, and a Vizsla. Came to the attention of Walt Disney Studios, moved to Hollywood, made it.

Now he says, "I am in more danger of being jailed for political reasons today than I was in 1956."

Well, these Hungarians are an emotional lot. Hubert's friend Doree says, "Hubert takes these things so much to heart!"

Robert Rush was one of the prime movers in the media case against Wells and other trainers. (I call it a media case because nothing ever came of it legally, nothing involving Wells, that is. Wells learned about the request for felony indictments from the newspapers.) A couple of years earlier, Wells was shooting a scene for a commercial involving a bear. Men from Rush's office showed up with shotguns that they proposed to point at the bear throughout the work.

Wells doesn't like having shotguns pointed at his animals. I do not know how to explain to you what it is to be a person whose beloved companions the state is at liberty to defame, impound, and destroy in the name of kindness.

There is a move on, as near as I can make out, to pass a "mall law" in Connecticut. This would outlaw the leaving of dogs in cars. My friends who just moved from Virginia to Arizona with their nineteen dogs report that there seems to be such a law in Texas, as they found stopping one evening at a motel there. They have a large van, with crates for the dogs; on the journey they stopped every so often to feed and exercise the dogs, a process that took two hours. They were tired by the time they reached this motel in Texas.

Were told by the motel owner that they couldn't stop there because it is illegal to leave dogs in cars in Texas. And of course there was no way, even with crates, even in Texas, they would be allowed to bring nineteen dogs into a motel room, especially since eighteen of them were either pit bulls or AmStaffs. So they drove on, to New Mexico, found a motel there in the wee hours, and overslept, which meant that their dogs suffered because the sun came out and heated up the van. (They had timed the stop in Texas in such a fashion that the dogs wouldn't have to be left in the van while the sun was up.)

This is in aid of kindness to animals, all of it.

I can't tell you much about my own idiocies, couldn't even if I were clear about what they are, and it is of course unfair of me to give you a view of mine enemy as he appears to me in his enemyhood without giving you a view of what I look like when I am the enemy.

I can't tell you about my idiocies because I would then have to tell you about the people who rescued me from them, and that is all a secret, but you should know that some people were brave for Bandit's sake, others for mine. And generous. Many people, in fact, but the wars are not over, and even if they were, some people are very secretive about their courage and generosity, which is roughly the way Hannah Arendt said it should be—at least, she has the idea that goodness that goes public must become the worst sort of wickedness. Or: Think of it often, speak of it never, as my mother used to say.

Courage and goodness are not exactly private, but they are often secrets, not that the acts of courage I know about would be any *surprise* to the familiars of the brave. It isn't that, it is as though the kind of public space in which knowledge of individual virtue is possible cannot be larger or more abstract than the kind of public space Bandit can guard, and this is a book so is not the kind of public space Bandit can guard. Or because a book, a nonfiction book, is a place where the soul cannot select her own society.

The people who were brave were less confused than most. And I have to tell you that the woman who said to me at one point, about an earlier battle in these wars, "Be careful. People who are kind to animals are not very nice," was not a dummy, knew some things. Also, that in Bandit's case and many, many others, there were acts of courage and generosity that were born in confusion and error, as though John Milton had been right when he argued against censorship on the grounds that it is our fate to discover what is good in the welter of what is evil.

Hannah Arendt, annoyingly, doesn't give any examples of what she means by "goodness," but I think that goodness cannot go public in part because it always entails some form of deep knowledge. Knowledge of dogs or of what you might call the politics of particular situations. The people who had genuine help to give were all in one way and another experts in the ways of the world as they relate to dogs, which means that they knew a lot about breeds and about kinds of dog work and wanted to know more, that they knew a lot about the current politics of relations between sundry dog and humane organizations at the local and the national level, and about patterns of friendship and power in various state and federal agencies, administrative departments, and legislatures.

The secrets in question, though, are not in the usual sense hidden—not as, say, the secrets of Watergate were hidden, even though there have been threats, mysterious events, several cases not in this part of the country in which a long series of expert witnesses canceled their appearances, citing the sudden death of an aunt or a broken leg or whatever.

People laugh when I tell them the dog wars are dangerous, and so do I—what is a humaniac beside the Ayatollah (unless the Ayatollah's behavior in asking for the death of Salman Rushdie for his unkindness to Muslims means that Rushdie is a pit bull and the Ayatollah was a humaniac). But I was threatened twice with action of the sort that puts you in jail. The threats were, if you like, silly, but they seem silly in retrospect and only because

Frank Cochran was there to see to it that nothing came of them. And it is not so funny, actually, or trivial, to receive a letter from the commissioner of agriculture threatening you with action if you take a dog into public, whether or not you have a judge's order saying that you can do that, not so funny to have Intino call and say, "The AAG is considering contempt of court." More importantly, it is not so funny that local dog wardens have and use the power to order an old man to build an expensive fence or have his dog killed.

The scars on Bandit's face and flank are also not so funny, though of course I don't know how they got there.

Bandit circling autistically at the back of his run when anyone but me approached was not so funny, is not trivial. Love does not matter to dogs nearly as much as trust does; it was trust that had broken down for him. And as I have tried to indicate with my sketchy discussion of Hollywood, earning an animal's trust is a long, hard work. It is also the major and I sometimes think the only activity that can be called kindness. That is wrong— there is also veterinary medicine and money. But animals take things personally or not at all, which means that you have to be kind to them individually, one by one, and there is no one who can do your kindness for you.

There is no one who can do your kindness for you, and kindness, deliberately setting out to do a kindness, is a confusing business. I know people who can manage to do it directly, or who seem to, but most cases in my ken entail knowing how to do something besides kindness. Train dogs, for example, or write poems, or run a kennel or cook or practice veterinary medicine, or shoe horses or labor in a research library or keep sheep.

Hannah Arendt's remark about the banality of evil is famous, and I have come to think that she may have had in mind the slipshod grammar, the motives neither high and noble nor interestingly debased, the indifference to accuracy about technical matters, the . . .

The slipshod grammar. For instance, "These dogs are bred to kill, and their training is part of their genetics."

What does one say about this?

But I was going to talk about the people who have been courageous in all of this. Like most people I have known who have shown heart and courage, like Bandit, they are capable of confusion. The usual story about people being brave in a political situation is much like the story Philip Hallie tells in the book *Lest Innocent Blood Be Shed,* a book about the French Protestant village of Le Chambon, which worked to give refuge to Jews during World War II. The good do not become afraid of mere public opinion or political pressure; they are like pastor André Trocmé as Hallie describes him, unafraid of arrest, not feeling confused, never being stupid, though perhaps wavering just a touch when he saw the camp he was taken to and here "felt fear pinch his heart for the first time."

Good people in the usual stories are never stupid or afraid. In the world Hallie describes, "God, the Devil, and halfwits of mind and heart were all struggling with each other to take over." Le Chambon was free of all of this, even mistakes: "Le Chambon had been spared the cretins."

But look: In 1987, according to the estimate of the Endangered Breed Association, 35,000 people took their bull breed dogs to pounds and humane societies to be killed, most of them pit bulls or something someone thought was a pit bull. There was television and newspaper coverage of people queuing up with their dogs to have them killed. They did this because they had read in the newspaper that their dogs were dangerous, liable to "turn on them" at any moment, or because their spouses and neighbors had read that, or because . . .

A man called me the other night from another part of the country because he was trying to understand what had happened to him. He had a pit bull named Chester, something over five years old. Guests had come to dinner. They were walking on a path in the garden when one of the guests picked up a garter snake and began tossing it around. This caused the guest's wife to shriek, so he threw the snake at her, and she shrieked even more, jumping about and waving her arms, and Chester bit her in the arm.

There was a suit, and a report of a dangerous dog, and then Chester's owner couldn't find any witnesses to help him, found plenty willing to testify about vicious dogs, began to feel hopeless and cornered, and . . .

After a while had Chester put down. Now visits his grave, begs his forgiveness, and calls me on roughly the other side of the country to ask me what happened, because I wrote an essay about pit bulls. He introduced himself and then said, "I am hoping you can tell me what happened." He told me what the experts had said, which was a familiar routine about how once dogs bite it changes their brain structure, and about how Chester was a dominant dog—one expert, a person who breeds Rotties, was disturbed because Chester didn't greet her elaborately. (People judge dogs by whether or not the dog wants to be petted, by them, including people who are outraged at the idea that women should want to be petted all the time.)

This man—a professional, a scientist, a good administrator of never mind what—sobbed, "He was my friend, and I killed him!" Killed his friend because the local humane society ordered him to.

And vowed to enter the wars, to protect other dogs and dog owners.

It took courage—I can't tell you enough about the courage for credibility without telling you who this man is—for him to call me, to face the fact that he had been separated from his own knowledge of his friend Chester. I can tell you this man's idiocy but not his courage, because he would get hurt if I told you his courage.

One combatant in the pit bull wars said, about the dogs who were being turned in for slaughter in the summer of 1987, "Good. They're better off dead than with such people."

Do you believe that?

That's how all this started, kindly people thinking that pit bulls were better off dead than with this or that kind of owner—rural Southern white owners, or urban black and Hispanic owners.

This man was relieved and astonished to learn that he wasn't alone. Queerly comforted to hear of Jake Wilder, the old man in Missouri, and of the man in Utah whose name I cannot reveal, and of the 35,000 dogs turned in by their owners in the summer of 1987.

There was the kennel full of Shar Peis in Ohio that were sold cheap because pit bulls were declared *prima facie* vicious and some local judge or hearing officer declared that the Shar Peis were pit bulls.

There was the law proposed in North Bergen, New Jersey, that banned pit bulls from the town and declared that a pit bull was "any dog bred or used to fight human beings or other animals." Every winter, hundreds of dogs entered in the Westminster Show in Madison Square Garden pass through North Bergen, New Jersey, because for many travelers that is the route to the Lincoln Tunnel.

In various communities there are moves to outlaw dogs on the streets and in the parks and all public places. In Southern California, there is a Dog Park: four acres set aside and cherished and guarded, where dogs can romp about, can even be off lead during certain hours. A great deal of energy is required on the part of a lot of people to keep those four acres free.

It used to bother me to see dead dogs and cats lying in the road. Still does, but recently I visited a small town in South Carolina. The area was fairly flat, and there were many small farms, the houses set back a few hundred yards from the road, and dogs would get onto the road and sometimes get run over. Something about this cheered me up, but I couldn't put my finger on it for a while until I returned to Connecticut, where I have not seen a dead dog on the road since I can remember, even though I live in what New Yorkers call "the country." Dead squirrels, possums, raccoons, but no dead dogs.

Then I worked it out. The presence of dead raccoons and such in Connecticut means—ah! It means that there are living raccoons around here and therefore that raccoons haven't been so thoroughly rescued as dogs have been. Indeed, it means that the wild animals in my little neck of the woods are in some ways more integrated into the *polis* than the (ultimately domestic) dog. If there were dead dogs on the road in South Carolina, that meant that there were still dogs running around, which meant that the local humane society hadn't yet rounded them all up and killed them.

This is the crux of the matter, of course, as far as the politics of the situation go. I suspect but am not certain that it is an illusion that there can be such a thing as a humane society, with or without capital letters. Because in a humane society, one governed by kindness without reference to goodness of the sort Nietzsche had in mind when he said he had destroyed the distinction between good and evil but not the distinction between good and bad, everyone has to be either a persecutor or a victim or a rescuer. None of this has anything to do with anything that excites my interest or the interest of any dog I have ever met.

In a humane and kindly society, all happiness would be ideologically unsound because happiness is extreme, fortuitous, personal, and a matter, mostly, of work.

If there is such a thing as justice, which I do not here disavow, things might be different. For me it remains the case that, as Stanley Cavell has said, "Society remains as mysterious to us as we are to ourselves, or as God is."

Coda:
A Thousand Dollars

"Where is that dog now?"
—MR. REDD

OUR STORY has no particular ending, and so no happy ending. There is, rather, a complex of prevented endings. Some of these prevented endings are happily prevented endings, some not. The state has not yet managed to execute Bandit, and the prospect of its doing so is an ever fading one. All of that is happiness. But Bandit has not been returned to Mr. Redd. And he never can be. Bandit's returning to the front porch on Henry Street, trained, restoring order there—this the state will adamantly prevent down to the end of time. That is an unhappily prevented ending, but it is not the only one. For example, Mr. Redd from time to time says I took his dog. Oh, people rush to my defense. They say, well, he is confused, so he cannot realize that I rescued his dog from the state, from the lethal injection. He may realize that in fact Bandit is now with me, that in fact I now own him, and have trained him, so that in so many ways he must be said to be *my* dog; he may even realize that in fact by now the transfer back to Henry Street would be as much of an upheaval for Bandit as the transfer away from it; but he cannot, my comforters say, realize that these were the only terms under which Bandit could remain alive.

But Mr. Redd stubbornly says that I took his dog. He also at one point thought that the film crew had taken his dog, and at another that the *Hartford Courant* had. He was wrong about that but right about this: I took his dog.

Now, I did not *mean* to take his dog. "My dog Bandit" has about it a helplessly doleful air. It was not my intention, not something I meant, for Bandit to be my dog. So here I am morally or ethically safe, and I am wrongly accused by Mr. Redd of having taken his dog. But as a poet and a dog trainer, I must tell the story of my having taken his dog as a story of my failure to do what was right in terms of both of those arts. Not my fault, perhaps, but my failure nonetheless.

There is another unhappily prevented ending, prevented by the muzzle requirement. That is the ending in which Bandit could continue his work, go to dog shows, win ribbons at obedience trials. The deepest evil was the removal of Bandit from the porch, all of the forces, some of them no fault of the state's, that removed him from that porch. But the nature of that evil is most baldly exposed, for those who know what dog training is, in the fact that he cannot go to a dog show. I would like to close by explaining what I mean by that.

In the sphere of morality, my good intentions are to the point. That is to say that there are rules to morality, and under the rules our good intentions get us off the hook, to some extent at least. Intentions may not save us, but they help, and my intentions were good in relationship to the old man. Not, of course, in relationship to Society and the Public, but I can't locate either of those entities so cannot have any intentions in relationship to them. I can have intentions in relationship to Mr. Redd and other moral creatures, and my responsibility for the effects of my actions is to some extent limited by the nature of my intentions.

As a poet and a dog trainer I am used to a different set of rules. The rules of art include this one: By the very fact of intending to make a painting or write a poem, you become responsible for everything that happens in your painting or poem. That does not mean that just anyone has the right to come up and demand an explanation of you—the responsibility is toward no one but the muse and the occasional ideal reader. Neither the muse nor the ideal reader can be predicted, so there can't be a law about what your responsibility is. Nonetheless, it is a large responsibility. Even if you intend only a small poem, a small clearing, you are responsible for everything that happens in that clearing. If, for example, you write a poem in which you refer to the pit bull of Jerusalem rather than the lion of Jerusalem because when you were in school your teacher made a mistake and said that it is a pit bull who guards the gate to the Old City, then you are responsible for the mistake and for mistaken meanings that spring from it, even though you were helpless to do otherwise.

Since we are human, finite, limited, we are in a way, even the greatest of us, always helpless to do otherwise. That is why the law and the courts cannot survey and judge art with even the relatively small but real degree of coherence they manage in other realms of behavior.

The responsibility of the poet—the responsibility of really, truly meaning what you say—is, in the words of Stanley Cavell, a terrible responsibility, but it is also a kind of relief to live in that terrible world, since there at least it is possible to determine what has happened. It is hard work, it takes a long time, and there are distressing facts about the ways meaning inevitably deteriorates that have been ably discussed in the last few decades, mostly under the misleading heading "deconstruction." Still, it is so close to possible to find out what is happening in a poem that I will go ahead and say that for all practical purposes it is often possible.

The responsibility of the poet—or perhaps the dancer—is a kind of responsibility some animals do not mind taking on: the responsibility of meaning each movement and action well, as in the case of the chimp named Willie, dedicated to meaning each of his movements in a certain way, along exact arcs of intention. And there is a possible justice made available thereby, as large as the possibility of injustice it suggests. There is relief in this possibility, because it is the possibility of clarity even if also of injustice, and clarity is a relief, but there is a burden in the injustice in question, since we can know more than dogs can know, and can therefore fail more horribly than they can. The possible injustice in question is our continual human failure to mean exactly what we say and do in what we say and do. It is as though the consequences of human error coming from our having meant well—that is, having wanted to do well, having wanted to be kind, but having failed to be kind—were always horrendous, as disturbing to the whole, as much a violation of the demands of life as the failure of harmonic coherence is a violation of the demands of music. It is as though our failures to mean well caused war.

In short: If life were like art, then Mr. Redd's disregard of my "good" intentions would be the rational response to my having taken his dog.

If life were like art, if life were a realm in which in merely intending to live, or even in merely staying alive, we shouldered terrible responsibilities for the coherence and justice (exactitude) of our actions, as though we were born into a poem we were answerable for, then all of the small failures that morality excuses or even erases would be inscribed as madness, as war, as man's inhumanity to man.

In a poem of thirty lines, ten syllables each, a missing syllable or a syllable with the wrong stress on it can alter the meaning of the whole. Or virtually destroy it. What if life were like that?

Well, it isn't, thank heavens. Or not quite.

Where does all this leave Bandit? Or dogs in general? Well, Bandit's in my kitchen. But I wish he were at a dog show. He isn't at a dog show because it is unclear whether or not the restrictions of July 29, 1988, the ones that include the requirement that Bandit wear a muzzle in public, have the force of law. I don't think they apply, since the agreement included the bit about the parties reviewing it after a year, and that review has not taken place, but I am unwilling to test this out. The image of Bandit being seized while we are out on the town green in Westbrook—a nice place to work dogs, as it happens—would make good copy, especially if the text were illustrated by photographs or a videotape of Bandit innocently retrieving and then being seized. I am sufficiently a child of the sixties to think it might be worthwhile being arrested myself for such a reason, whether deliberately or by accident, but they have me because I am not bold enough to offer Bandit as a hostage.

The possible but prevented happy ending I have in mind would have been for one thing less banal than the one we have. Not glorious, but less banal. Bandit, freed of the restrictions, having done respectably in a few rounds in the obedience ring, or maybe even flubbed a few, though not too badly—Bandit Is a Show Dog After All, as in the Tom T. Hall song about Lonesome George the Bassett Hound. If my Jeep were in better shape and I could devote six hours a day to the project of driving him out of state to work him, it might be managed, a photograph of Bandit with me and the judge, the judge holding at least a green ribbon reading "Qualifying Score," or maybe a blue or a red one.

These ribbons would have no official standing with the AKC, because no way is the AKC, which sanctions obedience trials, going to register Bandit. But they would be satisfying, because then I would be able to say something definite about the results of training him. That his score was 194, not bad for a bullheaded dog, though the judge was too lenient about his forging or other technical heeling faults (or too strict about them). I could tell you what Bandit's score was, and then everyone would have a clearer sense of "what happened to Bandit," a clearer answer to "Where is that dog now?" This is why it often turns out in one traditional form of the dog or horse story—*Big Red,* or *National Velvet,* or the Black Stallion books—that the central characters, human and animal, win at dog shows, field trials, racetracks, and horse shows. The love, passion, and difficulty are the reality of the story; the results of the competition tell you that they were, in fact, real. And it can happen in life, though it doesn't necessarily, that passion and effort and love and intelligence show up for a moment or so as a trophy at a dog show. They are not guaranteed by dog show trophies, any more than they are by anything else, but sometimes that is one way they show up, in fiction and in life.

This is true even in *National Velvet,* the only genuinely great feminist story for children in my ken, a book that told me more than any other book ever has about how one might go about finding one's intellectual or artistic courage in a sexist world.

One thing the story makes clear is that it helps to have, as I do, a courageous mother. The mother in the story, Mrs. Brown, is a Channel swimmer, and the family is not rich, but her daughter's ambitions are both literally and figuratively financed by what Mrs. Brown won swimming the Channel. This is a woman who was glad she had only daughters because she "understood the courage of women" but not the courage of men.

The horse is called The Pie, because he is piebald, and he is dangerous. So is Velvet Brown, who trains him. Disguised as a boy, she rides him in the Grand National, and wins—except that because she faints after crossing the finish line her banned gender is discovered. The Grand National, unlike the more genteel competitions sponsored by the AKC, was open to all horses, otherwise such a motley-coated animal would never have been allowed to enter—and that is part of the point, that the important competitions, which means the really difficult ones, like life itself, are open to anyone.

In any case, the official ruling, which is, roughly, that Velvet Brown was never in the race in the first place, has no effect on most people's judgment of what happened. Velvet and The Pie won. As in philosophy, where a contender such as Wittgenstein, a peculiar, eccentric person who was no fun at all at high table, who was a foreigner and after a while a Jew, is held, even by those who most profoundly resent his unmannerly refusals of the rules, to be clearly a winner, some say *the* winner. There were other noble contenders, but he won, this "Wittgenstein person," a pit bull of a person who grabbed hold of philosophy with all his heart and did not let go.

One of the interesting things about dog shows is that even though they are most easily understood as sports, they are also arts, which is why it is theoretically possible for every entry in a given class to "win" the same ribbon, the green ribbon awarded for a qualifying score. Another interesting thing about them is that for the dogs, they are sometimes, perhaps even often, artistic endeavors—the intentions of the dogs are not identical to the intentions of the judges, stewards, and handlers. Because I am a distractible and physically awkward person, liable to trip, wander off course, randomly change my speed and rhythm, I may know more about this than more graceful people, thanks to the numbers of dogs who have decided, by themselves, to be as powerful and graceful and beautiful as they can while dealing with my awkwardness. When I lose my concentration and my intended attempt at three smooth steps into the halt becomes a stuttering one and three-quarters steps and a bump, and the dog with me slides into the halt and saves both of us through his or her superior ability to intend to do this thing perfectly, I learn more about the power of a dog's intentions than I do in my more coordinated moments.

I do not mean that I am handicapped, only that, as every honest trainer knows, we are all in a way handicapped in relationship to dogs and horses, some of us more than others; for dogs with working hearts, the difficulties and triumphs even of what is called Novice Obedience become a thing that dismisses, absolves, and placates sorrow. Some dogs are able to shoulder such a responsibility. Bandit is one of them, a dog capable of a ready and willing entrance into a universe in which there are no excuses or explanations allowed.

The American Kennel Club's obedience regulations contain language that reveals the dual status of obedience trials. In a football or baseball game there is no requirement that the players look willing, or as though they are enjoying themselves. But the AKC's regulations say that the judge must carry a "mental picture of the theoretically perfect performance . . . which shall combine the utmost in willingness, enjoyment and precision on the part of the dog, and naturalness, gentleness, and smoothness in handling."

This is quite a requirement, as though a dog show were a place where the demands of art, its dilations of responsibility, and the demands of gentleness and kindness were collapsed into one, as though a dog show were an arena of moral art rather than a sport. The regulations require, for crying out loud, sincerity and cheerfulness as well as precision of execution, as though they were papal rulings gone berserk. (As though it were not enough for one to intend to do well by one's dog, or as though in intending to do well one offered oneself up to the sternest judgment. A judgment as stern as Mr. Redd's when he says, "You all had no right to take my dog.")

The requirement of willingness on the dog's part and "naturalness" on the handler's part is a case of the AKC giving itself airs, I often think. In any case, the postures one sees often in the ring are far from "natural"—there is a fad at the moment in heeling that entails the handler walking with his or her left hand carried on the midsection, as though nursing a stomach ache. As for the dog's willingness, this seems to be a case of the AKC intruding into areas that are none of its business, just as it is nosy, gossipy, of people to complain, as they do, that Beethoven or Wittgenstein or Michelangelo didn't seem to be enjoying themselves properly. The efforts of the great artist or thinker are sometimes distasteful to those around them, whether the nature of those efforts, the feeling that accompanies them, is understood or not, because virtually anyone can recognize, at least through their distaste and refusal, that the demands of the artistic or philosophical or scientific task, however arcane the problem may be, are simply the demands of any human heart written large enough for legibility. Mozart's success might be terrifying to people who read in it the nature of their own failure. This would be a weak reading, of course, since their failure is not what he wrote.

In the case of dogs in competition: Some dogs who cannot be said to be comfy in competition, dogs who are so "hot" to work, as we say, so full of desire for precisely that precision called for by the rules, work very fast. The intensity of their passion for the work shows as panting and a rapidly moving tail. These are the dogs that win approval for their "willingness." Other dogs, equally willing, show their willingness in a kind of meticulousness, more like the chimp Willie than like his energetic colleague Arthur.

The Indian sage Ramana Maharishi believed, against other Hindus, that animals are souls working off some aspect of Karma, and that some animals achieve Mukti, or liberation. And one has the distinct sense, with certain dogs, that in their

seriousness, in their refusal to jump about showing their willingness and pleasure, in their devotion to the task at hand, they
are indeed working on a spiritual problem. It would please me
if the AKC managed to show some respect for this phenomenon
in dogs, but of course it would please me in general if the AKC
managed to show some respect.

This business of judging a dog by the extent to which he
appears to be having fun is misleading in a number of ways.
Popularly, and sometimes in the show ring, a high, gay tail is
thought to be a sign of well-being and willingness in a dog. As
it happens, a dog whose heart is in her work will often carry the
tail lower—you can see this in a young sheepdog who starts to
"click," to get the point of the work; the tail moves down,
curved between the legs.

The tail is curved in concentration, as the back of Rodin's
thinker is curved in concentration; the dog does not look as
though she is having fun! Well, she isn't, and probably doesn't
want to. A passion for work is not necessarily "fun," though the
deep laughter that goes with artistic triumph is nonetheless a
true laughter. And some dogs with hearts so deeply meticulous
it would break yours if you knew about it respond to the sight
of the hurdles or the dumbbell or the tracking equipment by
setting themselves into as square and serious a position as they
can manage. On the way to a jump, you will sometimes see the
tail carried low in a dog who wants each paw to land exactly
here, exactly where the dog in his fastidious, tyrannically fastidious, heart intends it to land.

So I quibble with the AKC for insisting that "lack of willingness or enjoyment on the part of the dog must be penalized,"
for the same reason I become irritable with people who want to
penalize Wittgenstein or Beethoven, take off moral points, for
their lack of "enjoyment." Either this sport is serious or it is not.
If it is serious, then the dog who does the best job should win,
and if a dog who is tense about the show situation, or excessively worried or conscientious about the jumps, triumphs over
fear and turns in the most correct performance, that dog should
be honored.

If this sport is not serious, then each dog should come out and romp with the handler for ninety seconds, and the one who gives the most romp should win.

Be my quibbles as they may, the rules, in specifying will, or willingness, on the dog's part, are an acknowledgment, albeit a confused one, of the nature of the activity for the dogs. The confusion lies in holding the handler responsible for the dog's intentions in a way that discounts and belies the dog's moral powers—that is, the dog's ability to intend her actions. Dogs intend what they do, even when "pattern-trained" by handlers who do not know how much a dog can intend, even when the "utmost willingness" requirement prompts some handlers to induce artificial hyperthyroidism in their dogs—which, as a recent article in *Front and Finish* noted, causes anxiety rather than true willingness.

How would Bandit do in such a situation, one in which his cheerfulness was on the line—one in which cheerfulness is so important that there are seminars in training for "animation"? Well, he is like this: When we were working together regularly and the work was part of the continuing promise of work, he began to display mastery as zest. "Animation," if you like. This is the quality my friend Georgiana commented on after she watched him negotiate boulders and stone walls to retrieve. However, if he doesn't see the point of the work, he shows no zest, none; indeed he radiates an active immobility, a morose rebuff. He is a kind of all-or-nothing dog, so if I could work him and did my work well, the chances are that in the ring he would display sufficient "enjoyment" to satisfy the judge. It is not for his sake that I am expressing my quibbles with the AKC. Bandit isn't the world's foremost crowd pleaser, but he shows animation especially when the world becomes very certain, full of very difficult certainties. I am not saying that he *minds* having fun, only that fun isn't as much fun for him as it is for some dogs; it is difficulty that stirs that great soul of his.

Thus, in the facts of the judge and the apparatus around the judge at a well-run dog show, and especially in the training tested at a dog show, there is one possible scene of justice for Bandit, artistic justice, that is, rather than the sort Socrates was talking about. There are relationships between these two sorts of justice, at least in certain traditions, which is why the suppression of artists is associated with tyranny.

Hence it is not enough for me that Bandit is alive and comfy in my house. Hence, in the muzzle requirement, which prevents any more such justice for Bandit, you can read the meaning of the darker injustices I brood about. In the work he did with me in the spring and summer of 1988, Bandit earned the right to the justice of work, the only kind of justice he understands.

Of course, this was not an animal rights case. The rights under consideration were those of Mr. Redd, who does not care about these contemplations of mine and who complains that I took his dog. It was my intention to get his dog back to him, but I did not, and he mentions this, sometimes giving evidence of believing in my good intentions, sometimes not. The Bandit case is not, thank heavens, a work of art, for in art as at dog shows intention dilates responsibility absolutely, in art everything is given by what you intended to happen and the gap between that and what does happen. Mr. Redd's criticism would be a just one if this case had been a work of art.

A while ago a reporter named Joel Lang called up wanting to write a piece on Bandit for the Sunday magazine section of the *Hartford Courant*. I agreed, after warning him that the writing problems were, to put it mildly, a little sticky. He did a good job on a complicated feature, and Bandit's picture was on the cover of the April 29, 1990, issue, looking formidable as all get out, but not what you would call vicious.

During the fact-checking phase of the story and the gathering of photographs, Joel and a photographer named Steve Kemper drove down to Stamford to try to get a photograph of Mr. Redd. They didn't manage this—he wasn't in the mood—but Joel did talk to him for quite a while.

Joel called up the next day to say, "I don't want to put any moral pressure on you, but I thought I'd tell you how the conversation went."

Mr. Redd was not clear about the legal situation and events, expressed bafflement, as did everyone else in the case at one point or another.

He kept saying, "Where is that dog now?"

"Vicki has him."

"Oh, the nice lady with the curly hair, yes, that's good, she loves that dog."

Then, a few minutes later:

"Where is that dog now?"

"Vicki has him."

"Oh, that's good, because she really loves that dog. She feeds him real meat!"

Asked for his analysis of the case, Mr. Redd offered at one point, "It's just like in the South, the black man gets something good, the white man takes it away from him," said this more than two years after his defense of his dog had failed, the one that went: "The white ladies like him, too."

"The black man gets something good . . ." Curiously, curiously, the Fifth and Fourteenth Amendment rights that Mr. Redd's lawyer unsuccessfully appealed to are the ones that express Mr. Redd's view of Bandit. Bandit is "something good" he once had, something of value. The Constitution says that the state must not wantonly deprive citizens of what is of value. Bandit suffered, was harmed, was violated—but this was not an animal rights case, and because Bandit lives and responds, unlike a car and unlike a bank account, it is harder to explain this than it would be if he were inert.

Toward the end of the conversation, Mr. Redd said to the reporter, "I'll give you a thousand dollars to get that dog back for me."

Joel wondered if I might find another dog for him. But Bandit is irreplaceable, and now he has been thoroughly rescued, and, as Harold Bloom notes, "All of the world has become Babylon, permanently baffled," and not even a thousand dollars, not even all the gold in Jerusalem, will undo the damage, be enough to finance the paving of a road back to understanding.

Epilogue

SINCE THE HARDCOVER PUBLICATION of this book, the legal, policy, and enforcement crises it was written to address have reached epidemic and international proportions. Here, as in western Europe, Australia, the British Isles, Singapore, and Canada—and no doubt other places—there has been a proliferation of breed bans, an escalation of police and enforcement activities, and new laws and policies that impose criminal penalties, sometimes without the right to a hearing. These are leading dog people to realize that they inhabit police states of one sort and another. They always have, but the foggy and pacifying language of good citizenship and animal welfare has in the past kept most middle-class and upper-middle-class dog owners from realizing that if Mr. Redd, poor and black and elderly and politically incorrect, is not safe, no one is. As *Bandit* went to press I was involved in some cases, a few of them international, that would supply material for several dark books.

What I have just said sounds extreme. Well, we live in extreme times, times that are demanding extraordinary moral courage from vast numbers of people, not all of whom will rise to the occasion. However, some have, and more and more will. Hence there is reason to be both appalled and heartened. To believe that even as tragedies rise continually around us, we will learn to save our dogs by saving our own souls.

July 1992

Vicki Hearne 1946-2001

AFTER LONG ILLNESS, on the 21st of August 2001 my friend Vicki Hearne died. Although Vicki was nationally acclaimed as a poet and philosopher of animal consciousness, she was foremost a dog trainer who explained dog trainers' intuitive insights to the intellectual community. She studied dogs with Dick Koehler, philosophy with Stanley Cavell, and poetry with John Hollander. Vicki taught poetry at Yale and trained dogs nearby, specializing in dangerous and untrainable dogs.

Vicki's learning often astonished me. If Aristotle or Wittgenstein ever once referred to dogs—or ever had a thought that might advance our understanding of dogs—Vicki knew it.

Her famous book was *Adam's Task*, which is the finest study of human/dog interaction ever written.

During the worst of the Pit Bull terror, she rescued Bandit from the state, trained him and saved his life—and wrote about it all in the book you're now holding. (I once watched Bandit work; as Vicki said, Bandit was a dog who loved "Surmounting.")

In *Animal Happiness,* Vicki refuted the animal rights theorists and I've often photocopied her essay "Oyez À Beaumont" for friends devastated by the death of their dog. It is the only consolation I know.

Vicki Hearne loved language, clear thinking and dogs. She was intellectually fierce, gentle in person. As she once said of herself, Vicki had a terrier's heart.

Donald McCaig

Index

ABC News, 118–19
abuse. *See* submission
Adam, 218, 238
Adventures of Huckleberry Finn,
The (Twain), 51, 185
Adventures of Tom Sawyer, The
(Twain), 119, 150, 185
aggression, 38, 42–43, 45, 145–
48, 182
agitation, 37–40, 45, 47, 252–53
Ahlerich, 86
Airedale Terrier, 34, 58, 92, 146,
147, 149, 153, 168–69, 193,
195
Alaska, 210
America, 2, 63–68, 150, 176,
185–87, 195
American Bulldog, 34, 35–36,
47, 63, 65, 67, 112
American Bull Terrier, 31, 32.
See also American Pit Bull
Terrier
American Dog Breeders Associ-
ation (ADBA), 33, 34–35,
122, 176, 182
American Humane Association
(AHA), 266
American Jurisprudence: Trials,
103
American Kennel Club (AKC),
32–35, 126, 146–47, 176,
286, 288–91

American Pit Bull Dog, 47
American Pit Bull Terrier, 32–
36, 47, 67, 109, 111–15,
122–25, 144–45, 147–48,
168, 174–76, 181–88, 191–
93, 197–200, 229–30
American Society for the Pre-
vention of Cruelty to Ani-
mals (ASPCA), 119, 128,
132
"American Staffordshire Pit Bull
Terrier," 109, 112
American Staffordshire Terrier,
32–33
American Temperament Testing
Society, 246
Andersen, Kenneth, 254
Andrea da Firenze, 8, 177
Andrew Jackson, 34, 68, 185–86
Animal Actors, 249, 266, 268,
273
Animal Control (Riverside
County), 259
Animal Estate, The (Ritvo), 16,
141–42
Annie, 60–61, 67–68, 69, 192,
196–97, 232–36, 247, 265
Anthony, St., 30
anthropomorphism, 58, 163–64,
212
apes, 267
Apples, 259

Arendt, Hannah, 106, 127–28,
    186, 275, 276, 277
Argentinian Dogo, 47
Aristotle, 78, 84, 97
Arizona, 150, 274
Artegall, 97–98
Arthur, 269–70, 289
Arthur, King, 174
artificial intelligence, 74–75
"Artificial Nigger, The"
    (O'Connor), 114
Asali, 268
Ashley, 72
"A-Team, The," 66–67, 96, 158
Athens, 173
Atlanta, Ga., 214
At the Races, 192–93
Auden, W. H., 225
Austen, Jane, 209
Australian Terrier, 193
autism, 82, 112

Bail, L. Maugh, 149–50
Barker, Bob, 85, 266, 273–74
Bateson, Gregory, 110
Beethoven, Ludwig van, 289,
    290
Bella, 187
Bello, Robert, 19, 20, 26, 28,
    46, 52, 53, 247, 256
Benjy, 127
Bergh, Henry, 128
Bernard, George, 14, 46, 69,
    95–96, 100, 104, 129–31,
    132, 143, 253, 256, 257
Bernard, Lillian, 46, 99–100,
    104, 143, 150, 243, 249–52,
    253–54, 255, 257, 263
Big Red (Montgomery), 286
Bill Sykes's dog, 226

Bleak House (Dickens), 102, 120
Bloodhound, 184, 227
Bloom, Allan, 163, 164, 175–76
Bloom, Harold, 218–19, 239,
    293
Book of J, The (Bloom and
    Rosenberg), 218, 237–39
Border Collie, 36, 58, 169, 178–
    79, 181, 182, 212
Borzoi, 32, 179
Bouvier des Flanders, 170
Boxer, 175, 183, 229, 266
Bradford, England, 187
breed names and categories, 31–
    35, 47
Brisbin, I. Lehr, 188
Brooklyn, N.Y., 150
Buber, Martin, 57
Buck, 143
Buckingham Palace, 167
bull breeds, 32–37, 78, 106, 170,
    173, 191, 193. See also indi-
    vidual breeds
bulldog: as nickname for pit
    bull, 34, 174, 176, 177, 181,
    191
Bulldog Club, 178
Bullet, 129–31, 132
Bulletin of the New York Academy
    of Medicine, 20, 136
bull pup, 34
Bunyan, Paul, 66, 185
Burr, Leslie, 203
Bush, George, 195
Buster Brown, 184

Cain, 239
Cairn Terrier, 6, 193
Calico Silver, 2
California, 107, 128–29, 139,

149, 162, 237, 248–49, 258–
    59, 273, 280
Call of the Wild, The (London),
    82
Canine Control. *See* Connecticut
    Canine Control
Capitoline Pit Bull, 174–77, 183,
    188, 191–92, 193, 197, 198,
    199–200
Capitoline Wolf, 174–77, 183,
    190–91, 197, 198, 199–200
cart dogs, 36, 191
Cartwright, Nancy, 214
Cavell, Stanley, 3, 70, 71, 149,
    155, 157, 206, 208, 211,
    281, 284
"Celebrated Jumping Frog of
    Calaveras County, The"
    (Twain), 34, 68, 185–86
Centers for Disease Control
    (CDC), 138, 201
Cerberus, 2
Champion Bud, 184–85
Chester, 279
chimpanzees, 267, 268, 269
Churchill, Winston, 197
Claim of Reason, The (Cavell),
    70
Clifford, Donald, 15
Clovis, 88, 89
Cochran, Frank, 6, 104, 109,
    117, 128, 130, 240, 245,
    246, 253–60, 262, 277
Collie, 178–79, 181. *See also*
    Border Collie
Colorado, 161
Companion Dog, 126–27, 266
computers, 74–75
Connecticut, 10, 24, 26–27, 50,
    100, 154, 228, 274, 280–81

Connecticut Canine Control,
    24–25, 26–27, 47, 48, 241,
    245–46, 247, 253, 260. *See
    also* Intino, Frank
Connecticut Department of Ag-
    riculture, 26–27, 117. *See
    also* Connecticut Canine
    Control
Constitution (U.S.), 23, 101,
    102–3, 115, 120, 159, 161,
    293
Cookie, 52
Cooper, Diana, 59, 65–66, 68,
    187, 190, 238, 261
cops, 24–25, 95–99, 186, 241–
    42, 262
Corgi (Welsh Cardigan and/or
    Welsh Pembroke), 58
Cornell University, 188
Cover, Robert, 107–8, 111, 114,
    119
cows, 87–90, 100–101
Coyote (trickster god), 92–93
Cujo, 3, 15
cynicism, 13, 95–96, 129, 132,
    240

Dachshund, 32
Dalzel, Bonnie, 188
Darwin, Charles, 80
Davidson, Donald, 231
Davie, Donald, 104, 124
Dayton, Ohio, 11–13, 17–18
Dean, Harold, 53–54, 99, 206,
    243–44, 246, 255
Degas, Edgar, 188–90, 192–93,
    198
Derrida, Jacques, 173
Descartes, René, 222
Desdemona, 208

Dickens, Charles, 160, 226–27
Dickinson, Emily, 65, 66, 203
Diogenes, 129
Doberman Pinscher, 106, 180,
    193, 229
dog: history of term, 177–78
dog bites, 12, 23–24, 101, 134,
    135–56, 201, 244, 261–62
dogcatchers. *See* Connecticut
    Canine Control; Intino,
    Frank
dogfighting, 2–3, 33, 68, 118–
    19, 121–22, 124–25, 159,
    185–86, 194–95, 229
Dog in Action, The (Lyons), 181
Dogue de Bordeaux, 47
Dog World, 146
dominance, 71, 86–92, 121
Dominicanni, 8, 177
Dukakis, Michael, 195
Duncan, Robert, 209
Duty of Genius, The (Monk),
    110

Eachus, Jan, 187
Edgecliff Briar Hound, 209
Eldrige, Barbara, 220
Elective Affinities (Goethe), 67
elephants, 162, 267
Elizabeth II, Queen, 179–80
Elkhound, 94
Emerson, Ralph Waldo, 63
Eminent Dogs, Dangerous Men
    (McCaig), 180
Endangered Breed Association
    (EBA), 278
England, 15–16, 32, 141–42,
    178–80, 183–84, 187, 265
English Bulldog, 32, 34, 35,
    183–84

(English) bull terrior, 32, 174
Euthyphro (Plato), 104, 263
Eve, 218, 237

Faerie Queene (Spenser), 97–98
Fala, 185
Fallen Jockey, The, 188–90
feminism, 162, 202–3, 221
Ferorelli, Enrico, 64, 169–70
Fidelco, 154
Fouts, Roger, 272
Fox, Michael, 15, 237
Foxhound, 182
France, 32, 278
Francis of Assisi, St., 243, 246,
    257, 259
Francois, Linda, 104, 255, 257
French Bulldog, 32
Freud, Sigmund, 214
Front and Finish, 291
Frost, Robert, 71

gameness, 121–25, 193–98
gender, 201–39
genetics, 179–82
George, St., 205
Georgia, 136, 214
Georgiana, 61, 291
German Shepherd, 40–41, 71,
    80–81, 92, 139, 154, 167–
    69, 170, 172, 193, 195
Germany, 32, 105–6
Ginsberg, Professor, 249, 255
Glaucon, 163–65
Goethe, Johann Wolfgang von,
    67
Golden Retriever, 21, 197
Goodall, Jane, 267
Göring, Hermann, 105, 106, 264
Greensburg, Ill., 42

Greenwood, Kate, 35, 123
Greenwood, Ralph, 122–24
greyhounds, 61
Greystoke, 272
Griffin, Maureen, 220, 258, 259
guide dogs, 152, 154
Guidelines for Regulating Dangerous or Vicious Dogs, 158–61

Hall, Tom T., 286
Hallie, Philip, 278
Halpern, Diane F., 221
Handsome Dan, 34, 198
Hard Times (Dickens), 227
Harden, Mark, 268–73
Harris, Cheryl, 269, 272
Harris, David, 136, 139
Hartford, Ct., 49, 144. *See also* State Office Building
Hartford Courant, 53, 57, 206, 245, 255, 282, 292
Harwood, Pat, 187, 220
Hearne's Law, 18, 36–37, 272
Heidi, 161
Helmar, Phyllis, 34
Henry, Patrick, 122
Henry Street, 20–21, 22, 25, 40, 51, 115, 126, 155, 170, 171, 240, 256, 282
Hitler, Adolf, 105
hog dogs, 181
Hollander, John, 125
Hollywood, 3, 85, 248, 266, 268–73, 277
horror stories, 15–17, 106–7, 158, 180, 186–87, 212
horses, 59, 86, 188–90, 193, 203, 204–5, 210, 219–20, 235–36

hounds, 93–94
How the Laws of Physics Lie (Cartwright), 214
Hoyt, John, 15, 140
Human Condition, The (Arendt), 127
Humane Society of the United States (HSUS), 1, 14–15, 125, 138, 140–41, 158–60, 161, 162, 186–87, 215, 220, 237, 264, 265, 272
Humes, Valerie, 20, 64, 243, 257
Hungary, 274

Inn, Frank, 127
Intino, Frank, 47, 52, 104, 116–18, 157, 235, 237, 242–44, 246, 249–54, 256–57, 258, 261–63, 277
Irish Setter, 259
Irish Wolfhound, 209
Isaac, Virginia, 148, 149

J (poet), 218, 235, 237–39
Jack Russell, 193
Jekyll-Hyde syndrome, 1, 7, 10, 48, 49, 132, 195, 242, 263
Jessup, Diane, 148
Jiggs, 184
jive stories, 2–3
Jo, 145, 155
Job, 166
John Bull, 183–84
Johnson, Mr., 21, 22, 53, 118
Journal of the American Medical Association, 201
Journal of the American Veterinary Medical Association, 21
Joyce, James, 209

justice, 6–7, 97–98, 103–5,
    107–8, 112–13, 133, 158,
    240, 257, 262–63, 284,
    291–92

Kant, Immanuel, 5
Keesha, 83–84, 90–93
Kehoe, Dr., 113
Keller, Helen, 122
Kemper, Steve, 292
Khomeini, Ayatollah Ruhollah,
    17, 276
King, Martin Luther, Jr., 50,
    246
Klimke, Reiner, 86
Koch, Edward I., 140–41
Koehler, Dick, 27, 45, 104, 154,
    235, 237, 255, 257
Koehler, William, 48
Koehler Method of Dog Training,
    The, 150
Kristallnacht, 105
Kustner, Kathy, 203

Labrador Retriever, 167, 197,
    229
Lafayette, La., 124
Lake Charles, La., 50, 97, 119
Landrover Smith, 6, 268–69
Lang, Joel, 292–93
Lassie, 154
Lassie Come Home (Knight), 178
law, 102–3, 108, 111, 114–15,
    133
Leaves of Grass (Whitman), 64
Le Chambon, France, 278
Leibniz, Gottfried Wilhelm,
    79–80
Lest Innocent Blood Be Shed
    (Hallie), 278

Levine, Dr., 137
Lewis, C. S., 110
Lhasa Apso, 155–56, 182
Liberty, 48
Lightsay, B. W., 144–45
Lightsay, Laura, 145
Lincoln, Abraham, 64, 197
lions, 268
Little Vicious, A, 20, 64, 87, 243
Livy, 174, 176, 191
Lockwood, Randall, 15, 138,
    201, 215
London, Jack, 82, 143, 270
Lonesome George the Bassett
    Hound, 286
Lookout Mountain, 2
Lorenz, Konrad, 82
Los Angeles, Ca., 127
Louisiana, 50, 97, 119–20, 124,
    181
Louisiana, Catahoula, 181
Lovaas, Ivar, 82
Lucy Belle, 61, 232–33
Lynn, Ma., 266
Lyons, McDowell, 181

McBau, Judy, 136
McCaig, Donald, 180
McClean, Lily Mae, 20–21, 25,
    53, 157, 160
McDonald, Jeffrey, 98–99
Majchier, Vincent, 52–53, 206,
    255–56
Malamute, 48, 193
Maloney, Councilwoman, 135
Man o' War, 59
Marcus, Ruth, 221
Marxism, 51, 162
Masikio (Mouse), 269
Massachusetts, 34

mastiffs, 47, 177
Merrylegs, 227
Michelangelo, 66, 289
Milton, John, 99, 112, 235, 276
Miniature Poodle, 144
Missouri, 265, 280
Mr. T, 66–67
Molossian, 191
Monk, Ray, 110
Moses, 218, 219
Mozart, Wolfgang Amadeus, 75–76, 289
Mussolini, Benito, 200
muzzles, 216

National Velvet (Bagnold), 286–87
Nazis, 106, 186
New Haven, Ct., 224, 260
Newkirk, Ingrid, 81, 237
New Knowledge of Dog Behavior, The (Pfaffenberger), 152
New Mexico, 275
New York, N.Y., 2, 20, 113, 114, 135–36, 137, 139–40, 160
New York Times, 53
Nietzsche, Friedrich, 196, 198
1984 (Orwell), 171
Nordic breeds, 94
Noriega, Manuel Antonio, 213
North Bergen, N.J., 227, 280

O'Connor, Flannery, 114
Ohio, 12–13, 17–18, 280
Olde Bulldogge, 47
Oliver Twist (Dickens), 226
Olympic riding, 203
Othello, 206, 211
Our Gang, 3, 184

Our Knowledge of the External World (Russell), 54–55
Out of Africa, 268
Owens, Pat, 141

Panamanian defense dogs, 213, 262
paraphernalia laws, 107, 148–49
Paul, St., 190
Peck, M. Scott, 61
Peel, Sir Robert, 98
People, 141, 142
People for the Ethical Treatment of Animals (PETA), 81, 107, 127, 237, 265
Pete, 8–9
Pete the Pup, 3, 184
Pfaffenberger, Clarence, 152
Philadelphia, Pa., 142
Pie, The, 287
Pigot of Patshull, Lord, 193, 199
pit bulls, 1–2, 7–8, 12, 31–35, 54, 80–81, 100, 112–14, 135–38, 140–42, 181–87, 227, 229–30, 279–80. See also American Pit Bull Terrier; American Staffordshire Terrier; Andrew Jackson; Annie; Champion Bud; Chester; Jo; Puller; Rex; Sandy
Plato, 97, 133, 158, 263
Plott Hound, 67
Podjasky, Alois, 193
Pointer, 63, 183
police. See cops
police dogs, 11, 38, 39, 130–31, 147, 154, 167–68, 252. See also Schutzhund

Ponelli, Tom, 31, 37, 41–42, 44–45
Poodle, 21, 61
Powell, Effie, 1, 22–23, 53, 118, 152, 255
Primarily Primates, 85
Project X, 86, 266, 269–70, 272
Proverbs, 105
Psalms, 166
psychology, 162, 170, 213–17
Puller, 144–45, 154, 155, 156

Quayle, Dan, 195

rabies, 16, 141–42
Ramana Maharishi, 289
Raphael, 205, 224–25
Rather, Dan, 11–13, 16, 17, 18, 132
Reagan, Ronald, 186
Rebel terrier, 31
Redd, Lamon, 11, 19–20, 21, 22, 24, 25–26, 41, 43, 45–46, 49–50, 53, 64, 93, 101, 102, 108–9, 115–16, 119, 120, 125, 133, 157, 236, 237, 241, 243, 247, 254, 255, 282–83, 289, 292–93
Redford, Robert, 268
Reilly, Peter J., 244–45
Republic (Plato), 97, 131, 133, 158, 163–67
Rex, 32, 184, 197
Rhodesian Ridgeback, 182
Richmond, Va., 170, 185
Rin Tin Tin, 3, 18, 22–23, 38, 154, 169, 186
Ritvo, Harriet, 16, 141
Riverside, Ca., 139
Robinson, Wallace, 184

Rochester, N.Y., 7–9, 137–38
Rome, 94, 173, 174–75, 182, 191, 192
Romulus and Remus, 174, 190–91, 197
Roosevelt, Franklin D., 184–85
Roosevelt, Theodore, 32, 184, 197
Rorty, Richard, 170–71
Rosenberg, David, 218, 237
Rosie, 182
Rota, Gian-Carlo, 221–22
Rottweiler, 170, 174, 229, 279
Royal Society for the Prevention of Cruelty to Animals (RSPCA), 15–16, 36, 141–42, 187, 226, 265
Rush, Robert, 266, 273
Rushdie, Salman, 17, 276
Russell, Bertrand, 54–55, 56, 156, 192
Russia, 32
Russian Wolfhound. *See* Borzoi

Sachs *et alia,* 203–4
St. Bernard, 181
Salt Lake City, Utah, 122, 123
Samoyed, 94
Sandra, 249
Sandy, 182–83
San Mateo County, Ca., 107, 237
Schnauzer, 182
Schuaver, Cheryl, 269
Schutzhund, 40–41, 44, 145–46, 147–50. *See also* police dogs
Scotland Yard, 167
Scottish Terrier, 185
Screen Actors Guild (SAG), 266

Sex Differences in Cognitive Abilities (Halpern), 221
Shakespeare, William, 66, 156, 211. *See also* individual characters
Shar Pei, 13, 193, 280
sheepdogs, 166, 180, 181
Shepard, Charlie, 87, 100, 132, 195–96
shyness. *See* submission
Silver Trails, 46, 54, 99–100, 127, 130, 131, 143, 171, 243–45, 248, 249–52, 253
Simon, Officer, 53, 245
Sirrah, 6
"Sit!" command, 70–78
Skinner, B. F., 221
Socrates, 5, 97, 98, 99, 104, 131, 134, 163–67, 172, 173, 212, 240, 263
South Carolina, 280–81
Spenser, Edmund, 97–98
Spike, 118–19, 133
sporting breeds, 169
Sports Illustrated, 1, 142, 228
Staffordshire Bull Terrier, 33
"Staffordshire Pit Bull Terrier," 9
Staffordshire Terrier. *See* American Staffordshire Terrier
Stamford, Ct., 20, 28, 140
Stamford Advocate, 53, 242, 244–45, 246
Stamford Superior Court, 99
Stanford, Ca., 124
State Office Building (Hartford), 104, 113, 133, 154
Steinbeck, John, 184
Steinkraus, William, 203

Sterling Memorial Library (Yale), 192, 198, 199–200
Stern, Allen, 146–47
Stevens, Wallace, 6, 65, 66, 74, 111, 224
Stevenson, Robert Louis, 10
Stowe, Harriet Beecher, 49, 51, 120
Streep, Meryl, 268
Stubbs, Arthur "Stubby," 184–85
Stubbs, George, 193, 199
submission, 81–94
Sudan (lion), 268
Swett, Wallace, 85
Swinford Bandog, 47

Taxicab Geometry, 73–74
Teitleman, Robert, 53, 242, 258, 260
Tensas Swamp, 181
Terhune, Albert Payson, 178
terriers, 36, 168. *See also* individual breeds
Texas, 274–75
That Hideous Strength (Lewis), 110
Thoreau, Henry David, 63
Thurber, James, 32, 107, 175, 184, 197, 227, 266
Tierschutzverein, 105, 264
Tige, 184
Tolstoy, Leo, 190
Tony the Wonder Horse, 186
Toto, 6, 154
Tragesser, Robert, 27–28, 48, 69–70, 77, 256
training, 39, 44–46, 69–78, 81–94, 121, 127, 158–59, 162, 197, 198–99, 216, 266–73

Trattner, Alice, 249, 255, 274
Trigger, 186
Tufts University, 188
Turnipseed, Hayward, 214
Twain, Mark, 2, 6, 34, 49, 51,
    63, 66, 68, 103, 107, 120,
    185–86, 197, 209
Tyrone, 85

Uncle Tom's Cabin (Stowe), 51
Uniform Administrative Proce-
    dures Act, 1, 241
United Kennel Club (UKC),
    31–33, 34–35, 55, 176, 266
United States. See America
University of California at
    Davis, 188
University of Georgia, 188
University of Pennsylvania, 188
Utah, 122, 265, 280

Vandenberg, Mark, 18–19, 26,
    53, 127, 257
Victoria, Queen, 178, 179
Vietnam War, 186
Virgil (chimp), 269
Virginia, 50, 170, 184, 266, 274
virtù, 66–68, 93
vultures, 268

Wall Street Journal, 187
Wambaugh, Joseph, 98–99
Washington State University,
    188
Wells, Hubert, 86, 249, 266,
    268, 269, 272, 274
Welty, Eudora, 209

Westbrook, Ct., 285
West Highland White Terrier,
    161
Westminster Kennel Club, 280
Wethersfield, Ct., 100
Whitman, Walt, 63, 64, 66
Wilder, Jake, 265, 280
Williams, William Carlos, 66
Willie, 269–70, 272, 273, 284,
    289
Winkler, Hans, 203
Winski, Warden, 28–29, 31, 35,
    36, 37, 39–42, 44–45, 47,
    53, 248
Wittgenstein, Ludwig, 70, 74,
    78, 110, 111, 114, 166, 234,
    287, 289, 290
Wizard of Oz, The, 6, 154
Wizner, Steven, 101–3, 104, 118,
    119, 120, 129, 255
wolves, 78, 79–82, 90–94, 174–
    77, 191–92, 199, 249
Woolf, Virginia, 209
World War I, 32, 184
World War II, 119, 278
Wright, John, 15, 215

Yahweh, 218, 219, 238
Yale Law Journal, 102, 107
Yale University, 34, 101, 115,
    192, 198, 223
Yankee terrier, 31
Yeats, William Butler, 225
Yorkshire Terrier, 150
Youatt, William, 178

Zap, 213

COMMON READER EDITIONS

As booksellers since 1986, we have been stocking the pages of our monthly catalogue, A COMMON READER, with "Books for Readers with Imagination." Now as publishers, the same motto guides our work. Simply put, the titles we issue as COMMON READER EDITIONS are volumes of uncommon merit which we have enjoyed, and which we think other imaginative readers will enjoy as well. While our selections are as personal as the act of reading itself, what's common to our enterprise is the sense of shared experience a good book brings to solitary readers. We invite you to sample the wide range of COMMON READER EDITIONS, and welcome your comments.

www.commonreader.com